6$^{99}$

# Getting Started
# in Stocks

Also available from John Wiley & Sons

*Getting Started in Options, Second Edition* by Michael C. Thomsett
*Getting Started in Futures, Second Edition* by Todd Lofton
*Getting Started in Bonds* by Michael C. Thomsett
*Getting Started in Real Estate* by Michael C. Thomsett
  and Jean M. Thomsett

# Getting Started in Stocks

## Second Edition

### Alvin D. Hall

JOHN WILEY & SONS, INC.

New York · Chichester · Brisbane · Toronto · Singapore

*Library of Congress Cataloging-in-Publication Data:*

Hall, Alvin D.
    Getting started in stocks / by Alvin D. Hall.—2nd ed.
        p.   cm.
    Includes index.
    ISBN 0-471-02572-0 (pbk.; acid-free paper)
    1. Stocks.   2. Investments.   I. Title.
    HG4661.H28   1993
    332.63'22—dc20                                              94-326

Printed in the United States of America

10   9   8   7   6   5   4   3   2

This book is dedicated to the memory of four dear friends

*Richard Leigh Chittim*
Isaac Henry Wing Professor of Mathematics Emeritus
Bowdoin College
Brunswick, Maine

*Virginia Perkins White*
Chapel Hill, North Carolina

*Norman C. Robertson*
Chicago, Illinois

and

*John Davenport Neville*
Richmond, Virginia

# Acknowledgments

**A** fter more than 10 years of teaching much of the information contained in this book, putting my spoken words in writing proved an enlightening challenge. My classroom experience, and my inquisitive students, served me well. In preparing the second edition, I was greatly aided by the students in my "Beginning Stock Investing" class at The New School for Social Research in New York. Their eager, direct, and probing questions helped me to clarify and expand topics, making the book more useful for the audience for whom it is intended.

Additionally, I was served equally well by two groups of people. First, I thank my friends, especially those outside the securities industry, who read much of the original manuscript and were invaluable in helping me anticipate many of the questions and concerns of general readers. They are Roger Bakeman, Julie Hahnke, Van Morrow, and S. Gerald Saliman. Second, I am grateful to my professional colleagues whose comments and patience helped me keep the information and tone of this book "on the money." They are Edward S. Bradley, Douglas C. Carroll, John Keefe, Edward

Fleur, David Krell, and, most important, William A. Rini and Joseph A. Ross.

I truly appreciate the patience and understanding that Myles Thompson (my editor), Jacquie Urinyi, and Karl Weber at John Wiley & Sons, Inc. showed during the writing of this second, *and better* edition (and my other books). I also thank them for their ongoing support and belief in my future projects.

Bryan Forman—an art director, beginning investor, and reader of this book—worked with me to refine many of the illustrations that appear in the new edition. Like Trudy Lundgren, president of TypeRight Graphics, who created all of the illustrations for the first edition, Bryan endured my tendency to "make just one more little change" with humor and promptness. And finally, my thanks to Robin Schoen, my public relations consultant, whose creative and diligent work has helped expand the success of the first edition to more and more beginning investors.

# Contents

# Introduction:
# Investing in Stocks:
# The Fears, the Fantasies,
# the Facts

This book is a practical tool for anyone interested in stocks. Often those who are inexperienced in investments are left feeling confused when an experienced investor or professional tries to explain what stocks are, how they work, and how to use them to make money. This book is written to make you—a newcomer to the stock market or a person simply looking for straightforward, clear information—feel knowledgeable.

Almost everyone knows the word *stocks*, and almost everyone has a story about a friend, relative, or acquaintance who has invested in the market. Usually it is the amount of money this friend made—or lost—that influences an individual's perceptions of investing in stocks. Individual attitudes toward investing in stocks are as varied as the stories people tell. Some stories are of sudden riches, usually told with considerable pride and relish. Others are of huge losses and are often murmured in hushed tones, if at all. The three profiles that follow illustrate the diversity of feelings and experiences that people have about investing in stocks.

The first concerns a woman who worked as a middle manager in a small manufacturing company and decided to begin investing in stock early in her career. She was not rich. Often she could save only a few hundred dollars each quarter to invest. She had a clear goal in mind: to build a portfolio of what she decided were high-quality stocks—those that paid dividends regularly and whose issuers produced good products. Working with a broker, she researched the companies that interested her and bought 5, 10, or 20 shares as her income permitted. When she could, she reinvested the dividends in more shares. Over a number of years and after several stock splits, her holdings increased nicely, and the dividends from these investments began to provide her with a little discretionary income. With a small amount of this extra money, she began buying a few of what she called her "fun stocks": small, somewhat risky companies whose products interested her. Today, her retirement income comes primarily from the portfolio of stocks that she built. Looking back over her years of investing in stocks, she gives the following advice to beginning investors: buy quality. She readily admits that her "fun stocks" taught her how the stock market works, providing quick cash sometimes and harsh lessons at others. Her high-quality stocks, on the other hand, provided little action or excitement but have paid off handsomely in growth and steady dividends over the long run.

The second profile involves an art curator and author who invests his money only in art. His rationale is, "At least you have something to decorate the walls even if it loses its value." This person has never invested in a single stock. He is afraid of the market—a fear that comes from his boyhood. He remembers how his uncles, aunts, and cousins invested money in the market, certain that they were going to make a killing. More often than not, they got killed, losing all of their investment and then having to borrow money from relatives to cover their living expenses and losses. To him, stocks represent a sinkhole into which people pour fantasies of making it rich. Recently, however, some of his friends have done well investing in stocks, piquing his curiosity. He remains skeptical about investing, but he is interested in learning how stocks work and how his friends use them to make money.

The third profile is of a college professor and his wife, who runs a children's bookstore. Despite two incomes, they lived on a tight budget for several years in order to repay educational loans and save for a home. They now have some extra money, which they wish to invest. They are both intelligent people and are interested in stocks, but "we don't want to have to read *The Wall Street Journal* every day. We don't want to have to watch and listen to CNBC. How will we know what to buy? How will we know when to sell? Can we trust our broker? What are the chances that we will lose our hard-earned money? Is there any way we can protect ourselves against loss when we invest in stocks?"

The fears, insecurities, and questions contained in the second and third stories are typical of beginning investors. For some, this lack of knowledge combined with the seemingly formidable mystique of the stock market leaves them paralyzed at the starting line. They are unable to make even the simplest decisions and thereby miss good investment opportunities. Others take a more cavalier position, jumping, usually wallet first, into the pit with the bulls and the bears, hoping to learn as they go along.

If you have little or no investment experience, this book will demystify the stock market. In clear and easy-to-understand prose, you will obtain the fundamental knowledge that enables you to understand:

1. The various types of stocks and their characteristics.
2. The financial rewards and risk associated with each.
3. Basic stock analysis—those fundamental and technical factors within a company, within the stock market, and within the overall economy that influence the performance of stocks.
4. Conservative and aggressive strategies to follow in achieving your financial goals.
5. How mutual funds provide an indirect and "managed" way for an individual to invest in stocks.
6. A general understanding of investing in the international markets.

This book is not written in technical language. I assume that you have chosen this text seeking information that is presented and explained in clear, easily understandable English. The highly technical jargon, shorthand speech, and buzzwords that many people fearfully associate with Wall Street are absent.

Nevertheless, you will have to learn some words and phrases that describe various investment instruments, their characteristics, and the stock market itself. The first time each of these terms is used it will be defined in **boldface type** in the book's margin. When appropriate, I use a real-life example or illustration to expand and clarify the definition. The book contains a glossary of these and many other investment terms.

The text proceeds in five logical and cumulative steps designed to allow you to develop an overall knowledge of stocks, their markets, and their investment possibilities.

**Step 1: Setting your goals.** Clearly defined goals and limits of financial risk are essential to successful investing in stocks or any other security. To say that you "want to make money from investing" is an insufficient delineation of your goals. Are you investing for the short term or the long term? For a child's education or your retirement? To generate cash immediately or to build capital? How much money can you afford to invest without adversely affecting your life-style? How much of a return would you accept as reasonable for your investment? How much capital are you able and willing to risk? These are questions that you *must* answer *before* making any investment.

**Step 2: Choosing the right type of stock.** When most people think of stocks, they think of only two types: common and preferred. But there are at least 10 different categories of common and preferred stocks. All represent a direct investment in a company and entitle stockholders to receive dividends. The distinct characteristic of each type of stock can affect its performance and investment return in the market. Among the categories of common and preferred stocks that you will learn about in this book are:

- Blue chip stock
- Income stock
- Growth stock
- Penny stock

- Small-cap stock
- Straight preferred stock
- Cumulative preferred stock
- Callable preferred stock
- Convertible preferred stock
- Adjustable rate preferred stock

**Step 3: Formulating strategies.** How do you allocate your assets in order to achieve the goals you have set? There is a broad spectrum of relatively simple strategies, from very conservative to very aggressive, that beginning investors can use as models. This book discusses these strategies and shows how an individual stock or combination of stocks can be used to achieve your investment objectives. The models, of course, will be illustrative. You will find other securities that will enable you to accomplish the same goals.

**Step 4: Analyzing stock.** No whiz-bang computer program, accounting experience, or M.B.A. degree is necessary to analyze stock in which you wish to invest. The information you must have to make a sound investment decision can be contained in the security's prospectus, the company's financial statements, annual reports, and other publicly available documents. Both fundamental and technical analyses will be explained and illustrated. You will learn the meaning of such items as earnings per share, the price-earnings (P-E) ratio, retained earnings, the advance-decline theory, and the Dow Jones Industrial Average. I will show how this information fits into your investment decision-making process.

**Step 5: Reviewing alternatives.** Instead of purchasing individual stocks and building a portfolio, you may wish to invest in an existing portfolio managed by a professional. If this is the case, a stock mutual fund may be the right vehicle. Perhaps you want to participate in the profitable price movement of a stock without actually owning it. In this case, a stock-equivalent product, such as a warrant or option, may be suitable. At this last step, you will learn how to assess the benefits and risks of the various stock-derivative investment products compared with the actual stock itself. Stock equivalents, also referred to as stock-derivative products, have many of the investment dynamics of stocks but do not involve direct ownership of the stock itself. The investment instruments that will be explained are:

1. Stock mutual funds
2. Warrants
3. Rights
4. Stock options (calls and puts)

International investing using stock is covered in this book. With the increasing globalization of the securities industry and the growing importance of the Pacific Rim, Latin America, Eastern Europe and other emerging markets, many investment opportunities exist abroad. This book describes how to use international and global mutual funds as well as American depositary receipts and American depositary shares—stock-equivalent investment instruments—to accomplish your investment goals using the world markets.

With this book, you will come to understand the many investment instruments that come under the heading "stocks." You will gain the skill necessary to assess the broad range of investment possibilities that stocks offer and understand the rewards and risks associated with each. The final decision to invest will be yours, but at the very least you will be well informed by having read this book.

# CHAPTER 1

# Setting Your Goals: Assessing Risks and Rewards

"**I** just opened an account at a brokerage house. I work hard to earn my money, and I want to start making it work better for me by investing." A friend who has reached a point in his career where he has some discretionary income recently made this statement. When asked exactly how he plans to achieve the goal of "making his money work better" using stocks, he replied confidently, "Always buy low and sell high."

My friend's initial statement is the reason that most people begin investing in stocks. They have discretionary income—money in excess of that required for their living expenses, savings, and the necessary insurance coverage and cash reserves for emergencies—and want this money to earn more than it would in an account at a commercial or savings bank. Indeed, this is a good reason for investing in stock. Historically, stocks have provided a better return than most other types of investment. However, my friend's old chestnut of a response to the question of how he will achieve his goal indicates that he has given little, if any, thought to

**investment planning:** defining an investment objective and establishing the systematic approach to achieve it.

*investment planning.* Therein lies the potential for failure and disappointment.

When many people find they have "extra" money, the normal human response is to spend it. If they manage to restrain that urge, the next response is to invest the money in a get-rich-quick scheme. Both impulses often result in lost opportunities. Before making any investment, whether in real estate, art, antiques, bonds, or stocks, you must first evaluate your current and potential financial means, determine the goal or purpose of making the investment, and then design an investment strategy appropriate to these means to achieve the goals. Clear-headed assessment and planning are particularly important when you are considering investing in any securities that are inherently speculative, like stocks.

The six questions that follow are those that everyone contemplating investing in stocks should ask themselves before they make their first purchase. Under each question we explore the issues and topics that must be considered.

## HOW MUCH MONEY DO I HAVE TO INVEST?

**net worth:** the difference between the total value of a person's assets and possessions (e.g., home, land, savings accounts, investments) and the person's total indebtedness (e.g., mortgage, car loan, credit cards, school loans).

What you *want* to invest may be quite different from what you *have* to invest. Investment planning starts with reviewing your assets, liabilities, and future cash needs. Through this process, you determine your *net worth*. Thoroughness must be your guiding rule. Your assessment must include the following considerations:

1. Income: Salary, bonuses, and trusts.
2. Savings and other investments: Bank accounts, certificates of deposit (CDs), real estate, annu-

ities, mutual funds, stocks, bonds, and so forth.

3. Living expenses: The number of your dependents, food, utilities, housing costs, education costs, and vacations, for example.
4. Insurance coverage: Medical, disability, and life insurance, among others.
5. Retirement plan: Individual retirement accounts or plans provided by an employer.
6. Estate planning (a properly executed will is essential).
7. Discretionary income: That which is available after essential living expenses have been paid.

A review of your own budget may enable you to answer the "how much" question. If you are unable to assess your own financial position, seek the help of an objective, qualified investment professional. In addition to determining your net worth and capital available for investing, this process should enable you to establish what portion of this money should be liquid and what portion should be invested for the long term.

In the securities industry, much of the financial information enumerated above is requested on a brokerage firm's new account form. The broker uses it to create your *financial profile*, which becomes part of the information he or she considers when making investment recommendations.

**financial profile:** an assessment of an investor's assets, liabilities, investment objectives, and willingness to bear risk.

## HOW MUCH RISK AM I WILLING TO ACCEPT?

This is a complex question involving an understanding of the risk-to-reward relationship that is germane to all investing and an understanding of each person's investment temperament. The relationship between risk and reward is direct: the

**cash dividends:** part of a company's after-tax earnings that its board of directors decides, usually quarterly, to distribute to the shareholders.

**capital gain:** the profit that results when the proceeds from the sale of a stock are higher than the stock's cost basis.

**capital appreciation:** an increase in the market value of a stock or the overall market.

**total return:** the yield or percentage return on an investment that considers both the income made from dividends and the capital gains made on the stock's appreciation.

greater the risk, the greater the potential return from the investment; the lower the risk, the lower the return.

There are two types of returns that you can expect from investing in stocks: cash dividends and capital gains. *Cash dividends* are that part of a company's after-tax earnings that management decides to distribute to its stockholders. These payments are **not** automatic or guaranteed. This is true for both common and preferred stocks, as well as high-quality and low-quality stocks (see Chapter 2). A company's board of directors meets regularly (usually quarterly) to decide whether a dividend will be paid and, if so, the amount of it and when it will be paid.

*Capital gains* are the profits made from an increase in the market value of the securities. For the most part, the rise (or fall) of a stock's market value reflects the direct relationship between a company's performance and an investor's desire to own the stock. When investors believe that a company is developing well or is in a good position to do so, they buy the stock, hoping that the price will increase over time. An increase in the market value of a security is also called *capital appreciation*. The combination of the dividend income and the capital appreciation made on an investment constitutes your *total return*.

If you are seeking dividend income or capital gains from stock, you must be willing to accept some of the risks associated with this investment. Remember that all stocks are risky investments—and some are riskier than others. The biggest risk you face is the loss of the capital that you have invested because the company's stock becomes worthless. This is known as "capital risk." This risk is not just one risk; it takes several forms. Each is always present in the marketplace to a greater or lesser degree, depending on the type of stock.

Through *diversification* and *timing*, you can reduce the potential impact of these risks on your investments. The various forms of capital risk are:

**1. Business risk.** The company in whose stock you invest may not generate the sales and earnings growth as expected. Also the management of the company may not be able to bring the company to the next stage of development. As a result, the price of the security may remain low or even fall. At worst, the business may fail, and the stock will be worthless. Business risk plagues both new businesses and old businesses—for example, PanAm, Wang, and U.S. Steel.

**2. Stock-specific risk.** Also known as unsystematic risk, this is the risk associated with "putting all your eggs in one basket." If you buy only one stock—IBM or Philip Morris, for example—and the value of the stock drops 30 percent in one day, then you have lost 30 percent of your capital. You can protect yourself against this type of risk by investing in the stocks of a broad range of companies, industries, or geographical areas or by investing in different types of securities. This is known as diversification. In theory, diversification protects you because when one security's price is falling, another in the portfolio may be rising. The net result is that the two price movements offset each other. For an individual investor trying to accomplish this on his or her own, diversification has its drawbacks. It requires time spent analyzing stocks and actively managing the portfolio and more money spent on transaction fees.

**3. Liquidity or marketability risk.** When you are ready to liquidate or close out a securities position, you may discover that it is difficult to do. There may be too few investors in the market. This is known as a *thin market*. In this situation, you could incur high transaction fees closing out the

**diversification:** investing in different securities, different industries, or a mutual fund portfolio containing various securities in order to diminish the risk associated with investing in too few securities.

**timing:** attempting to buy or sell a security at the optimum moment in its price movement.

**thin market:** also called an illiquid market, a situation in which there are few buyers or sellers of a security and which is characterized by increased price volatility.

**bond:** a long-term debt security issued by a corporation, a municipality, or the U.S. government in which the issuer promises to pay the holder a fixed rate of interest at regular intervals and to repay the face value of the security at maturity.

**yield:** the percentage or rate of return that an investor makes on capital invested in a security or in a portfolio of securities.

position, which in turn would produce a lower-than-expected return or a greater-than-expected loss.

**4. Interest rate risk.** This risk affects all fixed-income securities—preferred stocks and *bonds*. The market price of these securities fluctuates inversely to changes in interest rates. When interest rates fall, the prices of outstanding fixed income securities rise. Conversely, when interest rates rise, the prices of outstanding fixed-income securities fall. The changes result from the forces of supply and demand. Fixed-income investors always seek securities that pay the highest *yield* commensurate with the level of risk they are willing to accept. When interest rates are falling, there will be greater demand for the older, already outstanding securities that pay high dividends or interest. When interest rates are rising, investors want to sell the low-yield securities they own and buy the newer securities that pay the better yield. During periods of interest rate volatility, this risk is most acute. For example, when you purchase a new issue, fixed-rate preferred stock, you run the risk that interest rates may rise shortly after you have bought the issue. The result would be an immediate loss, because the market value of the preferred would decline.

The early 1990s showed that common stock prices can be affected by interest rate changes. During this time interest rates were at an all-time low. Passbook savings accounts were yielding between 2.00 percent and 3.00 percent per year and certificates of deposit (CD) paid only slightly better. Seeking higher yields in exchange for a little more risk, investors transferred their savings and rolled over their CDs into mutual funds. As a result, mutual fund managers had more cash available to invest in securities. This increased demand from the fund managers for shares in which to invest this money as well as to set up new funds drove stock prices higher and higher. If interest rates were to increase, many investors would pull their money out of these mutual funds and invest it in safer instruments, such as CDs. The resulting lower demand for mutual fund shares and the resulting decreased demand for stocks by mutual fund managers could cause common stock prices to decline.

**5. Systematic risk.** Also known as market risk, this is the risk associated with the movement of the overall market. If the entire market declines, as it did on October 19, 1987, the value of all shares in your portfolio will likely decline. Diversification cannot protect you against this risk. *Hedging* is the protective strategy to use. (This is explained more thoroughly in Chapter 8.)

**hedging:** protecting against or limiting losses on an existing stock position or portfolio by establishing an opposite position in the same security.

**6. Inflationary or purchasing power risk.** Inflation erodes the purchasing power of money over time. The great attraction of investing in common stock is that this risk is minimized. Historically, stocks keep pace with inflation better than any other type of securities investment.

**7. Political risk.** This risk is most prominent when investing in the stock of companies located in politically unstable areas, such as Central America and Eastern Europe. Continued instability can severely reduce the productivity of the company whose stock you own. At worst, the country could decide to nationalize all businesses, in which case your investment would be lost.

**8. Taxation risk.** Under current tax laws, dividend income and capital gains on stocks are taxed at the same rate for individual investors. Changes in these rates could change the demand for stocks, making them more or less attractive as investment vehicles.

For a beginning investor, it might seem ironic that for only two potential ways of earning money from stock—dividends and capital gains—there are so many risks. This is why the next step in investment planning is important: Determining your attitude toward your money, in particular your discretionary income. Some individuals do not want to invest in anything where their capital is at risk. Others are all too ready to take unnecessary risks without the opportunity for commensurate rewards. Most people fall somewhere between these two extremes. Once you know your attitude toward your money and understand the risks associated with investing in securities, the next step is setting your investment goal.

My friend's goal of wanting to make his money work for him is far too general. Each investor must have clearly defined objectives before entering the stock market if he or she is to have a reasonable chance of achieving them. The ways that people with virtually the same financial profiles may want their money to work for them are as varied as their individual life-styles and ambitions. For example, a person whose goal is to generate current income from investing may purchase stocks that pay high dividends, such as utilities and blue chips. Another person's goal may be to build a portfolio of securities that will provide income for retirement. This person might invest in stocks whose market values and dividend payments are expected to increase over the long term. A third person may want to speculate in the market, buying and selling stock whose prices fluctuate broadly over the short term. The investment goal is important because it becomes the measure against which the performance of the selected investments is judged.

The most common investment objectives are income, conservative growth, aggressive growth, and speculation.

**Income.** Investors with this goal want to make current income from their investments. Typically, they use this money for some or all of their living expenses. Stocks that provide high dividend income, including high-yielding common and preferred stocks, are suitable for this objective. Most investors automatically assume that this objective is synonymous with conservative, safe investments. This is not necessarily true. Some very risky securities—*junk bonds* (a.k.a. high-yield bonds) or low-quality preferred stock, for example—provide high current income. If you are not interested in these kinds of speculative, income-producing securities, specify preservation of capital as a dual objective. If you want both income and preservation of capital, invest in securities that are relatively secure and stable—that is, those that are free from extreme price *volatility*. Suitable securities are those whose prices are relatively stable but still pay reasonable dividends, such as blue chip companies.

**junk bond:** low-quality (rated BB by Moody's, Ba by S&P, or lower), high-risk long-term debt security. To avoid the negative associations of the word "junk" more and more firms use synonyms such as high-yield bond, non-investment grade bond, and below investment grade bond.

**Conservative Growth.** Investors with this goal seek to build an investment portfolio that will make money over the long term by capital appreciation—hence, the use of the word "growth." Having taken a long-term view, these people do not want too much risk. They should understand that the security may not pay high dividends currently and its price will fluctuate over time. The overall expectation, however, is that the market value of the stock and its dividend payments will increase. This objective is also known as *wealth building*.

**volatility:** the relative amount or percentage by which a stock's price rises and falls during a period of time.

**wealth building:** an investment strategy designed to increase one's net worth over time.

**Aggressive Growth.** Securities that are expected to produce large short-term and long-term capital gains are suitable for investors with this objective. Current income from dividends is of little or no interest, and preservation of capital is a lower priority. Securities suitable for this objective are highly speculative. The high risk could yield high profits—or result in substantial losses.

**Speculation.** This is the objective of a person who buys and sells stocks often solely to profit from short-term price fluctuations. Most beginning investors are encouraged to "invest" in the market rather than speculate. The word "investing" suggests a longer-term view than does "speculation," which implies a total focus on short-term profits. Speculators do not expect to hold the securities for long periods.

Speculators are important to the functions of the market for all investors because their presence increases both the liquidity and efficiency of the market. Another view is that their presence brings undue volatility to the market, pushing stock prices up quickly in response to good news or driving prices down on bad news. Clearly speculation is the riskiest objective you can have.

Understanding your tolerance for risk and setting investment goals appropriate to that tolerance is not a simple task, and it is not static. As your financial means change, you will want to adjust your investment goals.

## ARE STOCKS APPROPRIATE INVESTMENT VEHICLES FOR ME?

In order to answer this question, you must have a basic understanding of the characteristics of stocks, bonds, and other investment instruments. This knowledge, provided in Chapter 2, must go beyond simply being able to compare the characteristics of various instruments. You must also know the alternatives or derivative products (mutual funds, options, and others) through which you can invest in stocks and bonds. And, to restate two points already made, you need a clear understanding of your investment goals and risk tolerance, in light of your age, the amount of money you have in savings, and other characteristics.

It is safe to say that either alone or as part of a portfolio of other securities, stocks can be an appropriate investment vehicle for accomplishing a broad range of investment objectives. However, investing in stocks is not suitable for all people, especially those whose primary objective is preservation of capital. Price fluctuation is an inherent characteristic of these securities. The stocks of even the most stalwart and successful companies (IBM, for example) can be subject to wide price fluctuations—a winner one day, a loser the next. If you do not want your money at risk, you will most likely find the stock market's volatility gut wrenching and will not be able to sleep at all, day or night.

At the other end of the risk spectrum are people who speculate in the stock market. They buy and sell constantly, seeing each rise and fall in a stock's price as an opportunity to make money. For these individuals, the market's volatility is as exhilarating as a ride on a giant roller coaster.

Most investors fall somewhere between these two extremes of the risk spectrum. They are willing to accept a moderate amount of risk in order to get a better-than-average, long-term return on their investment. For these people, investing in stocks is usually part of a mix of other investments—for example, money market or cash-equivalent securities, bonds, real estate, and annuities. Too often this combination of investments is totally arbitrary. Most investors give little thought to how a well-planned mix of investments can enable them to minimize certain risks and optimize their chances of obtaining their investment goals. The planned

**asset allocation:**
the systematic
placement of
investment dollars
into various classes
of investments,
such as stock,
bonds, and cash
equivalents.

and systematic division of money among various types or classes of investments with an eye toward achieving the optimal effective mix given a person's financial objectives is known as *asset allocation.*

Successful asset allocation is not a simple process. Its implementation requires evaluating and analyzing a good deal of information. The explanation presented here is designed to give you an overview and fundamental understanding of the process. At all times, keep in mind that there is neither a perfect asset allocation model for each economic condition nor a common approach to determining the optimal asset mix. The goal here is to present a basic approach that will enable you to understand the importance of asset allocation in your investment decisions.

Figure 1.1 outlines the four basic steps involved in asset allocation, proceeding from the general to the particular. Your first step is to determine the classes of assets in which to invest. By tradition, the three classes of assets usually are: (1) *cash equivalents*, safe, short-term investments such as money market funds and treasury bills; (2) stocks or equity securities; and (3) bonds or fixed-income securities. Other classes, such as fixed blend (listed in Figure 1.3) are created from combinations of the three traditional classes.

**cash equivalents:**
short-term
investments that
are virtually like
cash because of
their high liquidity
and safety.

Step 2 is to determine the amount of money to invest in each class. This decision involves more than assigning various percentages to each class in response to the bullish (buy stock) or bearish (sell stock) sentiments of market strategists. You must research such information as the historical performance of the various classes during certain economic conditions and the risk-to-reward relationship that influences the returns from investments. Always keep in mind the investment objective that the asset mix is designed to achieve.

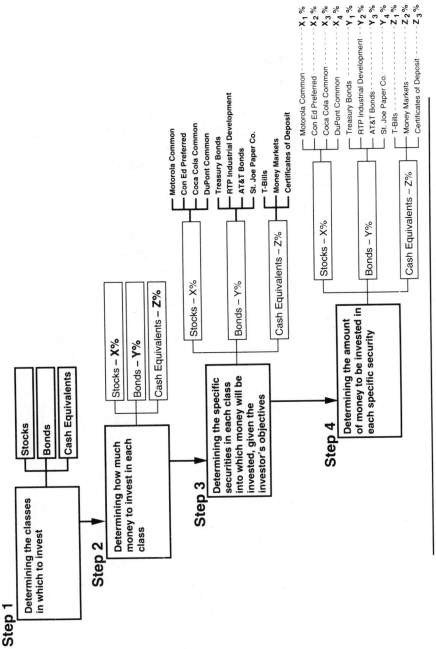

**Figure 1.1.** The four steps of asset allocation.

13

Clearly, there are economic conditions under which stocks will potentially provide greater returns than can be obtained from other investments. During periods when low interest rates result in low returns from fixed-income securities, people tend to invest more of their money in stocks, hoping that the total returns—from both dividends and capital gains—will exceed the returns from bonds. During periods of high inflation, usually characterized by high interest rates, stocks are less attractive investments; fixed-income securities are preferred because their fixed yields are higher.

There is no perfect asset mix for all investors. A "rule of thumb" that many investment advisors recommend investors keep in mind when using flexible asset allocation is that stocks should comprise a percentage of total assets equal to 100 percent *minus* your age. If you are 35 years old, for example, 65 percent of your investment assets should be in stocks or stock mutual funds.

There is also the "traditional and static" asset mix; it consists of 55 percent stocks, 35 percent bonds, and 10 percent cash equivalents. (See Figure 1.2.) The advantage of the static model is that your role in the initial decision-making process is essentially passive. However, you still have to choose the specific stocks, bonds, or mutual funds in each of the asset classes.

During the third quarter of 1993 when interest rates were low, *The Wall Street Journal* published the asset mixes recommended by the investment strategists at 12 brokerage firms. As Figure 1.3 shows, the percentage of assets recommended for stock investments ranged from 80 percent to 50 percent. (The average was approximately 64 percent.)

At step 3 in the asset allocation model (Figure 1.1), you identify the securities that belong in each

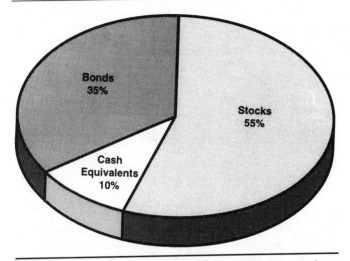

**Figure 1.2.    Traditional static asset allocation mix.**

class. When categorizing equities for this purpose, consider which stocks provide steady dividend income, which ones offer long-term capital appreciation, and which ones offset the risks associated with other types of securities in the mix.

In step 4, you determine the amount of money to allocate to each specific issuer's stocks and bonds.

The information contained in Figure 1.3 stops at the second step. The variations in performance documented in the chart show how choosing the right investments influences the return from each asset mix. At this point, you might wonder which allocation has provided the better performance over time: the traditional, static asset mix or the recommendations of the strategists. According to *The Wall Street Journal*, a majority of strategists' recommendations have always outperformed the traditional mix.

Few individual investors successfully accomplish asset allocation on their own. It is a complex process requiring diligent, careful analysis of fi-

# Who Has the Best Blend?

Performance of asset-allocation blends recommended by 12 brokerage houses in periods ended Sept. 30, 1993. Houses are ranked by 12-month performance. Also shown is the investment mix each house now recommends.

| | PERFORMANCE | | | RECOMMENDED BLEND | | |
|---|---|---|---|---|---|---|
| **BROKERAGE HOUSE** | **THREE MONTHS** | **ONE YEAR** | **FIVE YEARS** | **STOCKS** | **BONDS** | **CASH** |
| Kidder Peabody | 2.8% | **12.6%** | 86.7% | 70% | 30% | 0% |
| PaineWebber | 2.7 | **12.6** | 79.6 | 77 | 22 | 1 |
| Goldman Sachs | 2.7 | **12.3** | 84.6 | 70 | 25 | 5 |
| Dean Witter | 2.5 | **11.6** | 80.3 | 60 | 25 | 15 |
| A.G. Edwards | 2.9 | **11.3** | 75.8 | 65 | 30 | 5 |
| Lehman Brothers | 2.8 | **11.2** | 88.2 | 75 | 25 | 0 |
| Merrill Lynch | 2.6 | **11.2** | 82.2 | 60 | 25 | 15 |
| Smith Barney | 2.6 | **11.0** | 84.7 | 55 | 35 | 10 |
| Salomon | 2.4 | **10.6** | NA | 45 | 30 | 25 |
| Kemper | 2.2 | **10.2** | NA | 50 | 20 | 30 |
| Prudential | 2.4 | **9.8** | 93.7 | 80 | 0 | 20 |
| Raymond James | 2.4 | **9.6** | 76.2 | 60 | 20 | 20 |
| **COMPARISON YARDSTICKS** | | | | | | |
| Fixed blend* | 2.7% | **11.5%** | 83.8% | *Constant mix of 55% stocks, 35% bonds, 10% cash | | |
| Stocks | 2.6 | **13.0** | 98.2 | NA = Not applicable (not in study for full period) | | |
| Bonds | 3.4 | **11.5** | 73.5 | Note: Figures do not include transaction costs. | | |
| Cash | 0.8 | **3.2** | 36.0 | | | |

*Sources: Company documents, calculations by Wilshire Associates*

Figure 1.3.   Asset allocation recommendations from 12 brokerage firms during the third quarter of 1993. Reprinted by permission of *The Wall Street Journal*, © 1993 Dow Jones & Company, Inc. All rights reserved worldwide.

nancial information about the overall economy and the securities of specific companies. Individuals who build their own portfolios sometimes use the services of a professional investment adviser or fi-

Timing must take into account whether an investor's goals are long term or short term. In the first case, timing is a less critical issue. A long-term investor's focus is usually on fundamental factors: the increased value of an investment over time. This individual must understand that reversals are a normal part of the market's cyclical movement and must be prepared to wait them out. When you make long-term investments, avoid emotional, short-term responses to the periodic reversals of the market; otherwise you will lose through higher transaction costs, lost opportunities, and lost profits.

For short-term investors—traders or speculators—timing is everything. The old adage, "He who hesitates is lost," is most applicable. In a volatile market, a delay can quickly turn a gain into a loss—or you can suddenly find yourself on the wrong side of the market. Short-term trading is inappropriate for most beginning investors because commission costs are high and market expertise is critical.

## WHEN AND HOW SHOULD I REEVALUATE MY HOLDINGS AND INVESTMENT STRATEGIES?

The answer to this question depends on whether you are a speculator or a long-term investor. Speculative investing must be monitored closely— weekly, daily, or even hourly. It also requires discipline. The basic philosophy is to cut losses and let profits run. Many speculators and traders set limits—15 percent, 20 percent, or 25 percent—on the amount that the price of a stock can move against them before they liquidate the position. Regardless of any justification that they may have for wanting to hold an unprofitable position, disciplined traders get out of the market at the predetermined loss they are willing to incur on the investment. These investors do not try to recover their losses by waiting for the price of the stock to rebound; they simply cut their losses.

While speculators try to cut their losses quickly, they try not to take their profits too quickly. The old adage about "letting profits run" becomes their guideline. The combination of the two philosophies results in the gains made on the fewer winning positions exceeding the losses on the larger number of unprofitable positions. In fact, historical analysis of speculators' trades has revealed a surprising fact: the number of losing trades often outnumbers the profitable trades. To reiterate a point made earlier, successful speculation requires discipline and is usually not suitable for beginning investors.

Long-term investors must be disciplined in reviewing their financial holdings periodically—at least annually. Too often they relegate this responsibility to their broker, who is generally unaware of significant changes in a client's personal or financial circumstances. Many events can prompt a reevaluation of a person's situation—births, deaths, marriage, divorce, illness, job promotion, loss of job, inheritance, and others. Age is an important consideration, especially if a person believes that investments in equities always outperform other investments over time. The conventional wisdom is that younger investors should place more money in growth-oriented common stocks. (Remember the "rule of thumb" asset allocation mix recommended by many financial advisors: stock should make up a total percentage of your total assets equal to 100 percent *minus* your age.) Investors approaching retirement should shift more investment dollars into stable, income-producing securities. But there are no absolute percentages governing the amount that should be invested in each type of security at different ages.

A reevaluation takes you back to step 1 of the decision process, asking the question, "What are my investment objectives in light of these changes?" Remember that you are not trying to outsmart the market. You are simply refining or redirecting your long-term needs in light of new information. You may discover that your objectives have changed. For example, if there has been a birth in the family, it may be time to start considering long-term investing for the child's education. You may find that the objectives are the same but the portfolio has changed. If you are interested in establishing a portfolio of only blue chip stocks, you may discover that some of the companies' stocks have become speculative due to changes in the economy, increased competition, or changes in the company's management. In this case, it may be time to liquidate certain positions and acquire others. Or you may find that the investment climate has changed. Interest rates may be so low that buying preferred stocks offers no real gain, especially when compared to the rate of inflation. Common stocks, which are less interest rate sensitive, may provide a better total return. An investment review, either regularly or when and if personal or family circumstances change, is essential to achieving your investment goals.

# CHAPTER 2

# Common Stock and Preferred Stock

**equity securities:**
securities representing ownership in a business and the right to receive dividends.

**W**hen you buy a corporation's stock—either common or preferred—you become part owner of that company. This ownership is also referred to as having equity in a company; hence, stocks are called *equity securities*. As an "owner" of the company, you are entitled to share in the company's earnings through dividend payments and to benefit from the company's growth through the increase in the market value of the stock you own.

The percentage or proportion of this ownership depends on how many of the company's shares you own. If, for example, the company has 100,000 shares outstanding and you own 1000 of them, then you are a 1.0 percent (1000/100,000) shareholder of that company. If another investor owns 5000 of the same company's outstanding shares, that person owns 5.0 percent (5000/100,000) of the company.

Bonds, in contrast, do not represent ownership in a company. When you buy a corporation's bond, you become a creditor of the company, in effect, loaning money to the company by purchasing the bond. The company, in turn, promises to pay you interest on this loan at regular intervals—usually semiannually. The company also agrees to repay the principal or face value of the bond at a designated date in the future when the bond matures. At this time, all interest payments stop. Bonds, therefore, have a fixed term. Stocks, on the other hand, have an indefinite life, and dividend payments can continue for as long as you own the stock.

A company issues either stocks or bonds when it wishes to raise capital from public investors. This new money is usually earmarked for specific purposes, such as the research and development of new products, building new plants, acquiring new equipment, increasing production, or improving and developing new product distribution and sales systems. The decision to issue either stocks or bonds depends on the financial condition of the company and the general economy at the time. Some factors typically considered are the cost of borrowing money (interest rates), the amount of debt that the company is already carrying, and, especially for stock, the amount of control that the owner or board of directors of the company is willing to relinquish in exchange for the capital it receives from investors. A company that chooses to issue an equity security issues common stock first because this security is part of each company's capitalization.

## COMMON STOCK

*Common stock* is the most widely traded of all corporate securities. It offers investors great liquidity. On the New York Stock Exchange (NYSE), an average of 330 million shares are traded each day. On NASDAQ, the average daily trading volume is about 320 million. This trading volume is made possible by two factors: the public's demand for

**common stock:** an equity security that usually gives the holder the right to receive dividends and vote on company issues.

common stock and one of the primary characteristics of common stock, the ease with which ownership can be transferred from one investor to another.

In the United States, each publicly traded incorporated business is required to declare at least one class of common shares as part of its initial *capitalization*. The number of common shares is usually specified in the incorporation documents that the company files with a division of the Secretary of State's office. Once the business is incorporated, these shares are referred to as *authorized shares*. At this point, these shares have not been issued and do not trade. Only after they have been registered with the Securities and Exchange Commission and then distributed or sold to the public are these shares considered to be *issued and outstanding* and can then trade in the market.

**capitalization:** that part of a company's funds raised by issuing stocks and bonds.

**authorized shares:** the maximum number of common and preferred shares that a company is authorized to issue by its corporate charter.

**issued and outstanding:** authorized shares that have been distributed to investors and that may trade in the market.

## Rights of Common Stockholders

Common shareholders are granted certain rights or privileges by the issuing corporation. Many of these benefits, along with ease of transferability, make common stock an attractive investment.

### Right to Receive Dividends

All common shareholders have the right to receive dividends. These dividends are usually paid quarterly in cash, although a company may choose to pay a stock dividend, giving investors additional shares in the company in lieu of cash. A company does not pay dividends automatically. All dividends must be declared by the company's board of directors. A company is not required to pay dividends regularly in the same way that it is legally required to pay interest on bonds regularly. If the board decides not to declare a dividend, the common shareholders receive nothing during that quarter. Common stockholders cannot demand dividend payments even when the company is profitable.

Cash dividends are declared from the earnings that remain after the company has paid the required interest on any outstanding bonds, paid its taxes, and paid dividends on its preferred shares (if any of these securities are outstanding). The amount or percentage of these earnings that is paid out to common shareholders depends on the company's cash reserves, its needs, its reputation, and the philosophy of the board of directors regarding dividend payments. Older, more mature companies—those whose shares are called *blue chip* or *income stocks* such as Exxon, AT&T, General Electric, and Dow Chemical—and utilities tend to make regular and substantial dividend payments, partly because these companies have established a reputation for such payments. The main reason, however, is that as mature, well-established companies, the price of their stock tends to remain relatively stable, offering potential investors little opportunity for capital appreciation. These companies make their common stock attractive by providing investors with substantial current income through dividend payments.

Companies in new, expanding industries—those whose shares are called *growth stock*, such as Amgen, a biotechnology stock—usually pay low dividends—if they pay any at all. These companies typically retain the earnings that would be paid to common stockholders as dividends and reinvest them in the company, usually in research and development. As the company grows and becomes more profitable, the market price of its stock generally increases, benefiting stockholders. Overall, growth stocks tend to increase in price faster than income stocks—sometimes two or three times as fast. Investors interested in capital appreciation find growth stocks attractive.

**blue chip stock:** the shares of stable, profitable, and well-known public companies that have a long history of growth and dividend payments.

**income stock:** the shares of companies that make regular and substantial dividend payments to investors.

**growth stock:** stocks of new, expanding companies whose market values are expected to appreciate rapidly.

Some significant risks are associated with investing in growth stocks. Although their prices tend to rise faster than those of income stocks, they also tend to decrease faster, thereby increasing investors' chances of losing money. And because growth stocks pay little or no dividends, investors must be aware of the amount of time that their capital will have to remain invested in the company in order to achieve the desired price appreciation. During this time, investors receive little, if any, current income from the investment.

A company's board of directors may choose to pay a stock dividend instead of a cash dividend. This decision allows the company to save the cash or earnings that would have been used to pay the dividends.

A stock dividend may not satisfy the needs of persons seeking current income from their investment in common stock, but there are certain benefits to investors. First, stock dividends are not taxed at the time they are distributed. You pay taxes only after the stock is sold, which may be years after the date you received it. In contrast, you must pay tax on cash dividends in the year the company pays them. Second, as a result of a stock dividend, you own more of the company's shares at a lower *cost basis* per share.

**cost basis:** the price, for tax purposes, paid for a security, including commissions and markups.

To demonstrate this point, we use an illustration of a Corporate Dividend News table: (Figure 2.1). In the section of Figure 2.1 marked "Stock," Washington Federal Savings and Loan has declared a 10 percent stock dividend payable to all common shareholders. Let's consider an investor who already owns 100 shares that were purchased at $22 per share. (The total value of the investment is $2200.) After the stock dividend is paid, the investor will own 110 shares of Washington Federal Savings and Loan (10 percent more than before). Her cost basis for tax purposes will now be $20 per share. This new cost basis is computed by taking the total value of the original investment ($2200) and dividing it by the total number of shares the stockholder will own after the stock dividend. The stock will now provide a gain if the investor sells it at any price higher than $20 per share, the new cost basis.

Stock dividends have one particularly confusing feature that must be clarified. While a stock dividend results in an investor's owning more shares of a company's outstanding stock, the percentage of the total outstanding shares that the individual owns remains exactly the same. Each stockholder receives the same dividend percentage; however, the actual number of shares received depends on the amount of stock the individual owned when the dividend was paid. Continuing with the example, if another investor owns 1000 shares of Washington Federal Savings and Loan, he will receive 100 additional shares through the stock dividend. Each investor simply owns the same proportion of a larger number of outstanding shares.

Many investors are confused about when they must own the stock in order to be eligible to receive a cash or stock dividend. Four key dates must be understood in order to clarify this confusion; in chronological order, they are the declaration date, the ex-dividend date, the record date, and the payable date. Investors generally become aware of them in a slightly different order.

The *declaration date* is the day that the decision of the company's board of directors is announced to the public. This announcement notes the frequency with which it is paid ("Q" in Figure 2.1 stands for "quarterly"), the amount of the dividend that will be paid, the payable date, and the record date. All of these items are set by the corporation's board of directors.

The *payable date* is the date that the corporation

**declaration date:** the day that the board of directors announces the terms and amount of a dividend payment.

**payable date:** the date on which the cash or stock is paid to the investor who purchased the stock before the ex-dividend date.

# Dividends Reported January 20

## REGULAR

| Company | Period | Amt. | Payable date | Record date |
|---|---|---|---|---|
| Anchor BanCorp Wis | Q | .06 | 2-15-94 | 2- 1 |
| Arco Chemical Co | Q | .62½ | 3- 4-94 | 2-11 |
| ArizonaPubS pfW | Q | .453⅛ | 3- 1-94 | 2- 1 |
| ArizonaPubS adjpfQ | Q | 1.50 | 3- 1-94 | 2- 1 |
| Bear Stearns Cos | Q | .15 | 2-25-94 | 2-11 |
| Bear Stearns depB | Q | .49¼ | 4-15-94 | 3-31 |
| Bear Stearns depC | Q | .47½ | 4-15-94 | 3-31 |
| BearStearns adjpfA | Q | .68¾ | 4-15-94 | 3-31 |
| Bearings Inc | Q | .16 | 3- 1-94 | 2-15 |
| Burlington North | Q | .30 | 4- 1-94 | 3- 9 |
| Burlington No pfA | Q | .78⅛ | 4- 1-94 | 3- 9 |
| Capital Bancorp | Q | .17 | 2- 3-94 | 1-27 |
| Capital Bcp depshs | Q | .48¾ | 3- 1-94 | 2-22 |
| Carter-Wallace | Q | .0833 | 3- 7-94 | 2-11 |
| Century Bncrp clA | Q | .02½ | 2-15-94 | 2- 1 |
| F&C Bancshares | Q | .15 | 2-14-94 | 2- 4 |
| Fidelity Bancorp | Q | .07 | 2-10-94 | 2- 3 |
| 1stCommBcshs A | Q | .054 | 3-15-94 | 2-28 |
| 1st Intrst Bncp | Q | .50 | 2-25-94 | 2- 7 |
| Hilton Hotels | Q | .30 | 3-18-94 | 3- 4 |
| Kasler Hldg | S | .05 | 2-15-94 | 1-31 |
| Keystone Heritage | Q | .26 | 2-10-94 | 1-31 |
| McDonald's depshE | Q | .48¼ | p3- 1-94 | p2-14 |
| p-Corrected record and payable dates. | | | | |
| NrthwstNaturalGas | Q | .44 | 2-15-94 | 1-31 |
| Nthwest Nat Gas pf | Q | .59⅜ | 2-15-94 | 1-31 |
| Ogden Corp | Q | .31¼ | 4- 4-94 | 3-14 |
| Ogden Corp pfA | Q | .8376 | 3-29-94 | 3-14 |
| PPG Industries | Q | .54 | 3-11-94 | 2-22 |
| Pet Inc | Q | .08 | 4- 1-94 | 3-17 |
| Pitt-DesMoines Inc | Q | .22½ | 3-25-94 | 3-11 |
| Ply-Gem Indus | Q | .03 | 3- 4-94 | 2-10 |
| Providence F ⌐rgy | Q | .26 | 2-15-94 | 2- 4 |
| Quality Foo⌐ ⌐entr | Q | .05 | 2-18-94 | 1-28 |
| RJR Nabisco deppfA | Q | .20⅞ | 2-15-94 | 1-31 |
| RJR Nabisco deppfB | Q | .578⅛ | 3- 1-94 | 2-14 |
| RepubNY $1.9375pf | Q | .484⅜ | 4- 1-94 | 3-15 |
| RepublicNY$3.375pf | Q | .84⅜ | 4- 1-94 | 3-15 |
| Republic NY pfB | Q | .81¼ | 4- 1-94 | 3-15 |
| Security Svgs Bk | Q | .06 | 2-11-94 | 1-28 |
| Smith(AO) Corp | Q | .11 | 2-15-94 | 1-31 |
| Smith(AO) clA | Q | .11 | 2-15-94 | 1-31 |
| SouthCalEd 4.08%pf | Q | .25½ | 2-28-94 | 2- 4 |
| SouthCalEd 4.24%pf | Q | .26½ | 2-28-94 | 2- 4 |
| SouthCalEd 4.78%pf | Q | .29⅞ | 2-28-94 | 2- 4 |
| SouthCalEd 5.80%pf | Q | .36¼ | 2-28-94 | 2- 4 |
| Southwest Airlines | Q | .01 | 3-28-94 | 3- 4 |
| Southwest National | Q | .31 | 3-10-94 | 2-10 |
| Standard Fedl Bk | Q | .14 | 3- 1-94 | 2-15 |
| Susquehanna Bcsh | Q | .25 | 2-22-94 | 1-31 |
| Thiokol Corp | Q | .17 | 3-14-94 | 2-28 |
| Tidewater Inc | Q | .10 | 2-17-94 | 2- 3 |
| Time Warner Inc | Q | .08 | 3-15-94 | 3- 1 |
| Unifi Inc | Q | .14 | 2-10-94 | 2- 3 |
| Union Planters pfC | Q | .648438 | 12-15-94 | 2- 1 |
| Union Planters pfE | Q | .50 | 2-15-94 | 2- 1 |
| Utd Mobile Homes | Q | .10 | 3-15-94 | 2-15 |
| Univar Corp | Q | .07½ | 3- 1-94 | 2- 7 |
| Valero Energy | Q | .13 | 3- 9-94 | 1-31 |
| Wilmington Trust | Q | .25 | 2-15-94 | 2- 1 |

## IRREGULAR

| Company | Period | Amount | Payable date | Record date |
|---|---|---|---|---|
| Andover Bancorp | - | .10 | 2-14-94 | 1-31 |
| Co-Op Bank Concord | - | .05 | 2-15-94 | 1-31 |
| Courier Corp | - | .05 | 3- 4-94 | 2-18 |
| 1stCommerceBncsh B | - | .054 | 3-15-94 | 2-28 |
| Heritage Fed Bncsh | - | .11 | 2-25-94 | 2- 4 |
| Pinnacle West Cap | - | .20 | 3- 1-94 | 2- 1 |
| RFS Hotel Investrs | - | .23 | 2-15-94 | 1-31 |

## FUNDS · REITS · INVESTMENT COS · LPS

| Company | Period | Amount | Payable date | Record date |
|---|---|---|---|---|
| ColonialHiIncoMuni | M | .05¼ | 2-18-94 | 1-31 |
| Colonial Interm Hi | M | .058 | 2-11-94 | 1-31 |
| Colonial Muni Inco | M | .051½ | 2-18-94 | 1-31 |
| Ellsworth Convert | Q | .12½ | 2-21-94 | 2- 7 |
| First Boston Inco | M | .06 | 2-15-94 | 2- 1 |
| First Boston Strat | M | .06¾ | 2-15-94 | 2- 1 |
| KleinwrtBenAusInco | M | h.06 | 2-15-94 | 2- 3 |
| Mesa Offshore Tr | Q | h.012103 | 4-29-94 | 1-31 |
| Mesabi Trust | Q | .10 | 2-20-94 | 1-30 |
| Monmouth REIT | Q | .12½ | 3-15-94 | 2-15 |
| Sentinel Bond Fd | M | h.033 | 1-31-94 | 1-24 |
| Sentinel Govt Secs | M | h.04½ | 1-31-94 | 1-24 |
| Sentinel PA TxFr | M | h.053 | 1-31-94 | 1-24 |
| Sentinel Tax Free | M | h.05½ | 1-31-94 | 1-24 |
| Town & Country Tr | Q | .40 | 3- 1-94 | 2-10 |

## STOCK

| Company | Period | Amount | Payable date | Record date |
|---|---|---|---|---|
| Electro Rent Corp | | rr | 2-25-94 | 2- 7 |
| rr-Three-for-two stock split. | | | | |
| WashingtonFedl S&L | | 10% | 2-18-94 | 2- 1 |

## INCREASED

| Company | Period | New | Old | Payable date | Record date |
|---|---|---|---|---|---|
| BergenBrunswig clA | Q | .12 | .10 | 3- 3-94 | 2- 3 |
| Bryn Mawr Bank | Q | .15 | .10 | 3- 1-94 | 2- 4 |
| FamilyDollar Store | Q | .08½ | .07½ | 4-15-94 | 3-15 |
| 1st Alabama Bncshs | Q | .30 | .26 | 4- 1-94 | 3-17 |
| 1st Fed S&L E Hart | Q | .12 | .11 | 2-10-94 | 2- 3 |
| FirstFidelityBncp | Q | .42 | .37 | 2- 8-94 | 1-31 |
| Gallagher (AJ)&Co | Q | .22 | .18 | 4-15-94 | 3-31 |
| Massbank Corp | Q | .21 | .18 | 2-15-94 | 1-31 |
| Oneok Inc | Q | .28 | .27 | 2-15-94 | 1-31 |
| Pacific Gas & El | Q | .49 | .47 | 4-15-94 | 3-15 |
| Pinnacle Banc Grp | Q | .27 | .24 | 2-10-94 | 1-31 |
| Provident Bkshrs | Q | .09 | .08 | 2-11-94 | 1-31 |
| Republic NY Corp | Q | .33 | .27 | 4- 1-94 | 3-15 |
| Society Corp | Q | .32 | .28 | 3-15-94 | 2-28 |
| Sterling Bncsh Inc | Q | .10 | .09 | 2- 8-94 | 2- 1 |
| Union Planters | Q | .21 | .18 | 2-18-94 | 2- 4 |
| Watts Indus clA | Q | .11 | .09 | 3-15-94 | 3- 1 |

## FOREIGN

| Company | Period | Amount | Payable date | Record date |
|---|---|---|---|---|
| Tomkins PLC ADR | - | t.15½ | 4-18-94 | 2- 4 |

## LIQUIDATION

| Company | Period | Amount | Payable date | Record date |
|---|---|---|---|---|
| Natl Loan Bk | - | n.15½ | 2-15-94 | 2- 1 |
| n-Final liquidating distribution. | | | | |

## INITIAL

| Company | Period | Amount | Payable date | Record date |
|---|---|---|---|---|
| Allied Bnkshrs new | Q | .10 | 3- 1-94 | 2-11 |
| First USA new | Q | .02 | 2-10-94 | 1-31 |
| Network Imag pfA | - | r.26301 | 1-31-94 | 1-24 |
| r-Revised amount. | | | | |

A-Annual; b-Payable in Canadian funds; h-From Income; k-From capital gains; M-Monthly; Q-Quarterly; S-Semi-annual; t-Approximate U.S. dollar amount per American Depositary Receipt/Share.

\* \* \*

## Stocks Ex-Dividend January 24

| Company | Amount | Company | Amount |
|---|---|---|---|
| Aetna Life & Cas | .69 | Ford Motor depshs | 1.05 |
| Ameritech Corp | yy | Ford Motor depsh B | .515⅜ |
| yy-Two-for-one stock split. | | Genl Pub PLC | .42½ |
| Amway Asia Pac | .16 | Grand Metro PLC | t.599 |
| Boddie-Noell Rest | .31 | MuniYield AZ II | ¡22773 |
| BordenChem&Plas un | .18 | NBB Bancorp | .30 |
| CIM Hi Yld Secs | .07 | Nova Corp Alberta | b.06 |
| Cigna Hi Inco Shrs | .07½ | b-Canadian funds. | |
| Citicorp ser14 dep | .56¾ | Pall Corp | .09¼ |
| Citicorp ser16 dep | .50 | Phillips Gas pfA | .58¼ |
| Citicorp ser17 dep | .469 | Sysco Corp | .09 |
| Citicorp adj pf9 | .57 | Texaco Capitl MIPS | .143229 |
| Clorox Co | .45 | Weyerhaeuser Co | .30 |
| CompTelefChile ADR | t.4546 | | |
| EnrCpLLC8%MIPS | .166667 | t-Approximate U.S. dollar amount per American Depositary Receipt Share. | |
| Fluke Corp | .13 | | |
| Ford Motor Co | .40 | | |

---

**Figure 2.1.** Corporate Dividend News published daily in *The Wall Street Journal*. Reprinted by permission of *The Wall Street Journal*, © 1994 Dow Jones & Company, Inc. All rights reserved worldwide.

will pay the dividend to shareholders who are entitled to receive it. Typically, a shareholder receives the dividend check on the payable day. The *record date* is, in lay terms, the cutoff date that the company sets to determine who is eligible to receive the dividend. In short, an investor who owns the stock as of this date will receive the dividend. The list of eligible stockholders is compiled by the *registrar*, who is responsible for maintaining a complete and accurate record of who owns a company's stock, including names and addresses. When the record date is announced, the company instructs its registrar to compile a list of all individuals who own the common stock at the close of business on the record date. These persons, usually referred to as *holders of record*, are eligible to receive the dividend when it is paid. (A company can act as its own transfer agent, or it can hire an outside firm.)

Logically, there must be a date in the schedule on or after which a person buying the stock will not be eligible to receive the dividend. And logically, this date must be before the record date. This date is known as the *ex-dividend date*. (See the bottom section of Figure 2.1.) It is the first date that anyone buying the stock will not be eligible to receive the dividend that has been declared. In effect, the stock is now trading without ("*ex*" in Latin) the dividend. This date is not set by the company. It is set by the stock exchange for securities that trade there or by the National Association of Securities Dealers for stocks that trade in the over-the-counter market.

## Voting Rights

Common stock is sometimes referred to as voting stock because the right to vote is traditionally a characteristic of this security. Because of this right,

**record date:** the deadline date, set by the board of directors, on which an investor must be recorded as an owner of the stock in order to be eligible to receive the dividend payment.

**registrar:** a firm, usually a commercial bank appointed by the issuer of a security, that is responsible for keeping an accurate list of all stockholders' names and addresses.

**holder of record:** the person whose name appears as the owner of the security on the company's records, usually as of the record date.

**ex-dividend date:** the day, set by the National Association of Securities Dealers, or an exchange, that the bid price of the stock is reduced by the dividend amount. Anyone purchasing the stock on that day or later will be ineligible to receive the cash dividend.

**proxy:** a form by which an investor votes *in absentia* by transferring voting authority to another party.

**statutory voting method:** a procedure whereby a shareholder must divide his or her total votes equally among the directorships being decided; the standard voting method in most corporations.

**cumulative voting method:** a procedure whereby a shareholder can place his or her votes on directorships in any combination he or she chooses.

common stockholders have the greatest control over the management and policies of a company. They decide a broad range of issues, including changes in the corporate charter, the authorization or issuance of new stock, reorganizations, mergers, and, perhaps most important, the election of the company's board of directors, which is responsible for setting the management direction of the company, reviewing overall performance, and determining the dividend that the company will pay to its common stockholders.

Most elections and policy decisions occur at the company's annual meeting, which most investors do not attend. As a result, most shareholders vote by *proxy*. When it is time for the shareholders to vote, the company that issued the common stock sends proxy materials—a voting card and information about the persons nominated to directorships or about the issues being decided—to either the customer (if the stock is held in the customer's name) or the brokerage firm (if the stock is held in "street name"—the name of the brokerage firm holding it on the customer's behalf). In the latter case, the broker distributes the proxy materials to the customer who, in turn, checks his or her choices, signs the proxy form, and returns it to the firm, which places votes in accordance with each customer's choices. If the customer does not return the proxy, the brokerage firm will usually vote in accordance with the recommendations of the current management.

Two methods of voting are available to common shareholders: the *statutory method* and the *cumulative method*. A company's charter decides which method will be used before the shares are sold or distributed to the public.

In order to understand the difference between the two methods, consider the following scenario. There are three positions open on a company's board of directors, and 10 people are running for these positions. You own 100 shares. Under the statutory voting method, you can cast 100 votes for each of the positions being decided. You must choose three candidates and cast 100 votes for each of those three. This is the only way you can cast your votes. You cannot pool the votes, casting all 300 for one candidate; nor can you split your votes, giving 50 votes to one candidate, 250 to a second candidate, and none to the third. This method, the oldest and the more common, clearly gives control to stockholders in direct proportion to the amount of stock they own.

Under the cumulative voting method in the same situation (you own 100 shares and are voting in an election for three positions on the board of directors), you can pool or split your votes as you wish. You can cast all 300 votes for one candidate, 150 votes for two of the candidates, or 200 for one candidate and 100 for another. But you are limited to casting your votes for the number of positions being decided.

Clearly the cumulative voting method is advantageous to small shareholders. By banding together and agreeing to place all of their votes behind one individual, for example, small shareholders have a better chance of electing someone to the board of directors who represents or is sympathetic to their interests and concerns. Under the statutory method, the people owning the most shares—usually family members and their handpicked board members—control the company. Exactly the same voting methods are used to decide issues involving the firm's management, such as whether the company should issue new shares or split its stock.

The right to vote can be banded together in another way called a *voting trust*. This is usually established when a company has been in financial difficulty for a period of time and board members want to concentrate voting power so that they can

**voting trust:** a trust, usually having a maximum life of 10 years, established to control the voting shares of a corporation.

make changes in corporate policy quickly. The board sets up a voting trust at a commercial bank and asks common stockholders to deposit their shares into the trust. The bank serves as the trustee of the account. In exchange for each common share deposited in the account, the bank issues a *voting trust certificate* (VTC) to each shareholder that gives the holder all the rights and privileges of a common stockholder except the right to vote. This privilege now belongs to the trust, which is controlled by the board of directors.

**voting trust certificate (VTC):** negotiable certificates showing that common shares have been deposited into a voting trust and that shareholders have forfeited their right to vote.

Voting trusts are established for a fixed period of time—anywhere from 5 to 10 years. Once investors deposit shares into a voting trust, they cannot withdraw them until the trust is dissolved. This restriction does not adversely affect the marketability of the voting trust certificates. They have the same liquidity and ease of transferability that the common shares have. If investors did not deposit all of the shares into the voting trust, then a broker must be careful when purchasing the company stock for a customer to determine if the customer wants to buy the common stock or the voting trust certificates.

### Right to Maintain Proportionate Ownership in the Company

**preemptive right:** an entitlement giving existing stockholders the right to purchase a proportional amount of new common shares before they are offered to other investors.

Under many companies' charters, existing common stockholders have the right to maintain their proportionate ownership of the outstanding stock when new shares are issued. If, for example, you own 10 percent of a company's outstanding common shares and the company issues 500,000 additional shares, you automatically have the right to purchase 10 percent, or 50,000, of the new shares. This privilege is known as the *preemptive right*. Under its terms, a company must offer all new common shares to existing stockholders first. The distribution to existing stockholders of the privilege to purchase these additional shares is handled through a process known as a *rights offering*, which is discussed in detail in Chapter 8.

### Limited Liability and Last Claim to the Company's Assets in a Liquidation

If a company in which you own stock goes bankrupt or the investment proves bad, your total loss as a common stockholder is limited to the amount that you paid for the security. Neither the corporation, the banks from which it borrowed money, the companies to which it owes money, nor the bondholders have any claims on your personal assets.

Additionally, if a company goes bankrupt, you have a claim against the company's remaining assets; however, yours is the last behind all other types of securities and creditors. The priority of claims when a company is dissolved are:

**1.** Wages and taxes
**2.** Secured bondholders
**3.** General creditors and unsecured bondholders
**4.** Preferred stockholders
**5.** Common stockholders

In practical terms, there are usually no assets left when the common stockholders' claims are finally reached.

## Valuation of Common Stock

Two terms—*par value* and *market value*—often confuse new investors as to the "real" value of common stock. The par value of common stock is set at the time the company files its incorporation papers or the stock is authorized. It is an arbitrary value

**rights offering:** an offering of new shares to existing shareholders. The method and terms by which preemptive rights are distributed to existing shareholders are explained in the prospectus that accompanies the offering.

**par value:** for common stock, an arbitrary value assigned to the stock at the time it is issued.

**market value:** the price of a stock determined by the forces of supply and demand in the marketplace.

that is of virtually no importance to investors. Originally, it represented the value of the company's assets underlying each share. Today, par value serves some bookkeeping purposes for the issuing company. For example, some states' incorporation fees are based on this value. To avoid excessive fees, a company puts a low par value or even no par value on its stock. Both Exxon and McDonald's common shares, for example, have no par value. Therefore, the par value of common stock has no relation to a stock's issue price, potential earnings, dividend policy, or market value.

The public offering price of a new issue of common stock is set by the underwriter who helps the company price the issue and sell it to the public. In setting the price of a new issue, the underwriter considers the amount of capital that the company wishes to raise, the number of shares being offered to the public, the company's earnings record, and the anticipated dividends, as well as the price and earnings of the stock of similar companies. It also considers the indications of interest that it receives from sending out a preliminary prospectus, or *red herring*, for the issue.

**red herring:** jargon for the preliminary prospectus, which is often used to get an indication of the public's interest in a security before the price is set and the security is issued.

Throughout the underwriting process, the investment banker does a delicate balancing act. At the same time that the underwriter wants to get the issuer the maximum proceeds or capital from the sale of the new issue, the firm also wants to establish an offering price that is attractive to investors, thereby achieving the complete sale of the issue. Often, the public offering price of a new issue is established as much by the underwriter's considerable intuitive judgment, based on the information and facts it is evaluating, as by hard financial data.

Once underwriter and issuer have sold the new shares to the public at the offering price, their market value in the secondary or aftermarket is determined totally by the forces of supply and demand.

Hence, it changes constantly. If investors lose confidence in a stock due to reduced dividends or poor sales and begin to sell it, the market price will decline. Conversely, if they view the stock favorably and start to buy it, the price will rise.

There are actions that companies can legally take to influence the value of their stock in the secondary market. If a company feels the price of its stock is too high and wants to increase the marketability of its shares to investors in a broader economic range, it may initiate a *stock split*. In 1992, Coca-Cola announced a two-for-one stock split. Its stock was trading at approximately $82¾ per share. An investor owning 100 shares (total value $8275) before the split owned 200 afterward. The share would have an adjusted market value of approximately $41⅜ per share ($82¾ ÷ 2). For shareholders, there is no change in the total value of their investment in the company or in the percentage of ownership in the company's stock. Each investor's equity is simply spread over more shares.

**stock split:** an increase or decrease in the number of a company's authorized shares that results in no change in the total value of the investor's holdings.

The overall impact of a stock split is usually beneficial to shareholders because this action tends to be viewed positively by the market. First, the company's board of directors often increases the amount of the dividend per share, thereby increasing investors' yield or return on the investment. Second, the stock's lower price tends to increase demand for the security because it is now affordable for a larger pool of investors.

The type of stock split just described is called a "positive stock split" and is used more frequently by companies than a "negative" or "reverse stock split," in which the company reduces the number of shares outstanding—for example, a one-for-two stock split. A company takes this action when the price of its shares is too low, and it is in danger of being delisted by a stock exchange.

Another action that a company may take to in-

**tender offer:** a limited-time offer by a company to purchase its own shares or another company's outstanding shares, usually at a premium to their current market value.

**treasury stock:** stock that has been repurchased by the corporation that issued it.

fluence the price of its stock in the market is to buy back stock that it has already issued to the public. It can repurchase the stock through a *tender offer*— a formal offer to purchase stock from investors at a fixed price (usually the current market price)—or it can buy its stock in the open market. The stock that the company buys back after it has already been issued is called *treasury stock*. It is no longer part of the company's issued-and-outstanding shares and therefore has none of the rights and privileges of such shares. Treasury stock receives no dividends, has no voting rights, has no preemptive rights, and is not considered when the company calculates its earnings per share.

Most investors are unaware of the existence of treasury stock; however, it can have an impact on the return on their investment. By repurchasing its own stock in the open market, a company reduces the number of shares outstanding. Hence, dividends are spread over fewer shares, resulting in an increased return for investors.

What does a corporation do with the shares of treasury stock? It may simply hold them. After repurchasing them at a relatively low market price, it may hold them for a while before reissuing them to the public at a higher price in order to raise additional capital. It may distribute the treasury stock to key employees as part of their bonus plan or to any employee as part of the company's employee stock option plan (ESOP). Once distributed, these shares again become part of the company's issued-and-outstanding common stock, receiving all the benefits and privileges of such stock.

## Classes of Common Stock

All incorporated businesses are required to issue at least one class of common stock; traditionally these

**NEW YORK STOCK EXCHANGE**

| 52 Weeks Hi | Lo | Stock | Sym | Div | Yld % | PE | Vol 100s | Hi | Lo | Close | Net Chg |
|---|---|---|---|---|---|---|---|---|---|---|---|
| 75 1/2 | 50 | GenElec | GE | 2.04 | 3.1 | 14 | 8931 | 67 5/8 | 66 5/8 | 66 7/8 | + 5/8 |
| 8 5/8 | 3 7/8 | GenHost | GH | .34 | 5.0 | 32 | 114 | 6 3/4 | 6 5/8 | 6 3/4 | ... |
| 16 1/8 | 7 3/4 | GenHouse | GHW | .32 | 2.0 | 12 | 64 | 15 7/8 | 15 1/2 | 15 7/8 | + 3/8 |
| 57 3/4 | 35 3/8 | GenMills | GIS | 1.28 | 2.2 | 21 | 1836 | 57 3/8 | 56 1/4 | 57 1/8 | + 1/2 |
| 50 1/2 | 30 3/8 | GenMotor | GM | 1.60 | 4.2 | ... | 8471 | 38 1/8 | 37 1/2 | 37 3/4 | + 1/4 |
| 45 7/8 | 40 3/4 | GenMotor pf | | 3.75 | 8.4 | ... | X8 | 45 | 43 3/4 | 44 1/2 | + 1/4 |
| 60 1/4 | 55 | GenMotor pf | | 5.00 | 8.6 | ... | X3 | 58 1/4 | 58 1/4 | 58 1/4 | - 1/2 |
| 47 | 27 7/8 | GenMotor E | GME | .64 | 1.6 | 20 | 2461 | 41 | 39 3/4 | 40 3/4 | +1 |
| 82 5/8 | 82 1/8 | GenMotor E pf | | ... | ... | | 1473 | 83 1/4 | 80 3/4 | 83 | + 7/8 |
| 23 5/8 | 16 1/4 | GenMotor H | GMH | .72 | 3.7 | 11 | 58 | 19 3/4 | 19 3/8 | 19 1/2 | ... |
| 47 7/8 | 38 1/2 | GenPubUtil | GPU | 2.60 | 5.3 | 10 | 550 | 48 5/8 | 47 7/8 | 48 5/8 | + 7/8 |
| 99 7/8 | 69 | GenRe | GRN | 1.68 | 1.8 | 14 | 1416 | 95 1/4 | 92 3/8 | 95 1/4 | +31/8 |
| 59 3/8 | 31 3/8 | GenSignl | GSX | 1.80 | 4.5 | ... | 282 | 40 3/4 | 39 7/8 | 40 1/8 | + 1/8 |
| 6 7/8 | 3 | Genesco | GCO | | ... | 100 | 847 | 4 | 3 7/8 | 4 | ... |
| 14 3/4 | 8 | GenevaSteel | GNV | | ... | 5 | 133 | 13 3/8 | 13 3/8 | 13 3/8 | − 1/8 |
| 5 1/4 | 1 1/2 | GenRad | GEN | | ... | ... | 139 | 2 7/8 | 2 5/8 | 2 5/8 | − 1/4 |
| 42 3/8 | 33 1/8 | GenuinePart | GPC | 1.45 | 3.6 | 15 | 535 | 40 5/8 | 40 | 40 1/8 | + 1/8 |
| 16 3/8 | 4 7/8 | GeorgiaGulf | GGC | | ... | 5 | 1650 | 15 1/4 | 14 7/8 | 15 | −1/8 |
| 48 1/2 | 25 3/8 | GenPacific | GP | 1.60 | 3.7 | 10 | 1995 | 43 1/4 | 42 3/8 | 42 3/4 | − 1/2 |
| 5 | 1 1/8 | FlowInt | FLOW | | ... | 14 | 87 | 2 9/16 | 2 3/8 | 2 3/8 | ... |
| 14 | 5 7/8 | FlowMole | MOLE | | ... | 23 | 2351 | 14 3/4 | 14 | 14 5/8 | + 7/8 |
| 17 | 11 1/8 | FoodLion A | FDLNA | .15 | .9 | 31 | 1137 | 17 | 16 3/8 | 16 7/8 | + 3/8 |
| 17 | 10 3/4 | FoodLion B | FDLNB | .15 | .9 | 32 | 1064 | 17 1/8 | 16 5/8 | 17 | + 1/4 |
| 8 1/2 | 4 3/4 | FoothillBcp | FOOT | .16 | 2.4 | 6 | 9 | 6 3/4 | 6 3/4 | 6 3/4 | + 1/2 |

*Left annotations:* Classes of GM Common Stock (GenMotor GM, GenMotor E GME, GenMotor H GMH); Classes of Food Lion Common Stock (FoodLion A FDLNA, FoodLion B FDLNB)

**Figure 2.2.   Classes of common stock.**

shares have voting rights. A corporation also can issue other classes of common stock. General Motors (GM, GME, GMH) and Food Lion (FDLNA, FDLNB) illustrate this point (Figure 2.2). These other classes may offer investors a different set of privileges, such as a different annual dividend rate, or, as in the case of General Motors, each class may be backed by a different division or subsidiary of the corporation.

The most typical difference is that one class of common shares has the right to vote and another does not. The voting rights are concentrated in the class of common shares held by family members or board members who wish to maintain control of the company. The example most often cited is Ford Motor Company, which has two classes of common stock outstanding: Class A and Class B. Class A, which trades in the open market and represents more than 90 percent of the company's total outstanding shares (both A and B), has only limited voting rights. Class B controls 40 percent of the total voting rights, although it makes up less than 10 percent of all outstanding common shares and does not trade publicly. It is held by the Ford family and key board members, thereby ensuring the family's control of the company.

Although the ability or inability to vote is usually the difference among various classes of common stock, this is not uniformly true. Similarly, you cannot tell from the sequence of the letters—Class A, Class B, Class C, or the General Motors E and H shares—which class has certain privileges. Wise investors carefully read the prospectus of each class of common stock to find out the exact privileges granted. Another source of information is Standard & Poor's Corporate Records, a reference service that contains detailed information about more than 12,000 publicly held companies. The "Stock Data" section for each corporation's financial coverage contains, among other useful information, a description of the privileges and features of each class of common stock that the company has issued.

Class is a way of distinguishing the different issues of common stock distributed by one company, but the common stock of different companies is often grouped together based on different features, such as dividend payment history, potential for capital appreciation, and reactions to the economy and business cycles. Growth stock, income stock, and cyclical stock are examples of these groupings, some of which are defined below:

**Defensive stock.** This is the stock of a company that will not be affected adversely during a recession or downturn in the economy. The demand for this company's products remains relatively constant even in a worsening economy. Examples are stock issued by utility companies, food companies, and pharmaceutical companies.

**Cyclical stock.** The market value of these securities moves directly with the rise and fall of the economy—the business cycle. As the economy strengthens and businesses expand, their prices rise. As the economy contracts or a recession occurs, their prices fall. The term "cyclical stock" is almost a synonym for the common shares issued by companies that produce durable goods or companies in the home-building industries.

**Countercyclical stock.** The prices of these companies' shares move opposite to the business cycle. When the economy is contracting, these shares increase in price; when the economy expands, their prices fall.

**Established growth stock.** Apple Computer is a classic example of an established growth company. Typically, stock issued by the company has traded in the market for several years, showing steady increases in earnings and dividend payments. Often there have been several stock splits during this period. The company remains in a growth position because it continues to build market share for its products in its particular industry.

**Emerging growth stock.** This is stock issued by a newly underwritten company. Initially financed by *venture capital*, this company has no track record of steady growth, earnings, or dividend payments. It does, however, have an interesting idea or product.

**Penny stock.** Technically, penny stock is a common stock whose market value is less

**venture capital:** money invested in a new, unproved, and risky business or enterprise.

than $5. Many penny stocks trade at less than $1 in the market. These shares are issued by small companies that may have a new product or idea that shows some growth potential. Characteristically these issues have few assets other than the potential of the idea. These securities are very risky.

**Letter stock.** This is common stock that is not freely or easily transferable because it has been issued privately by a company and has not been registered with the Securities and Exchange Commission. These securities are most often sold to sophisticated investors with substantial financial resources. The persons agree, usually in writing, not to resell the securities except under certain circumstances and only after holding them for a designated period of time.

Many of these groupings are confusing to beginning investors. In Figure 2.3, these and other types of common stock are categorized under two headings intended to clarify these groupings: stocks that reflect the state of the company's growth and stocks that reflect the business's reactions to the general economy or business cycles.

## PREFERRED STOCK

Preferred stock gets its name from two characteristics in which it has preference over (is senior to) common stock:

1. A company must pay dividends to its preferred shareholders before it can pay any dividends to its common shareholders.
2. If the company goes bankrupt, preferred shareholders' claims on the company's assets are

| Reflecting the State of the Company's Growth | Reflecting Reactions to the Economy |
|---|---|
| Blue Chip stock | Cyclical stock |
| Income stock | Counter-cyclical stock |
| Established-growth stock | Defensive stock |
| Emerging-growth stock | Speculative stock* |
| Penny stock | |

* Speculative stock is used to denote those companies that go through "feast or famine" cycles that reflect the rise or fall, respectively, of the business cycle.

**Figure 2.3.  Categories of common stock.**

considered before those of the common shareholders.

Although preferred stock is categorized as an equity security, it has features that are similar to both common stock and bonds (debt securities). Like common stock, it represents ownership in the corporation; however, the owners of preferred shares are more like silent partners. Typically they have no voting rights and therefore no voice in the management of the company. (Some companies permit limited voting by preferred shareholders or grant them voting rights under certain circumstances. These are usually detailed in the prospectus for the security.) Preferred shareholders have no preemptive rights. The company is not required to offer new preferred shares to existing shareholders before the securities are sold to the public.

Like common stock, preferred shares have the right to receive dividends. Usually paid quarterly, these dividends must be declared by the company's board of directors; however, the amount or percentage is fixed when the security is issued to the public. The dividend payments remain the same for as long as the security is outstanding. In this way, a preferred stock is like a bond on which the interest rate is set at the time the security is issued and remains the same throughout its life. Unlike a bond, a preferred share does not have a maturity date; it has an indefinite life.

The amount of the dividend that the investor receives is based not only on the fixed amount or percentage; it also depends on the par value of the preferred. Most preferred shares have traditionally been issued with a par value of $100. Today, most preferred issues are assigned a $50 or $25 par value in order to make them attractive to a broader range of investors. Like the interest on a bond, the amount of the annual dividend is a percentage of par value. A "10 percent preferred" with a $100 par value pays investors $10 annually (10 percent of $100) or $2.50 quarterly. (This same stock is also referred to as a "$10 preferred.") Par value is important to preferred stock in the same way it is important to bonds. It is not, as with common shares, an arbitrary value of no importance to investors.

Because the dividend rate on preferred stock is fixed, the forces that affect its issue price and market price are different from those that affect common shares. Most new issue preferred shares are sold to the public at par value. The amount or percentage of the fixed dividend reflects the financial health of the issuer, as well as the prevailing interest rates at the time the security is issued. The preferred rates are usually higher, reflecting the increased risk associated with corporate securities as compared with, for example, the risk of U.S. government securities. If investor confidence flags severely, as it did with several commercial banks in poor financial condition in early 1990, a corporation may be forced to offer dividend rates that are substantially higher than prevailing interest rates in order to sell its new issue preferred.

Although the market price of preferred stock is generally considered to be fairly stable, it is sensitive to interest rate changes. As interest rates rise, the market value of outstanding preferred stock with a fixed dividend rate declines. Conversely, as interest rates fall, the market value of outstanding preferred shares rises. The following example illustrates this point.

You own a portfolio consisting of 10 percent (or $10) preferred shares, each having a current market value of $100. (The securities are trading at their par value.) Interest rates in the broad market decline to 5.0 percent—half of the rate on the preferred that you own. Because the outstanding preferred pays a higher dividend rate than investors can earn by purchasing newly issued, interest-sensitive securities, they will be willing to pay a *premium* for the already outstanding preferred. In theory, the market price on the outstanding preferred would nearly double, because the 10 percent rate is twice as attractive as the 5.0 percent current rate. Consequently, the preferred will trade at $200 per share, twice its par value.

**premium:** the amount by which the market value of a preferred stock exceeds its par value.

If, on the other hand, interest rates rise, the outstanding preferred would be less attractive to investors. They could purchase new issue preferred stock and bonds that would pay a better annual dividend. The subsequent lower demand for the outstanding preferred would result in a decrease in its market price. It would sell at a *discount*.

A change in interest rates is not the only factor that influences the price of preferred stock. Investor confidence is another. The market value of an issuer's outstanding preferred will trade at lower

**discount:** the amount by which the market value of a preferred stock is below its par value.

prices in response to flagging investor confidence. If a company is experiencing financial difficulty, its board of directors may choose to suspend all dividend payments or make only partial payments to its preferred shareholders. Current stockholders may begin to sell their shares at the same time that new buyers, also wary, choose to purchase the shares of other companies. The resulting decreased demand will cause the price of the security to decline.

Remember that the market value of common stock is determined by the same forces of supply and demand. Additionally, it is affected by the company's performance and its earnings. Common shares offer investors two opportunities: (1) participation in the company's increasing earnings through increasing dividends payments and (2) participation in the company's increasing worth through the increasing market value (capital appreciation or capital gains) of its common shares. These growth opportunities are generally not available to purchasers of preferred stock. This is one of the trade-offs that preferred shareholders make in exchange for both their preferential status and their fixed dividend payments. Nonetheless, preferred stock is considered safer than common stock. It is suitable for investors seeking safety of principal and predictable dividends. It is, however, somewhat less liquid than common stock because there is less preferred stock issued by companies.

## Types of Preferred Stock

Broadly speaking, four types of preferred stock are regularly issued today:

**1.** Cumulative preferred
**2.** Adjustable rate preferred (ARP), of which there

are two types—money market preferred and auction rate preferred

3. Convertible preferred
4. Callable preferred

Some characteristics may be shared among the various types. For example, most preferred stock issued today is callable, usually at a premium to its par value. Each feature was created in order to increase the marketability of the security, to facilitate a quick response to changes in the marketplace, or to satisfy investor demands.

## Cumulative Preferred

If a company fails to pay dividends on *cumulative preferred*, the missed payments accumulate as arrearages. The shareholder has the right to receive all the accumulated back dividends before any dividends can be paid to common shareholders. In most cases, these arrearages are paid. However, if a company fails to pay them or offers only a partial settlement, cumulative preferred shareholders have no legal recourse. Today, most preferred stock is issued with the cumulative feature. Issues without this feature are known as "noncumulative preferred."

**cumulative preferred:** if dividend payments are missed, holders of these shares have a right to receive all back dividends before any dividend payments can be made to common shareholders.

## Adjustable Rate Preferred

*Adjustable rate preferred* (ARP) shares do not pay a fixed dividend. Instead, as the name suggests, the dividend rate is reset periodically. The new rate is usually reset at a slight premium to some standard rate (such as the discount rate on 90-day U.S. government treasury bills) or a rate determined by a formula adopted by the issuer. Some adjustable rate preferred issues have provisions that permit the issuer to adjust the dividend rate every 49 days.

**adjustable rate preferred:** a preferred stock whose dividend is adjusted periodically to reflect changing interest rates.

**money market preferred:**
adjustable rate preferred whose dividend is adjusted to reflect short-term interest rates.

**auction rate preferred:**
adjustable rate preferred shares whose dividend is adjusted periodically by the issuer offering rates to which the shareholders must agree.

**convertible preferred:**
preferred stock that shareholders can convert into a fixed number of common shares.

**conversion ratio:**
the number of common shares that an investor receives when converting a preferred stock.

Given this frequency, the reset rate usually reflects short-term interest rates instead of long-term rates. This type of ARP is known as a *money market preferred*.

Another recent variation on this theme, and currently the most widely issued, is the *auction rate preferred*. Like money market preferred, the rate is reset every 49 days; however, the issuer proposes dividend rates, which the shareholders may accept or reject. If the shareholders reject the offer, the corporation has two options: raise the rate to a level that the holders will accept (which can sometimes be quite high if investors have lost confidence in the company) or buy back the issue at its par value.

ARPs, especially money market ARPs, have a distinct advantage for investors. Because the rate is reset every 49 days, the interest rate risk associated with preferred stock is minimized. The market price of the stock still moves in opposite directions to changes in the interest rates. The degree of its movement is decreased by the fact that every 49 days, when the rate is adjusted to the prevailing market rate, the preferred trades again at par value. In short, investors can sell adjustable or auction rate preferred every 49 days at the security's par value.

### Convertible Preferred

Holders of *convertible preferred* stock have the right to convert their shares into another security—usually the common stock of the same issuer. The terms and conditions of the conversion are set by the issuer when the security is first sold to the public. For example, a company issuing new $50 par value convertible preferred sets the *conversion ratio* at 5:1. This means that whenever you choose, you can covert one share of preferred stock into five shares of common stock. This ratio is fixed. It does not change with the market value of the preferred or of the common stock. It will, however, be changed if the common stock splits or pays a stock dividend.

The choice to convert is purely yours. When is it advantageous to convert? The example that follows illustrates such an opportunity.

You purchase a $100 par value convertible preferred stock with a conversion ratio of 10:1. For every preferred that you own, you will receive 10 shares of common when and if you convert. If the market price of the preferred is $100 per share at the same time that the market value of the common is $10 per share, the securities are described as trading at *parity*. This means that the market value of the convertible preferred equals the total market value of the 10 shares of common stock. In this case, $100 would be the parity price of the preferred if $10 is the price of the common stock. "Parity price" and "market price" are not synonymous. They are the same only when the preferred and common are trading at parity, which is not often. Usually convertible securities trade at a premium over the price of the common stock.

Because convertible preferred stock can be turned into common stock, the prices of these two securities tend to move in tandem. Given the many different forces at play in the market, the prices do not always move at the same time or in the same direction. Sometimes the preferred's market price may be above the parity price. When this occurs, the preferred is said to be "trading at a premium." At other times, the market price of the preferred may be below parity with the common, trading at a discount. For holders of a convertible preferred, the price disparity presents an opportunity to profit.

Continuing with our example, the market price of the preferred drops to $85 per share on word that interest rates are increasing at the same time

**parity:** when the total market value of the common shares into which a security can be converted equals the market value of the convertible security.

that the market price of the common rises to $11 per share based on reports of increased sales and earnings for the company. Based on the price of the preferred, the common would have to be trading at $8.50 ($85/10) in order to be at parity. However, its market price is $11 per share. If you owned or bought the preferred, you could convert into the common, acquiring the common at a cost basis of $8.50, and then sell the stock at its market price of $11.00. You would have a $2.50 per share profit on each share of the 10 common shares.

Explained from another point of view, the market price of 10 shares of common would be $110 ($11 × 10 shares). The total parity price of the common upon conversion would be $25 higher than the market price of the preferred $85. The $25 difference represents the total profit you would make by converting the preferred and then selling the common shares at the current market price.

**arbitrage:** the simultaneous purchase and sale of securities in different markets in an attempt to profit from short-term price disparities.

In reality, the price disparity between an issuer's convertible preferred and its common stock exists for only a short period of time—seconds in fact. *Arbitrage* by professional traders who watch the market closely for these opportunities cause the two prices to return quickly to parity. Hence, it is rare that a preferred would trade at a discount to parity. It is also virtually impossible for individual investors to profit from the situation illustrated above.

**straight preferred:** a synonym for "nonconvertible preferred."

Still, convertible preferred stock is advantageous because it allows you to convert to common shares when their capital appreciation and dividend payments exceed your return from the fixed-rate preferred stock. Convertibility offsets the fact that *straight preferred* does not offer much growth potential to investors.

The conversion feature is also beneficial to the issuer. Because the shareholders have the potential to participate in the company's growth, convertible securities often have a lower fixed dividend rate when compared to other preferred stock.

### Callable Preferred

This stock has a *call feature* that gives the issuing company the right, at its option, to recall its outstanding preferred stock and repay the stock's par value to shareholders. Sometimes the company pays investors a slight premium over par value when the stock is called. A company will most likely exercise this call provision when interest rates in the general market are significantly lower than the dividend rate it is paying on an outstanding preferred issue. Suppose, for example, that Chrysler issued preferred stock with a 14 percent dividend rate in 1982. If it were to issue the same stock today, it could issue it with a 9 percent dividend rate because interest rates have fallen significantly since that time. Clearly, the 5 percent difference would represent a significant savings for Chrysler. If the preferred had a call provision, Chrysler would most likely issue new shares at the lower rate and use the proceeds to "call" the outstanding, high-dividend preferred.

**call feature:** a provision that permits the issuer to repurchase preferred stock, usually at a premium to its par value.

Calling a high-dividend preferred represents a savings to the issuer. Conversely, it represents a loss of income for investors. If the Chrysler shares had a $50 par value, an investor owning the 14 percent preferred would have received $7 dividend annually (14 percent of $50). A person who bought the new issue would receive only $4.50 annually (9 percent of $50). The premium that a company offers shareholders when it calls its preferred is small compensation for the loss of income.

Clearly, investors and issuers have opposite opinions on callable preferred stock. Investors do

**call protection:**
the period of time
following the
issuance of a
security when it
may not be called.

not like having their high-dividend preferred called when interest rates drop. During periods of high interest rates, the public is more willing to purchase a company's noncallable preferred. The issuing company, on the other hand, wants to retain the right to call the issue and save money, if and when interest rates fall. The compromise is preferred stock with *call protection*. When issuing new preferred, the company makes the shares noncallable for the first five years of its life. (The length of the call protection varies, although five years is standard.) Afterward, the shares are callable at a premium over its par value as compensation to holders of the called issue. The premium is usually highest in the first year of the call. It then drops or, to use an industry phrase, "is scaled down" each subsequent year until it reaches par value.

The following example illustrates this concept. On July 1, 1992, a company issues preferred stock at $50.00 per share. (Remember that preferred is issued at its par value.) The issue has a five-year no-call provision; thus, it cannot be called until after July 1, 1997. At that time, the shares are callable at a 5 percent premium over its par value, or $52.50. The provisions of the call state that in each subsequent year after the initial call, the premium will drop by 1 percent. On July 1, 1998, the premium drops to 4 percent, or $52.00. On July 1, 1999, the premium drops to 3 percent, or $51.50. By the year 2002 and in all subsequent years, an investor who tenders shares in response to the call receives only par value ($50.00) for the stock. This compromise allows companies to take advantage of changes in interest rates. At the same time, investors know that they will receive the fixed dividend for the minimum period specified in the terms of the call protection.

A call provision can affect the market price of a preferred stock when interest rates fall. Combining the two examples used earlier, we can illustrate when and how this occurs. Let's postulate that Chrysler issued 14 percent preferred ($50.00 par value) with a five-year call protection. By July 1, 1997, Chrysler could distribute new preferred at 9 percent due to a drop in interest rates. The outstanding 14 percent shares would be very attractive to investors, who would be willing to pay a premium for the high dividend rate. If there were no call provisions on the shares, their theoretical market price at this time would rise to a little more than 77¾. It would be unwise to purchase the preferred at this price when it is callable at $52.50 per share. If this did happen, you would have an immediate loss of approximately $25.25. While stock might trade above the call price if interest rates drop early in the call protection period, as the end of this time approaches, the market price of the common would move closer and closer to the call price. Once the company can issue a call, the preferred will not trade above its call price. The call price therefore acts as a ceiling on how far the market price of preferred stock can rise in response to a decline in interest rates.

## Classes of Preferred Stock

A preferred stock with features and a dividend rate different from other outstanding preferred by the same issuer is not referred to as being a different class, as common stock is. It is simply a different issue. Most companies have only one issue or class of common stock outstanding, but many have several issues of preferred stock trading in the market at the same time, as Commonwealth Edison does (Figure 2.4). Among the preferred issues the utility company has outstanding are $1.90 preferred, $2.00 preferred, and $8.40 preferred. If you checked Standard & Poor's Corporate Record, you might find

## NEW YORK STOCK EXCHANGE

| 52 Weeks | | | | | Yld | | Vol | | | | Net |
| Hi | Lo | Stock | Sym | Div | % | PE | 100s | Hi | Lo | Close | Chg |
|---|---|---|---|---|---|---|---|---|---|---|---|
| 8 5/8 | 3 3/4 | ChockFull | CHF | .24t | 3.1 | 15 | 102 | 7 3/4 | 7 5/8 | 7 3/4 | + 1/8 |
| 17 5/8 | 9 1/8 | Chrysler | C | .60 | 4.2 | 48 | 2847 | 14 1/2 | 14 1/8 | 14 1/4 | − 1/4 |
| 29 | 9 | CircuitCty | CC | .10 | .6 | 11 | 640 | 17 1/4 | 16 7/8 | 17 | − 1/8 |
| 70 7/8 | 35 3/4 | Circus | CIR | | | 24 | 1035 | 66 3/4 | 64 1/2 | 66 3/4 | +17/8 |
| 25 1/4 | 10 3/4 | Citicorp | CCI | 1.00 | 6.8 | 26 | 6662 | 14 7/8 | 14 1/2 | 14 5/8 | ... |
| 63 | 39 1/4 | Citicorp pf | | 6.00e | 10.9 | ... | 47 | 54 7/8 | 54 1/2 | 54 7/8 | + 1/8 |
| 72 | 46 1/2 | Citicorp pfA | | 7.00e | 10.8 | ... | 1 | 64 3/4 | 64 3/4 | 64 3/4 | − 1/4 |
| 103 1/2 | 70 1/4 | Citicorp pfB | | 9.28e | 10.3 | ... | 1 | 90 | 90 | 90 | +37/8 |
| 24 5/8 | 17 | Citicorp pfC | | 2.28 | 10.0 | ... | 42 | 23 1/8 | 22 5/8 | 22 7/8 | + 3/8 |
| 45 3/8 | 32 1/8 | Clorox | CLX | 1.44 | 3.8 | 15 | 1478 | 39 1/2 | 38 3/8 | 38 3/8 | −1 1/8 |
| 28 5/8 | 14 7/8 | ClubMed | CMI | .30 | 1.3 | 8 | 90 | 22 5/8 | 22 1/8 | 22 3/8 | + 1/8 |
| 55 1/2 | 37 1/8 | CocaCola | KO | .96 | 1.8 | 27 | 7967 | 54 7/8 | 54 1/8 | 54 3/4 | + 1/2 |
| 19 3/4 | 12 1/4 | CocaColaEnt | CCE | .05 | .3 | 29 | 1424 | 19 | 18 1/4 | 19 | + 1/2 |
| 77 3/8 | 56 | ColgatePalm | CL | 1.80 | 2.4 | 17 | 698 | 76 3/4 | 76 1/4 | 76 3/8 | ... |
| 22 1/4 | 16 1/8 | CommerclMtls | CMC | .52 | 2.5 | 12 | 12 | 20 7/8 | 20 5/8 | 20 3/4 | ... |
| 19 3/8 | 4 1/2 | Commodorelnt | CBU | | ... | 14 | 3875 | 18 3/8 | 17 5/8 | 17 7/8 | − 1/2 |
| 40 | 27 1/4 | ComwEd | CWE | 3.00 | 7.71 | 78 | 2616 | 39 3/8 | 39 1/8 | 39 1/8 | − 1/4 |
| 40 | 28 5/8 | ComwEd pf | | 1.42 | 3.5 | ... | 6 | 40 3/8 | 40 3/8 | 40 3/8 | + 3/8 |
| 22 1/8 | 19 | ComwEd pr | | 1.90 | 9.2 | ... | 36 | 20 7/8 | 20 3/4 | 20 3/4 | − 1/8 |
| 23 1/8 | 19 7/8 | ComwEd pr | | 2.00 | 9.0 | ... | 3 | 22 1/8 | 22 1/8 | 22 1/8 | ... |
| 26 1/4 | 24 | ComwEd pr | | 2.37 | 9.2 | ... | 6 | 25 3/4 | 25 7/8 | 25 5/8 | + 1/4 |
| 30 | 26 1/8 | ComwEd pf | | 2.87 | 9.8 | ... | 8 | 29 5/8 | 29 3/8 | 29 3/8 | + 1/8 |
| 95 1/4 | 84 | ComwEd pf | | 8.40 | 9.1 | ... | z4050 | 91 7/8 | 91 1/2 | 91 7/8 | +17/8 |
| 37 3/8 | 29 1/8 | ComwEngy | CES | 2.92 | 8.9 | 15 | 106 | 32 7/8 | 32 1/4 | 32 7/8 | + 3/4 |

Issues of Commonwealth Edison Preferred Stock

**Figure 2.4. Various issues of preferred stock from Commonwealth Edison.**

that each issue has a distinct combination of features. For example, one issue might be a straight cumulative preferred, another might be a cumulative convertible preferred, and still another might be an auction rate callable preferred.

### Preferred Stock Today

To this point, this discussion of preferred stock has presented the basic or classic concepts that have always been associated with this security. Many outstanding preferred issues have these characteristics, but many of the shares issued today have new features that represent significant changes. Three of these are important to investors who are considering purchasing these securities.

In theory, preferred stocks have an indeterminate life, but this is becoming less and less true. Today most preferred stock is issued with a *sinking fund provision*. Like a covenant on a bond, this provision allows the issuer to retire the shares after a period of time, usually 8 to 10 years after they were issued. During each year the preferred is outstanding, the corporation deposits money into an escrow account that will be used to retire the preferred.

**sinking fund provision:** a feature that permits a company to redeem or repurchase an outstanding preferred issue or bond using money that it has deposited into an escrow account.

The second characteristic is that fewer and fewer companies are issuing preferred shares with fixed par values of $100, $50, or even $25. Companies are issuing no par value preferred. In this case, the dividend is a fixed dollar amount, not a fixed percentage of the par value.

And finally, fixed-rate preferred is being replaced increasingly by adjustable and auction rate preferred. This feature allows the issuer to reset the dividend periodically based on the prevailing interest rate and the financial condition of the company. The percentage or amount of the dividend is usually reset every quarter.

Individual investors are no longer the largest purchasers of preferred shares. Tax breaks have made it very attractive for one company to invest in the preferred stock of another corporation. Under the Internal Revenue Service's corporate dividend-received exclusion rule, 70 to 80 percent of the dividends that a domestic company receives from investing in an equity security of another domestic corporation is excluded from taxation. The exact percentage excluded depends on the percentage of a company's stock the investing corporation owns, and not all dividends are excludable. To be eligible for this deduction, the Internal Revenue Service requires a 46-day holding period for the investing corporation. Hence, the 49-day readjustment period for adjustable rate preferred is designed to make the stock eligible for the dividend-received exclusion. If the investing corporation does not like the new rate, it can sell the preferred it is holding and still qualify for the exclusion on the dividends received. For a corporation, this type of tax benefit is available on few other investments.

## SUMMARY

Common stock and preferred stock are both negotiable equity securities, but in many ways they are different. In many ways, preferred stock is being given features that are closer and closer to those of a bond. It is each distinct feature or combination of features that makes common and preferred suitable for a broad range of investment objectives. As we explore the ways these investments are analyzed and used, you may want to refer back to this chapter to clarify any points that may be confusing.

# CHAPTER 3

# The Basics of Buying and Selling Stocks

**B**uying stocks is what most people think of as investing (or speculating) in the stock market. The securities industry jargon for buying stock includes the phrases "establishing a *long position*" and "going long" (the stock). You buy securities when you believe the price will, over time, rise above the price originally paid for the stock and produce a profit. In general, the shorter the period of time during which you expect to profit, the more speculative, or risky, the investment is considered to be. When you sell stocks that you own, the action is called *selling long*; you are liquidating a long stock position.

Another way of speculating in stocks is by *selling short*. You use this strategy when you are bearish on a stock—that is, you believe the price of a stock will decline. Through a broker, you borrow shares, from either another investor or a brokerage firm, and sell them in the market. (The process whereby the firm borrows and lends the securities is unimportant to you as an investor.) Your objective is eventually to buy back the same number of borrowed shares at a lower price than you originally received when they were sold and then return

**long position:** phrase denoting ownership of a security, which includes the right to transfer ownership and to participate in the rise and fall of its market value.

**selling long:** selling securities or liquidating stock positions that an investor owns.

**selling short:** strategy investors use to profit from a price decline; involves selling securities that the investor does not own, with the *intent of replacing the securities at a lower price.*

**covering:**

*eliminating a short position by buying the shares that have been sold short and delivering them to the lender.*

the shares to the lender. This strategy is called a "short sale" because you do not own (i.e., have borrowed) the securities that you have sold. When you eventually buy back the borrowed stock and close the short position, this transaction is known as *covering* a short sale.

To illustrate selling short, let's say you believe that Digital stock, which is trading at $45 per share, is about to decline. In order to profit from this situation, you sell short 100 shares of the stock at $45, receiving proceeds of $4500. (Commissions are deducted from the sale price.) Digital then declines to $30 per share, and you cover the short position, paying $3000 to repurchase the 100 shares. (Commissions are added to the purchase price.) Having sold short the stock at $45 per share and then bought it back at $30 per share, you have a gross profit of $1500.

Selling short is a complex and risky strategy. When you sell short, you want the stock's price to decline. If the price rises, you are subject to unlimited potential loss. (Short sales are explained in more detail in Chapter 4.) It is important for you, as a beginning investor, to have a clear and basic understanding of the jargon used for buying (long, cover short) and selling (selling long, selling short) stocks so that you will understand some of the investment strategies discussed in this chapter.

## INVESTMENT ACCOUNTS

Opening an account at a brokerage firm is a simple procedure. You begin by filling out a new account form. Typically, you must provide at least the following information on this form: your name, address, social security or tax identification number, confirmation that you are of legal age, citizenship, the name of your bank (or other brokerage firm if appropriate), name of your employer, and your investment objectives. If you are married, the firm may request the name, address, social security number, and employer of your spouse. Additional information, such as your approximate net worth or annual income, may be requested in order to fulfill the firm's requirements for opening a new account. This additional information varies slightly among brokerage firms, but each firm requires potential customers to provide sufficient information so that it can "know the customer." In general terms, this means the broker handling the account, and the firm, must be familiar with a customer's financial means, fiscal responsibility, and investment objectives in order to transact business properly with the client. This information is also used by the broker to make recommendations to the investor.

A new account form is required for all customer accounts. Cash accounts and margin accounts are the two most common types used to trade securities.

## Cash Account

Most investors trade stocks using a *cash account*. In this account, you can buy any stock by depositing 100 percent of the shares' market value or you can sell long (liquidate) stocks that are fully paid. When stocks are bought or sold in a cash account, settlement typically occurs five business days after the date of the transaction. This is known in the securities industry as *regular way settlement*. [**Note:** There is a proposal pending to shorten regular way settlement to three business days after the trade date.] On the settlement date (the due date) you must pay for the purchased stocks in full. If you sold long stocks, the certificates must be delivered to the broker on or before that date, at which time the sales proceeds are released to you. In many cases, the firm already has the certificates, which it has been holding for you.

**cash account:** an account in which an investor buys securities by paying for them in full or sells securities fully paid.

**regular way settlement:** the normal settlement method for stock transactions, occurring five business days after the trade date. (See Note in Text.)

Should you fail to pay for the stock or deliver the certificates on the settlement date, the brokerage firm may liquidate the position. Following this forced liquidation, the firm freezes your account for 90 days. This means that you can trade in the account only by depositing "good funds"—cash, a certified or guaranteed check, or federal funds—before any trade will be executed.

If the forced liquidation results in a loss, you are liable. In order to recoup the loss, the firm may demand additional cash from you, legally attach any *cash balances* that you may have in other accounts, or liquidate other securities positions already in the account.

**cash balances:**
cash deposits in an account at a brokerage firm that are uninvested or awaiting investment.

You cannot use the proceeds from the sale of a stock to pay for an earlier purchase of the same stock. You must first pay for the purchase before any proceeds from the sale can be withdrawn or used. For example, a customer buys 200 Duracell common shares at $20 per share on Monday. Regular way settlement on this purchase will occur on the following Monday—five business days after the trade date. By Thursday, the third day after the purchase, the price of Duracell has risen to $27 per share, and the investor sells the 200 shares. The customer has a $1400 profit ($7 × 200 shares). In order to receive the profit, the investor must first deposit $4000 in the account on the Monday following the purchase in order to settle the initiating transaction. The sales proceeds will be credited to the account on the settlement date of the closing transaction—the following Thursday. To reiterate, investors are prohibited from buying stocks, selling them profitably before settlement, and then using the proceeds to meet the cash deposit required to settle the initial transaction.

Some of the transactions that you can make in a cash account include:

1. Buying fully paid stock
2. Selling fully paid stock
3. Buying rights (see Chapter 8)
4. Buying warrants (see Chapter 8)
5. Buying options (see Chapter 8)

In the last three cases, the positions can also be liquidated in a cash account.

When you buy securities in a cash account, the stock certificates can be issued in one of two ways: in your name or in *street name*. If they are issued in your name, the *transfer agent* prints your name on the certificate and sends it to you for safekeeping. This process can take several weeks. Therefore, if you plan to sell the shares quickly, you would be ill-advised to have certificates issued in your name.

If the certificates are issued in street name, the name of your brokerage firm appears on them. The certificates are held in safekeeping by the firm for you. The name of the individual investor is un-known to the corporation that issued the shares. The issuing corporation's records show the broker-age firm as the *holder of record*; however, your name appears in the firm's record as the *beneficial owner* of the stock.

Many investors believe it is safer to have the stock certificate issued in their names because it proves they own the stock. This is not true. A per-son who is the beneficial owner of a stock held in street name receives the same legal protection, benefits, and privileges as a person whose stock is in customer name. The brokerage firm must promptly credit all dividends to investors' accounts and promptly forward all corporate communica-tions—proxies and annual reports, among oth-ers—to investors.

There are advantages to leaving securities in street name. The process of selling the securities is

**street name:** industry term describing securities owned by an investor but registered in the name of the brokerage firm.

**transfer agent:** usually a commercial bank or trust company responsible for cancelling old certificates and issuing new certificates. Also responsible for mailing dividends and other important information and documents to the shareholders.

**holder of record:** the name of the owner of a security as it is recorded in the records of the transfer agent or issuer.

**beneficial owner:** the investor who owns securities held in street name.

simplified, in part because the firm does not have to get your signature on the certificates. Since the securities are in its name, the firm simply sells them on your behalf. A security held in street name is also less likely to be lost or damaged because the firm keeps them at a central depository, such as the Depository Trust Company (DTC). Replacement of a lost or damaged stock certificate is costly.

Perhaps the only investor who benefits from having securities issued in his or her name is a large investor who uses the services of several brokers. The advantage here is that he or she can choose the broker through whom the trade is initiated and liquidated.

**book entry only:** securities for which no certificates are issued.

**registrar:** usually a commercial bank that is responsible for maintaining an accurate list of the names and addresses of a company's stockholders.

Many companies, especially those trading on international exchanges such as the Tokyo Stock Exchange, do not issue stock certificates at all. Instead, ownership of shares in the company is in *book entry only* form. The number of shares that an investor owns is listed in the computer records of the *registrar* or transfer agent for the issuing company. When the shares are bought or sold, no certificates change hands. The change of ownership is simply recorded in the registrar's records. The issuance of book-entry securities reduces the amount of paperwork associated with stock transactions and provides better safeguards for the securities. In the United States, this form of ownership is being accepted only slowly by people who invest in stocks. In the debt markets, particularly Treasury bills, Treasury bonds, and municipal bonds, book-entry ownership is more widespread.

**margin account:** an account in which an investor buys (or sells short) securities by depositing part of their market value and borrowing the remainder from the brokerage firm.

## Margin Account

In a *margin account*, you do not pay in full for stocks that you buy or sell. Under current Federal Reserve Board rules, you must deposit half (50%) of the stock's market value at the brokerage firm. The remainder you borrow from the brokerage house. If, for example, you have $3000 to invest and use a cash account, you can buy only $3000 worth of securities. If you buy the securities on margin, you can purchase $6000 of securities. This *leverage* enables you to double the purchasing (or selling) power of every dollar invested in stocks. It also doubles the returns you can make for each dollar invested.

**leverage:** the purchase (or sale) of a large amount of stocks using a small amount of the investor's money. The rest of the money is borrowed from the brokerage firm.

The risks associated with margin trading are also increased by leverage. You lose twice as fast because there is less money backing the position. Moreover, you must also pay interest on the loan from the brokerage firm. A greater profit is necessary for you to break even.

Trading stocks on margin is more speculative than trading them fully paid. The mechanics of trading stocks on margin are set forth in detail in Chapter 4, but there are some basic concepts that beginning investors need to understand at this point. Any stock can be bought or sold in a cash account, but not all stocks can be traded on margin. Common and preferred stocks that are "marginable" include:

1. All stocks listed on an exchange
2. All NASDAQ National Market—the 2700 largest, most active over-the-counter stocks trading on the NASDAQ Stock Market.
3. All other over-the-counter (OTC) stocks (NASDAQ Small Cap Issues and the "Pink Sheet" Stocks) contained on the Federal Reserve Board's margin stock list

All other stocks can be bought or sold only in a cash account, where you must deposit 100 percent of their market value.

When you buy or sell shares on margin, the certificates are always held in street name. They cannot be issued in your name because the brokerage firm has a lien (margin loan) against the value of the securities. The firm does this to protect itself. If the market value of the securities declines and you fail to deposit the additional money requested by the firm—a *maintenance call*—in order to maintain adequate equity in the account, the broker can liquidate the securities without your signature. You are liable for all losses resulting from this forced liquidation.

**maintenance call:** a demand from a brokerage firm that an investor deposit sufficient funds in a margin account to restore it to the minimum margin requirement.

Some transactions involving stock and equity derivatives can be performed only in a margin account. These include:

1. Buying stocks on margin
2. Selling stocks short
3. Writing uncovered stock options (see Chapter 8)

## TRADING STOCKS

### Sizes of Trades

**round lot trade:** a trade involving 100 shares of stock.

Stock trades are described as round lots or odd lots. A *round lot trade* in stock is usually for 100 shares or multiples thereof. This is the most common trading unit on the stock exchange floor and in the over-the-counter market. However, there are some preferred stocks on exchanges that trade in round lots of 10 shares. The technical term for these stocks is *cabinet stocks*. Because they do not trade frequently and their prices are usually high, like Berkshire Hathaway whose price is approximately $18,000 per share, the exchange established smaller round lot units for these stocks.

**cabinet stock:** exchange listed stock that trades in 10-share round lots and does not have an active trading market.

**odd lot trade:** a stock trade involving between 1 and 99 shares.

Any trade for 1 to 99 shares of a stock (or for 1 to 9 shares of cabinet stock) is called an *odd lot trade*. Many small investors trade in odd lots because they lack the funds to buy round lots. Overall, the price at which these trades are executed tends to be higher because they are executed separately from round lot trades. Most frequently, they are grouped with other odd lots in order to form a round lot, and then the trade is executed. As a percentage of dollars invested, commission costs on these transactions are also higher.

## The Trading Markets: Exchange and Over-the-Counter

As beginning investors soon discover, there is not just one stock market in which all securities are bought and sold. Stocks and bonds trade in two markets: on a *stock exchange* or in the *over-the-counter (OTC) market*. Collectively these markets are called the secondary or *aftermarket*. When new issues are distributed or sold to the public, this activity takes place in the *primary market*. Although the impact of these distinctions is of little import to most people's investment decisions, this is nonetheless important information to know.

### Exchange-Listed Stocks

Commonly referred to as *listed stocks*, these are the approximately 4300 common and preferred stocks that trade on the floors of the exchanges in the United States. The seven largest exchanges are:

1. New York Stock Exchange
2. American Stock Exchange
3. Chicago Stock Exchange
4. Pacific Stock Exchange
5. Philadelphia Stock Exchange
6. Boston Stock Exchange
7. Cincinnati Stock Exchange

Generally listed stocks are the outstanding shares of the best-capitalized and most widely held

**stock exchange:** an auction market in which exchange members meet in a central location to execute buy and sell orders for individual and institutional customers.

**over-the-counter (OTC) market:** a decentralized, negotiated market in which many dealers in diverse locations execute trades for customers over an electronic trading system or telephone lines.

**aftermarket:** a collective term for the markets— exchange and over-the-counter— in which stocks are bought and sold after they are issued to the public. Proceeds from trades in this market go to the investors.

**primary market:** the market, either

**exchange or over-the-counter,** in which securities are first issued to the public, with the proceeds going to the issuing corporation.

**listed stock:** a company whose stock meets the listing requirements of one of the exchanges and has been accepted by the exchange to trade on its floor.

**floor broker:** an exchange member and an employee of a member firm who executes buy and sell orders on the trading floor of an exchange.

**trading post:** the designated place on the exchange floor where a particular stock trades.

**specialist:** an exchange member firm located at the trading post, responsible for

U.S. companies (such as AT&T, IBM, and 3M) and some large foreign companies (such as Glaxo, British Airways, and Sony). Approximately 2200 of these and other companies' common and preferred stocks trade on the New York Stock Exchange, the largest and oldest exchange in the United States.

A company's stock trades on an exchange for two reasons: (1) the company and its shares meet the exchange's listing requirements, and (2) the company wants the prestige of having its securities traded in the same place as those of the biggest and best corporations in the country. The criteria for being listed on an exchange include consideration of the following items:

- A company's aggregate before-tax earnings
- The number of publicly held shares
- The number of shareholders
- The stock's trading volume
- The price of the security
- A national interest in trading the security

Each exchange sets its own listing requirements. Hence, the same stocks do not trade on all of the exchanges, although there is some overlap.

When you place an order to buy or sell a listed stock, the broker or registered representative records your instructions on an order ticket, which the firm transmits electronically to the floor of the exchange. There, a *floor broker* receives the order, takes it to the *trading post* where the stock trades, and executes it with the *specialist* or another floor broker. Once the transaction is completed, the price at which the order is executed is reported on the *ticker*. Confirmation and the details of the execution are sent by computer to the brokerage firm and the registered representative, who notifies you. A written *confirmation* of the execution is sent to you on the next business day.

When buying or selling listed securities, the brokerage firm always acts as an *agent* or middle-man between you and the buyers and sellers on the exchange floor. Specialists and floor brokers are prohibited from trading directly with the public. As compensation for its role in executing the order, the brokerage firm charges its customers a *commission*. When you buy stock, the brokerage firm adds the commission to the purchase price of the securities. When you sell shares, the commission is deducted from the proceeds that you receive. The amount of the commission must be disclosed to you on the written confirmation.

### Over-the-Counter Stocks: NASDAQ and the Pink Sheets

If a company's common or preferred stock does not trade on an exchange, then it is said to trade in the over-the-counter (OTC) market. The OTC market is not a centralized market; there is no trading floor on which orders are executed. Across the United States and around the world, thousands of brokerage firms trade by telephone or use an interdealer electronic computer system known as the NASDAQ (National Association of Securities Dealers Automated Quotation) Stock Market to buy and sell securities out of their own inventories. More than 20,000 stocks trade in the OTC market.

Today, however, the term "over-the-counter" is being redefined by NASDAQ. Describing itself in advertisements as "The NASDAQ Stock Market" and featuring the names of some of the largest companies in America that trade over its electronic system, NASDAQ is presenting itself as being on par with and more forward-thinking than the tradi-

maintaining a fair and orderly market in the stock(s) assigned to it.

**ticker:** the electronic display that continuously shows the stock symbols and prices at which each successive order is executed. Also called the ticker tape or the consolidated tape.

**confirmation:** a notice sent from the broker to the customer on the day after the trade date that gives the details of the execution of an order.

**agent:** a registered person who acts as the intermediary in the purchase or sale of a security and charges a commission for the service. A synonym for "broker."

**commission:** the fee charged by a broker or agent for executing an order for a customer.

**Pink Sheets:**
sheets listing the bid and ask prices of certain over-the-counter stocks, mostly low-priced and foreign issues. Named for the color of the paper and published each business day by the National Quotation Bureau.

tional stock exchanges. NASDAQ would also prefer that the phrase "over-the-counter" be used only in reference to the non-NASDAQ traded stocks that are listed on the *Pink Sheets* (see Figure 3.3).

From the more traditional point of view, the over-the-counter market for stocks is a tiered market, consisting of three distinct segments. The approximately 2700 best-capitalized and most-active OTC stocks are known as NASDAQ National Market Issues. (See Figure 3.1.) Of the stocks in this group, nearly 1000 meet the NYSE's listing requirements. However, the companies' boards of directors have chosen to keep their stock trading in the NASDAQ market, preferring the way trading is conducted over the NASDAQ system to the way trading is conducted on an exchange. The listing requirements for a company's stock to be placed in the National Market Issues group are similar to those for equity securities trading on a stock exchange, including shareholder approval to issue additional shares, prohibitions against shareholder disenfranchisement, annual shareholder meetings, and an independent board of directors. As Figure 3.1 shows, the NASDAQ National Market Issues listings in the financial press are identical to the listings for NYSE-traded stocks.

The second tier of OTC stock is listed under the heading NASDAQ Small-Cap Issues (See Figure 3.2). There are approximately 1700 stocks in this tier. The companies' stocks do not meet the listing requirements for those in the National Market Issues tier. In fact, the requirements to be included in this group are significantly lower than those in the first group. These companies are considerably less capitalized (having fewer assets and revenues), have fewer shares outstanding, and have a lower price per share. In short, stocks in this group are more speculative.

# NASDAQ NATIONAL MARKET ISSUES

Quotations as of 4 p.m. Eastern Time
Thursday, November 4, 1993

| | 52 Weeks Hi | Lo | Stock | Sym | Div | Yld % | PE | Vol 100s | Hi | Lo | Close | Net Chg |
|---|---|---|---|---|---|---|---|---|---|---|---|---|
| | | | **-A-A-A-** | | | | | | | | | |
| s | 13¼ | 5⅝ | ABS Ind | ABSI | .20 | 1.6 | 20 | 24 | 12⅜ | 12 | 12⅜ | + ⅜ |
| n | 23¾ | 15 | ABT BldgPdt | ABTC | | ... | ... | 398 | 23¾ | 22¾ | 23¼ | ... |
| s | 22 | 10½ | ACC | ACCC | .12 | .6 | 70 | 1034 | 21 | 20¼ | 20¼ | ... |
| n | 46¾ | 10¾ | ACX Tch | ACXT | | ... | dd | 201 | 37 | 35¾ | 35¾ | − ½ |
| s | 44 | 18⅛ | ADC Tel | ADCT | | ... | 32 | 2287 | 35½ | 35 | 35⅛ | − ⅜ |
| | 17¼ | 5½ | **ADESA** | **SOLD** | | ... | 27 | 1831 | 16¾ | 15½ | 15¾ | −1½ |
| | 8¼ | 5 | **AEL Ind A** | **AELNA** | | ... | dd | 420 | 8¼ | 7⅜ | 8¼ | +1 |
| | 20 | 9¾ | AEP Ind | AEPI | .05e | .3 | 18 | 11 | 18½ | 17¼ | 18½ | ... |
| n | 11¼ | 7 | AER EngyRes | AERN | | ... | ... | 384 | 11¼ | 10¾ | 11 | + ¼ |
| | 33½ | 21 | AES Cp | AESC | 1.00 | 3.1 | 18 | 427 | 33½ | 32 | 32 | − ⅞ |
| ▲ | 29¼ | 6⅛ | AGCO Cp | AGCO | .04 | .1 | 33 | 9167 | 31¼ | 29 | 30 | +1 |
| n▲ | 42 | 24½ | AGCO pf | | 1.63 | 3.8 | ... | 1587 | 44¼ | 42¼ | 42¾ | +1⅜ |
| n | 27½ | 20⅛ | AMCOR Ltd | AMCRY | .51e | 1.9 | ... | 7 | 27½ | 27½ | 27½ | ... |
| n | 17¼ | 15¼ | APS Hldg | APSI | | ... | ... | 278 | 16½ | 16⅛ | 16¼ | − ¼ |
| n▼ | 12¾ | 9⅜ | **A PeaInPod** | **APOD** | | ... | ... | 691 | 9½ | 8¾ | 8¾ | − ⅝ |
| n | 19 | 14 | A+ Comm | ACOM | | ... | ... | 713 | 18 | 17¼ | 17¼ | − ¼ |
| | 6 | 1⅞ | ARI Netwk | ARIS | | ... | dd | 130 | 4⅞ | 4½ | 4⅞ | + ⅛ |
| | 28⅛ | 9½ | ASK Grp | ASKI | | ... | cc | 216 | 14 | 13⅝ | 13⅝ | − ⅜ |
| | 24¼ | 12¾ | AST Rsrch | ASTA | | ... | dd | 6655 | 21 | 20¼ | 20¾ | + ¼ |
| | 9 | 5¼ | ATSMed | ATSI | | ... | dd | 181 | 6⅛ | 5⅞ | 6⅛ | + ¼ |
| | 6⅛ | 3 | AW Cptr A | AWCSA | | ... | 9 | 32 | 4 | 3¾ | 3¾ | ... |
| s | 13⅛ | 6 | AamesFnl | AAMS | .30 | 3.0 | 10 | 432 | 10½ | 10 | 10⅛ | − ⅛ |
| n | 13¾ | 7 | AaronRents B | | .08 | .7 | ... | 10 | 11 | 10½ | 11 | + ⅜ |
| | 8 | 4 | Abaxis | ABAX | | ... | | 23 | 7½ | 7 | 7 | ... |
| | 25½ | 14¼ | AbbeyHlthcr | ABBY | | ... | 25 | 609 | 22¼ | 21 | 22¼ | ... |
| | 12¼ | 6¼ | AbingtnSav | ABBK | | ... | 14 | 66 | 11½ | 10¾ | 11⅛ | + ⅛ |
| | 15½ | 7 | **Abiomed** | **ABMD** | | ... | dd | 50 | 9 | 8 | 8 | −1 |
| | 6½ | 4 | AbramsInd | ABRI | .12f | 2.2 | 8 | 6 | 5½ | 5½ | 5½ | ... |
| | 12½ | 6¾ | **AbraxasPete** | **AXAS** | | ... | dd | 3197 | 11¼ | 9¾ | 9⅞ | −1⅜ |
| n | 16½ | 4½ | AbsolutEntn | ABSO | | ... | ... | 277 | 8½ | 8 | 8¼ | − ¼ |
| | 12⅛ | 3¼ | AccessHlth | ACCS | | ... | 41 | 115 | 9¼ | 8⅞ | 9 | ... |
| s | 31¾ | 8 5/32 | **AcclmEntn** | **AKLM** | | ... | 40 | 7872 | 27¾ | 25¾ | 25⅞ | −2 |
| n | 17½ | 6¾ | **AceCashExp** | **AACE** | | ... | 29 | 1151 | 11⅝ | 10¾ | 10¾ | − ¾ |
| s | 17½ | 12¾ | Aceto | ACET | .28 | 2.2 | 32 | 39 | 13 | 13 | 13 | − ½ |
| | 20¾ | 11 | **AcmeMetals** | **ACME** | | ... | 25 | 51 | 15¼ | 14½ | 14⅝ | − ⅞ |
| n | 20½ | 10½ | Actel | ACTL | | ... | ... | 1755 | 13 | 11⅝ | 12½ | − ¼ |
| n | 7 | 4½ | ActionPerf | ACTN | | ... | ... | 572 | 5 9/16 | 5¼ | 5 7/16 | − 1/16 |
| n | 1¾ | 9/16 | ActionPerf wt | | | ... | ... | 60 | 1¼ | 1 3/16 | 1 3/16 | − 1/16 |
| s | 24¼ | 12¼ | Acxiom | ACXM | | ... | 36 | 80 | 23 | 22¾ | 22¾ | ... |
| s | 16⅞ | 9¼ | **AdacLabs** | **ADAC** | .48 | 3.6 | 13 | 1052 | 14⅛ | 13⅜ | 13⅜ | − ⅞ |
| | 7½ | 3¼ | Adage | ADGE | | ... | 33 | 113 | 6⅜ | 6 | 6 | − ¼ |
| | 37¼ | 18½ | **Adaptec** | **ADPT** | | ... | 16 | 22058 | 35 | 31⅛ | 31⅝ | −3 |
| | 18¼ | 12¼ | AddintnRes | ADDR | | ... | cc | 372 | 17½ | 17¼ | 17¼ | − ¼ |
| | 26½ | 11½ | **AdelphiaComm** | **ADLAC** | | ... | dd | 92 | 25¼ | 24 | 24 | −1¼ |
| | 26½ | 15¼ | AdiaSvcs | ADIA | .16 | .7 | 15 | 31 | 22 | 20¾ | 21½ | −1 |
| s | 37 | 14½ | AdobeSys | ADBE | .20 | 1.0 | 18 | 9156 | 20½ | 19½ | 19¾ | − ⅜ |
| | 6¼ | 1¼ | AdvaCare | AVCR | | ... | dd | 1093 | 2 | 1 13/16 | 1 15/16 | + 3/32 |
| | 15 | 6⅜ | AdvCircuit | ADVC | | ... | 9 | 1048 | 11⅝ | 10⅞ | 11⅛ | − ¼ |
| ▲ | 22¾ | 10¼ | AdvRoss | AROS | | ... | 27 | 70 | 23 | 22 | 23 | +1 |
| | 5⅞ | 1 15/16 | AdvIntrvnt | LAIS | | ... | dd | 32 | 2⅞ | 2⅝ | 2⅝ | − ⅛ |
| | 5 9/16 | 2½ | AdvLogicRsrch | AALR | | ... | dd | 480 | 3⅝ | 3¼ | 3½ | − ⅛ |
| | 9¾ | 5¼ | AdvMktg | ADMS | | ... | 13 | 3 | 7⅛ | 7⅛ | 7⅛ | − 3/16 |
| | 10⅛ | 5⅛ | AdvPolymer | APOS | | ... | dd | 365 | 5⅝ | 5¼ | 5¼ | − ¼ |
| | 13⅛ | 6½ | AdvPromoTch | APTV | | ... | ... | 606 | 12 | 10¾ | 11¼ | ... |
| | 2⅛ | ⅝ | AdvSemi | ASMIF | | ... | ... | 22 | 1⅝ | 1½ | 1⅝ | + ¼ |
| | 24½ | 15¼ | AdvTchLab | ATLI | | ... | dd | 147 | 17 | 16¼ | 16¾ | + ¼ |
| | 14½ | 6½ | AdvTissue | ATIS | | ... | ... | 4076 | 9¼ | 8⅞ | 9¼ | + ¼ |
| s | 46¾ | 15¾ | **Advanta A** | **ADVNA** | .17 | .4 | 22 | 5086 | 43½ | 40¼ | 40¼ | −3⅛ |
| s | 38½ | 14 | **Advanta B** | **ADVNB** | .20 | .6 | 19 | 2986 | 36 | 33½ | 33½ | −3 |
| | 28¼ | 16 | AdvntgBcp | AADV | | ... | 12 | 487 | 27 | 24½ | 25 | −1¼ |
| | 20¾ | 8½ | AdvntgHlth | ADHC | | | 12 | 85 | 12¾ | 12 | 12½ | − ½ |
| | 15/16 | ½ | Alpharel wt | | | ... | .. | 20 | ½ | ½ | ½ | |
| | 6¼ | 3¼ | **AlpineLace** | **LACE** | | ... | dd | 1540 | 6 | 4⅞ | 5½ | + ⅝ |
| | 2⅜ | 13/32 | AltaGold | ALTA | | ... | dd | 543 | 1½ | 1¼ | 1 15/32 | + ⅛ |
| | 4½ | 2½ | Altai | ALTI | | ... | 33 | 15 | 3¾ | 3⅝ | 3⅝ | − ⅜ |
| | 15¾ | 7¼ | Alteon | ALTN | | ... | ... | 33 | 8⅝ | 8½ | 8⅝ | − ⅛ |
| | 33⅝ | 11 | AlteraCp | ALTR | | ... | 34 | 5169 | 26¾ | 25¾ | 25⅞ | |
| s | 24½ | 3⅛ | Altron | ALRN | | ... | 21 | 771 | 16½ | 15½ | 15¾ | + ¼ |
| ▲ | 6 | 2¾ | **AMBAR** | **AMBR** | | ... | dd | 25 | 6¼ | 5½ | 6¼ | + ½ |
| | 18½ | 4½ | AmbersStr | ABRS | | ... | 10 | 432 | 5¾ | 5⅜ | 5½ | |
| | 28¾ | 20 | AmcoreFnl | AMFI | .72f | 2.8 | 12 | 33 | 26¼ | 26 | 26 | − ⅜ |
| | 23½ | 17¼ | AmerianaBcp | ASBI | .80 | 4.0 | 10 | 4 | 20¼ | 20¼ | 20¼ | − ⅜ |
| | 2 | ⅞ | AmeribcInv | AINVS | j | ... | dd | 150 | 1 7/16 | 1 7/16 | 1 7/16 | − 1/32 |
| | 30 | 23 | AmFstFnlFd | AFFFZ | 1.60 | 6.4 | ... | 90 | 26 | 25 | 25 | − ½ |
| | 11¾ | 9½ | AmFstPfFd | AFPFZ | 1.06 | 10.2 | ... | 90 | 10⅜ | 10 | 10⅜ | − ¼ |
| s | 7¾ | 5½ | AmFstTxEx | AFTXZ | .54b | 8.2 | ... | 490 | 7 | 6⅝ | 6⅝ | − ¼ |
| | 10 | 7¾ | AmFstTxEx2 | ATAXZ | .75 | 8.1 | ... | 159 | 9½ | 9 | 9¼ | .. |
| | 65 | 16¼ | AmOnline | AMER | | ... | cc | 512 | 62¾ | 61 | 62 | + ½ |
| | 7½ | 2¾ | AmSvcGp | ASGR | | ... | 10 | 1326 | 3⅜ | 3 | 3 | |
| | 4⅝ | 3¾ | AmAllSeasFd | FUND | .25e | 6.1 | ... | 153 | 4 5/16 | 4⅛ | 4⅛ | |
| | 37 | 21½ | AmBcp | AMBC | 1.00 | 2.9 | dd | 9 | 37 | 34½ | 34½ | ... |
| | 30¾ | 20⅜ | AmBkrsIns | ABIG | .68 | 2.7 | 9 | 919 | 25⅜ | 24¾ | 24⅞ | − ¼ |
| | 7½ | 3½ | AmBiogen | MABXA | | ... | ... | 511 | 6 | 5¾ | 5 13/16 | − 3/16 |
| | 18½ | 10½ | AmBusnInfo | ABII | | ... | 19 | 518 | 15 | 14¼ | 14⅝ | |
| | 26 | 15 | AmCtyBsJnl | AMBJ | | ... | 22 | 1 | 24½ | 24½ | 24½ | − ¼ |
| | 7¾ | 2½ | AmClaimEval | AMCE | | ... | 15 | 126 | 3½ | 3¼ | 3½ | + ⅛ |
| s | 33 | 7¼ | AmColloid | ACOL | .20 | .9 | 32 | 1383 | 24½ | 23½ | 23½ | − ½ |
| | 13½ | 2¾ | **AmDentalTcn** | **ADLI** | | ... | dd | 7 | 3⅝ | 3¼ | 3¼ | − ⅜ |
| | 14½ | 6 | AmEcology | ECOL | | ... | 10 | 33 | 12 | 11½ | 12 | + ½ |
| | 7½ | 3 7/16 | AmEducation | AMEP | | ... | 14 | 461 | 4 5/16 | 4 | 4⅛ | |
| | 12¼ | 6¼ | AmFedBank | AMFB | .10e | 1.0 | 7 | 47 | 11 | 10½ | 10½ | |
| | 2¼ | ¼ | vjAmFilmTech | AFTIQ | | ... | ... | 343 | 9/16 | 17/32 | 9/16 | ... |
| s | 20½ | 10 | AmFrtways | AFWY | | ... | 33 | 175 | 20¼ | 19½ | 20 | + ½ |
| s | 33½ | 22½ | AmGreetgs | AGREA | .50 | 1.7 | 18 | 4130 | 30 | 29½ | 29¾ | − ⅛ |
| | 26 | 15½ | AmHlthcp | AMHC | | ... | 26 | 717 | 25⅞ | 24¾ | 25¼ | ... |
| | 3⅛ | 1⅝ | AmHldg | HOLD | | ... | 12 | 42 | 1⅞ | 1¾ | 1¾ | ... |
| | 16¼ | 5¾ | AmIndemFnl | AIFC | .12 | 1.0 | 4 | 2 | 12½ | 12½ | 12½ | − ½ |
| s | 21 17/32 | 3¾ | **AmIntPetrol** | **AIPND** | | ... | dd | 422 | 4⅝ | 4 | 4⅛ | − ⅜ |
| | 28½ | 23½ | Am Life pf | ALHCP | 2.16 | 7.9 | ... | 4 | 27⅝ | 27¼ | 27¼ | − ¼ |
| | 23¾ | 14⅞ | AmMgtSys | AMSY | | ... | 23 | 58 | 22⅛ | 21¾ | 21¾ | − ¼ |
| | 13⅜ | 5¾ | AmMedElec | AMEI | | ... | 22 | 947 | 13¼ | 12⅜ | 12¾ | − ¼ |
| | 27¼ | 2¼ | **AmMobSys** | **AMSE** | | ... | ... | 1845 | 25¾ | 20½ | 21 | −4⅜ |
| | 63¼ | 43 | AmNatlIns | ANAT | 2.20f | 3.7 | 8 | 14 | 60½ | 58½ | 59 | −1½ |
| | 1⅜ | ⅛ | AmNuclear | ANUC | | ... | dd | 17 | 9/32 | 5/32 | 5/32 | − ⅛ |
| n | 13 | 9¼ | **AmOilField** | **DIVE** | | ... | ... | 918 | 11½ | 10¼ | 10¾ | −1⅛ |
| | 37¼ | 11 | AmPacCorp | APFC | | ... | 26 | 875 | 12½ | 11¾ | 12¼ | − ¼ |
| | 4 | 1½ | AmPhysnSvc | AMPH | | ... | 6 | 140 | 2½ | 2⅜ | 2½ | ... |
| s | 24¾ | 9⅝ | AmPwrConv | APCC | | ... | 44 | 10648 | 21¾ | 19¾ | 20½ | −1 |
| | 7¾ | 5½ | AmRecCtrs | AMRC | .22 | 3.4 | 17 | 14 | 6½ | 6½ | 6½ | ... |
| | 24½ | 13½ | AmResident | AMRS | | ... | 9 | 453 | 19⅞ | 19 | 19¾ | + ¼ |
| n | 14½ | 10⅜ | AmSaftyRazr | RAZR | | ... | ... | 54 | 13¼ | 12¾ | 12¾ | − ½ |
| s | 20⅜ | 6⅞ | AmSavFla | ASFL | | ... | 8 | 151 | 18⅛ | 17⅞ | 17⅞ | ... |
| | 11¼ | 5½ | AmSftwr A | AMSWA | .32 | 3.9 | 43 | 3269 | 8⅛ | 7⅝ | 8⅛ | + ⅛ |
| s | 21¼ | 6 | AmStudios | AMST | .08 | 1.3 | 30 | 188 | 6¾ | 6¼ | 6¼ | .. |
| | 27¾ | 15½ | AmSuprcnd | AMSC | | ... | ... | 45 | 24¼ | 24 | 24 | − ¼ |
| | 14⅞ | 6½ | **AmTrvlrs** | **ATVC** | | ... | 11 | 568 | 12⅞ | 11⅞ | 12⅛ | −1 |
| | 6⅜ | 4½ | AmUtdGlbl | AUGI | | ... | 19 | 1062 | 5 15/16 | 5⅝ | 5 15/16 | + 3/16 |
| | 16¼ | 7¼ | **AmVngrd** | **AMGD** | | ... | cc | 116 | 15½ | 14½ | 14½ | −1½ |
| | 35½ | 17¾ | AmeriFed | AFFC | .60a | 1.8 | 11 | 121 | 33¼ | 32¾ | 33¼ | + ⅜ |
| | 12¼ | 4 | AmhostProp | HOST | | ... | 91 | 244 | 6⅝ | 6⅛ | 6⅜ | + ⅛ |
| s | 16½ | 9½ | Ameriwood | AWII | | ... | 10 | 338 | 14½ | 14¼ | 14½ | + ¼ |
| sn | 26¾ | 11¾ | AMFED Fnl | AMFF | .10r | .4 | ... | 733 | 25½ | 24¾ | 24¾ | − ⅝ |
| | 78 | 31 | Amgen | AMGN | | ... | 15 | 13534 | 46¼ | 43¾ | 44 | −2 |
| | 2⅞ | 1⅛ | Amistar | AMTA | | ... | dd | 20 | 1⅝ | 1⅝ | 1⅝ | ... |
| | 43 | 15½ | Amoskg | AMOS | | ... | 16 | 442 | 39½ | 39½ | 39½ | + ⅛ |
| | 8⅛ | 3 | **Ampex** | **AMPX** | | ... | dd | 655 | 4 | 3⅛ | 3⅛ | − ⅞ |
| sn | 8⅛ | 5 | **Amrion** | **AMRI** | | ... | ... | 951 | 7½ | 6¾ | 6¾ | − ⅜ |

**Figure 3.1. A listing of NASDAQ National Market Issues from *The Wall Street Journal*. Reprinted by permission of *The Wall Street Journal*. © 1993 Dow Jones & Company, Inc. All rights reserved worldwide.**

# NASDAQ SMALL-CAP ISSUES

Figure 3.2. A listing of NASDAQ Small-Cap Issues from *The Wall Street Journal*. Reprinted by permission of *The Wall Street Journal*, © 1993 Dow Jones & Company, Inc. All rights reserved worldwide.

The lowest level of OTC stocks—all of which are non-NASDAQ stocks—are listed on the Pink Sheets (See Figure 3.3.) Published daily by the National Quotations Bureau in Cedar Grove, New Jersey, the Pink Sheets list in alphabetical order the company's name, the last reported price of its stock (when available), and the name of the brokerage firm that makes a market in the stock. In many cases, there will be no price for a stock on the Pink Sheets because it has not traded recently. A broker must call the market maker at the phone number provided on the sheet to find out the current and accurate market price of the stock.

Although the stocks of many large companies trade over the counter, overall the market is one of growth stocks. Generally, the listing requirements for stocks to trade OTC are more lenient than those of the exchanges. Typically the OTC markets' requirements involve lower price per share, lower after-tax earnings and net worth for the company and fewer outstanding shares. As a result, the majority of the companies whose shares trade in this market are newer, smaller, and less well capitalized. Many investors will interpret this description as meaning that the over-the-counter stocks are riskier. Although this is often true, many larger, well-capitalized companies like MCI, Apple Computer, Intel, McCormick Spice Co., and Microsoft choose to keep their stocks in this market. This is done because the listing fees in the OTC market are lower than those of the stock exchange and some companies prefer the OTC's market maker system (explained later) over the exchange's specialists system.

Customer orders are executed differently in this market. As with listed issues, a registered representative records your order on an order ticket. The ticket is sent to the trading desk within the brokerage firm where a trader ''shops'' among the stock's *market makers* for the highest *bid price* if you wish to

**market maker:** an NASD member firm that disseminates bid and ask prices at which it stands ready to buy stock into and sell stock from its inventory at its own risk. Synonymous with "dealer."

**bid price:** the highest price at which a market maker offers to purchase an OTC stock from an investor who wishes to sell.

# "Pink Sheets"®

## February 3, 1994

Published daily, except New York Stock Exchange holidays by:

# National Quotation Bureau, Inc.

### △ AN INFOBASE HOLDINGS COMPANY

150 Commerce Road, Cedar Grove, N. J. 07009-1208

Telephone 201-239-6100     FAX 201-239-2908     Listing Department 201-239-5300

| SECURITY | SYMBOL | FIRM NAME | TELEPHONE | BID | ASKED |
|---|---|---|---|---|---|
| A & A FOODS LTD | ANAFF | WK VOL- 1165 HB- 2 7/8 LB- 2 1/2 | | 2 9/16 | 2 11/16 |
| A & W BRANDS INC | | JB RICHARDS SECS CRP CHGO | 800 621 5253 | | |
| | | GABELLI & CO INC RYE | 914 921 5154 | | |
| | | MAYER&SCHWEITZER INC J CY | 800 631 3094 | | |
| AAA TRAILER SALES INC | *AAAT | CARR SECS CORP NY CARRB2F | | | |
| A A IMPORTING CO INC | *ANTQ | CARR SECS CORP NY | 800 221 2243 | | |
| | | HERZOG HEINE GEDULD NY | 212 962 0300 | | |
| | | A G EDWARDS & SONS ST L | 800 325 8197 | .001 | W/O |
| | | CARRO.08FHRZGO.10F | | | |
| M- AAON INC | AAON | WK VOL- 3334 HB- 10 3/4 LB- 9 3/8 | | 9 3/4 | 10 |
| A B C INVESTMENT CO | | CARR SECS CORP NY | 800 221 2243 | | |
| M- ABC RAIL PRODUCTS CORP | ABCR | WK VOL- 1102 HB- 18 5/8 LB- 17 1/2 | | 17 | 17 3/8 |
| A.B.E. INDUSTRIAL HOLDING | *ABEH | CCCO.05FHRZGO.05F | | | |
| M- AB ELECTROLUX CLASS B ADR | ELUXY | WK VOL- 404 HB- 45 LB- 40 1/8 | | 51 1/4 | 51 5/8 |
| ABN AMRO HOLDING NV ADR | *ARBLY | ARNHOLD&S BLEICHROEDER NY | 212 943 7518 | | |
| | | MERRILL LYNCH PFS NY | 212 449 4093 | | |
| | | FBCOB363/8O365/8 | | | |
| ABQ CORP | *ABQC | HRZGO1/16FMASHO.05F | | | |
| M- ABS INDUSTRIES INC | ABSI | WK VOL- 12 3/4 LB- 11 1/2 | | 13 1/2 | 14 1/2 |
| M- ABT BUILDING PRODS CORP | ABTC | WK VOL- 1113 HB- 27 1/4 LB- 25 1/2 | | 28 3/4 | 29 1/4 |
| M- ACC CORP | ACCC | WK VOL- 10925 HB- 21 LB- 18 | | 19 3/4 | 20 1/4 |
| M- ACE CASH EXPRESS INC | AACE | WK VOL- 290 HB- 12 1/4 LB- 11 | | 11 1/2 | 12 |
| ACNB CORP | *ACNB | WH NEWBDS DV FAHSTK PHILA | 800 682 5381 | | |
| | | FAHNB411/2FFBWAB421/2FO451/4FFJMCB421/2FO443/4FHILLB421/4F | | | |
| | | BOENNING&SCATGO W.CONSHKN | 800 883 8383 | 22 | |
| AG ARMENO MINES&MNRLS INC | AROYF | WK VOL- 972 HB- 1 3/8 LB- 1 1/16 | | 1 9/16 | 1 11/16 |
| A G BAG INTL LTD | AGBG | WK VOL- 15211 HB- 1 9/16 LB- 1 1/4 | | 1 3/8 | 1 1/2 |
| A G BAG INTL LTD 94 WTS | AGBGW | WK VOL- 138 HB- 1/16 LB- 1/32 | | 1/32 | 1/16 |
| M- AGCO CORP DEP SHS | AGCOZ | WK VOL- 1962 HB- 52 LB- 49 3/4 | | 52 | 52 3/4 |
| | | TUCKER ANTHONY&R L DAY NY | 212 225 8140 | | |
| | | GRACE BROTHERS LTD CG | 312 868 0294 | | |
| | | WG TRADING CO LP N HIL NY | 516 684 3580 | | |
| | | O'CONNOR & ASSOCIATES CG | 800 641 2509 | | |
| M- AGCO CORP | AGCO | WK VOL- 8114 HB- 40 LB- 37 3/4 | | 39 1/4 | 39 1/2 |
| AGP & CO INC | AGPC | WK VOL- 4246 HB- 1 11/16 LB- 1 5/16 | | 1 5/16 | 1 7/16 |
| AGS COMPUTERS INC | *AGSC | MAYER&SCHWEITZER INC J CY | 800 631 3094 | | |
| M- AG SVCS AMER INC | AGSV | WK VOL- 57 HB- 19 3/4 LB- 18 3/4 | | 18 3/4 | 19 3/4 |
| AIC INTERNATIONAL INC | *AIIN | BISHOP ROSEN & CO INC NY | 212 602 0681 | | |
| VJ AIM TELEPHONES INC | | BISHOP ROSEN & CO INC NY | 212 602 0681 | | |
| A I N LEASING CORP | *AINS | DATKO.015FWIENO.01FU | | | |
| A.I. SOFTWARE INC A | *AIIAF | ALEXB3/4O7/8 | | | |
| ALC COMMUN CORP A PR | | CARR SECS CORP NY | 800 221 2243 | | |
| | | SHERWOOD SECS CORP DENV | 800 525 3499 | | |
| | | BEAR STEARNS & CO NY | 212 272 5100 | 25 3/4 | 27 |
| | | PARAGON CAPITAL CORP NY | 212 785 4700 | | |
| ALC COMMUN CORP 97 WTS | *ACMMZ | TAFT SECURITIES CG | 312 696 2050 | | |
| | | BEAR STEARNS & CO NY | 800 964 6403 | | |

**Explanatory Notes**

BW   Bid Wanted

CPN   Coupon (for Tranche securities)

M    Included on Federal Reserve list of marginable securities

MAT   Maturity date (for Tranche securities)

OW   Offer Wanted

UNS   Unsolicited

VJ   In bankruptcy or receivership or being reorganized under the Bankruptcy Act, or securities assumed by such companies.

The Nasdaq Stock Market **trade prices** are the prior day's close. **WK VOL** number of securities traded for the prior week, updated each Mon. The **HB** (high bid) and **LB** (low bid) for the week are also provided for all Nasdaq securities.

---

**Figure 3.3.** **The Pink Sheets Listing. The Pink Sheets list the bid and ask prices of certain over-the-counter stocks, mostly low-priced, thinly traded domestic issues, and foreign issues (ADRs). The sheets are published and distributed to brokerage firms each business day and are named for the color of the paper on which the information is printed. Reproduced with permission of National Quotation Bureau, Inc. All rights reserved.**

sell the security or the lowest *asked price* if you want to buy the security. Market makers are the firms that buy and sell out of their own inventories. Here, again, the firm acts as an agent in the transaction. It adds commission to the asked price you pay when buying stock and deducts the commission from proceeds it receives for selling the stock for you.

If the firm is a market maker for the stock that you wish to buy or sell, then it can execute the trade out of its own inventory of the security. In this case, the firm is not acting as an agent; it is acting as a *dealer* or "principal" in the trade. A market maker's or dealer's role in the over-the-counter market is similar to that of a specialist on the exchange; however, the exchange specialist cannot trade or deal with the public and carries no accounts for the public. A market maker can deal with the public. Like a department store, the over-the-counter market maker buys securities into its inventory and then sells them out of it. The firm charges a *markup* on the ask price of the stock when you are buying. When you sell OTC stocks, the market maker *marks down* the bid price.

The amount of the markups or markdowns is disclosed on only the *NASDAQ National Market Issues*. The markups and markdowns on other OTC stocks—those on the Pink Sheets or listed under the heading "NASDAQ Small-Cap Issues—are not disclosed to you. You would therefore not know the profit that the dealer is making on the transaction. Your confirmation for a trade in these stocks would show a "net price." It must also disclose that the firm "acted as a principal in the transaction and is a market maker in the security."

A brokerage firm is prohibited from acting as both a broker (agent) and a dealer (principal or market maker) in the same OTC trade. Hence, for executing a customer's order, a firm can either

**asked price:** the lowest price at which a market maker offers to sell stock to a buyer. Also known as the "offer price."

**dealer:** a NASD member firm that makes a market in an OTC stock. Also called a "principal" or a "market maker."

**markup:** the amount or percentage added to the ask price when a customer buys an OTC stock from a firm acting as a principal or market maker in the transaction.

**markdown:** the amount or percentage subtracted from the bid price when the customer sells OTC stock to a market maker or principal firm.

**NASDAQ National Market Issues:** the approximately 2700

most active and best capitalized OTC stocks.

charge the customer a commission or a markup (or a markdown) but **never** both.

The National Association of Securities Dealers (NASD), the regulatory body of the over-the-counter market, does not set a minimum or maximum limit on commissions or markups. In general terms, the law simply states that all markups and commissions must be "fair and reasonable" considering the circumstances of the transaction and the services provided. Full-service brokerage houses that offer customers research and investment advice charge higher fees than do discount firms, which offer few services beyond order execution.

## New Issue Stock

**initial public offering (IPO):** the first time that a company issues or sells its stock to the public.

When a company issues stock to the public for the first time, the issuance is called an *initial public offering (IPO)*. If the same company later issues more shares to the public, these new shares are simply referred to as *new issues*. In both cases, the proceeds from the sale of the stock go to the issuing company, which uses the services of an *underwriter* (also known as an investment banker) to set the *public offering price* and promote the sale of the stock to the public.

**new issues:** securities offered for sale by the issuer in the primary market (for example, an initial public offering).

Typically you can purchase a new issue only from a brokerage firm that is a member of the underwriting group. These are the only firms that have the new shares to sell. No commission is added to the stock's public offering price when you buy a new issue. This is a *net transaction*. The underwriter's compensation is built into the issue price. Investors purchasing a new issue must receive a copy of the issuing company's prospectus at or prior to receiving confirmation of the trade. Most initial public offerings occur in the over-the-counter markets because start-up companies do not meet the strict listing requirements of the exchanges.

**underwriter:** a brokerage firm that assists the issuer of a new security in setting the offering price and in marketing the securities to the

Once the new shares are issued (sold) to the public, investors immediately begin to trade (sell and buy) the shares in the secondary or aftermarket—that is, on the floor of the exchange or in the over-the-counter market. The profits from trades in these markets do not go to the issuing company; instead they go to the investors.

If, immediately after issuance, the price of the shares in the secondary market exceeds their public offering price, the stock is described as a *hot issue*. For example, Snapple issued new shares in November 1992 at a price of $22 per share. By the end of the first day's trading in the secondary market, investor demand for the stock had driven the price up over 35 percent. Investors lucky enough to buy the shares at the initial offering price had an immediate and substantial gain.

Most new issues, however, do not become hot issues. More commonly, all of the shares are sold at their offering price in the primary market, and then the price declines slightly once they begin trading in the secondary market. This price decline is caused by speculators who sell off their shares if the stock does not become a hot issue.

New issues can fail to attract enough interest for underwriters to be able to sell the issuing company's shares. In this case, the issue can be withdrawn from the market. Anyone who bought shares of the failed offering gets his or her entire investment back from the underwriter.

Knowing the difference between the exchange market and the over-the-counter market and how trades are executed in each enables you to understand better the information that is disclosed on the confirmation. Additionally, this knowledge helps clarify how a stock's liquidity in the market affects the cost of a trade—both the price at which an order is executed and the commissions or markups charged on a transaction.

public. Also known as an "investment banker."

**public offering price:** the price at which a security is sold to the public by its underwriters.

**net transaction:** a trade, such as the purchase of a new issue, in which the buyer or seller is not charged a commission or additional fee.

**hot issue:** a newly issued stock that immediately begins trading in the secondary market at a price higher than its public offering price.

## Types and Uses of Orders

Most investors use only a few of the many types of orders available. The three most frequently used orders are market orders, limit orders, and stop orders. Knowing how each of these orders is executed, the results that each order can produce, and the risks associated with each is key to using them effectively.

Throughout this discussion, keep some basic facts in mind. If no time limit is specified on an order, it is a *day order*. If it is not executed or cancelled by the end of the trading session in which it was placed, it expires. If you want an order to stand in the market longer, one of the following time limits or notations must be specified when the order is placed:

**GTW**—good through the week
**GTM**—good through the month
**GTC**—good 'til canceled

**day order:** an order to buy or sell securities without a time notation; if it is not executed or canceled, it expires at the end of the trading session during which it was placed.

If either of the first two time limit notations is used, the order will be canceled by the brokerage firm on the last trading day of the week or month, respectively, when the order is placed. An order with the GTC notation is also called an *open order* and theoretically can remain unexecuted in the market for years. However, most brokerage firms require a GTC order to be renewed or confirmed monthly or quarterly. The exchanges require semiannual reconfirmation.

**open order:** remains valid until it is executed or canceled; same as a good 'til canceled order.

### Market Order

**market order:** an order to buy or sell stock immediately at the best available market price.

Investors use *market orders* most frequently to buy or sell stocks. When you call your broker and say, "Buy 200 shares of Motorola" or "Sell 100 shares of Home Depot," you are placing a market order. You specify both the stock and the number of shares but not a price or time. The stock is bought or sold at the market price of the security when the order

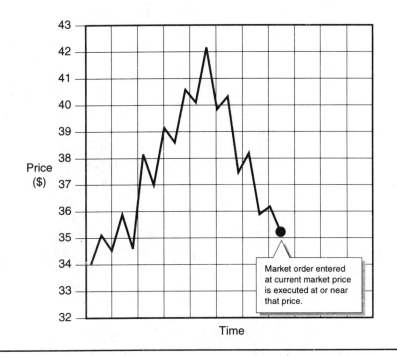

**Figure 3.4.  Price movement and current market price of ABC common stock.**

reaches the exchange floor or the over-the-counter trading desk.

Figure 3.4 shows that ABC stock is trading close to $35 per share (indicated by the bullet on the line graph). If you enter a market order to buy or sell ABC, it would be executed near $35 per share.

An investor placing a market order knows that it will be executed promptly—usually within a few minutes (or even seconds) after it is placed—unless there is a thin market for the stock. In this case, execution may take much longer. It is understood that a buy market order will be executed at the lowest available price and a sell market order will be executed at the highest available price at the time.

A broker cannot and does not guarantee a specific execution price on a market order. This point confuses many investors who call their brokers, request a price quote on a stock, and then place the order to buy or sell. They are usually surprised to find out that the order is not executed at the price that the broker quoted over the phone. Investors must keep in mind that the broker or account executive does not execute the order directly. They write the order ticket and place the order. The order is then executed at the best price available when it reaches the trading floor (for exchange-traded stocks) or trading desk (for over-the-counter stocks). In the short time between the phone conversation with your broker and the order reaching the trading area for execution, the price of an actively or heavily traded stock will most likely have changed.

Many investors still believe that all orders are sent to a floor broker, who yells and gesticulates in a crowd of other floor brokers in an attempt to get an execution. This image is no longer true. Today most investors' market orders are routed through computerized order execution systems. The New York Stock Exchange's system is known as Super-DOT ("Designated Order Turnaround"). The over-the-counter market's system is called SOES—an acronym for "Small Order Execution System." The orders are executed automatically at the best available prices reported in the system.

### Limit Order

**limit order:** an order to buy stock (buy limit) at a specified price or lower, or to sell stock (sell limit) at a specified price or higher.

When you place a *limit order*, you specify the price at which you want the order executed. It is understood that the order will be executed only at the stated limit price or better. The limit price is never the same as the stock's current market price. It is always "away from the market"—either above (on sell limit orders) or below (on buy limit orders) the current price. You believe the stock will move to the specified price within a reasonable period of time, at which point the order will be executed. The length of time that a limit order stands in the market after it has been entered depends on the time limit instructions given—GTW, GTM, or GTC. If no time is specified when the order is placed, the order is a day order and will be canceled at the end of the trading session if it is not executed. The following examples illustrate how buy limit and sell limit orders are used and executed in the market.

**Buy Limit Order.** A buy limit order is used to buy stock at a price that is below the current market price. Perhaps you observe that ABC common stock is trading at $34 per share. You want to purchase the stock but only if the price is $32 or lower. You believe that the price will decline to this point during the next few weeks before rising due to the increased demand resulting from the attractive low price, so you enter the following buy limit order: "Buy 100 ABC at $32 GTC." Note that this order is placed "away from"—specifically below—the stock's current price, as Figure 3.5 illustrates.

If and when the price declines to or below the limit price, the order will be executed and the stock purchased at $32 or lower. The risk for you is that the buy limit order may not be executed at all. If the stock does not trade down to at least $32, the limit price, the order will not be executed.

No investor would ever place a buy limit order above the current market. Because the stock's price would already be below the limit price, the order would be executed immediately, defeating the purpose of a limit order.

**Sell Limit Order.** A sell limit order is used to sell stock at a price that is higher than its current market price. For example, you own 100 shares of ABC, which is trading at $37 per share. You believe the

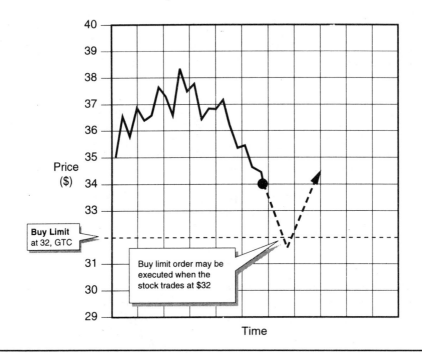

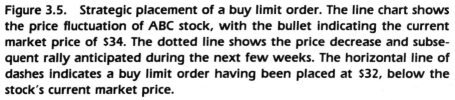

**Figure 3.5.   Strategic placement of a buy limit order. The line chart shows the price fluctuation of ABC stock, with the bullet indicating the current market price of $34. The dotted line shows the price decrease and subsequent rally anticipated during the next few weeks. The horizontal line of dashes indicates a buy limit order having been placed at $32, below the stock's current market price.**

stock will reach a peak price of nearly $40 per share during the next few days and then decline. Wanting to sell near the high, you enter the following sell limit order: "Sell 100 ABC at $39 GTC." As Figure 3.6 shows, the sell limit price is entered above the stock's current market price.

If and when the stock's price rises to or above the limit price, the order will be executed and the stock sold at $39 or higher; your objective will be accomplished. If the price never rises to the limit price, the order will not be executed. This is your risk.

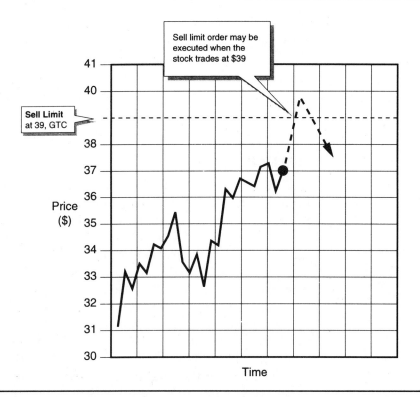

**Figure 3.6.    Strategic placement of a sell limit order. The line chart shows the price fluctuation of ABC stock, with the bullet indicating the current market price of $37. The dotted line shows the price increase and subsequent price decline expected to occur. The horizontal line of dashes shows a sell limit order having been placed at $39, above the stock's current market price.**

No investor would place a sell limit order below a stock's current market price. An order entered at this position would be executed immediately because the stock's market price would already be above the order's limit price. The objective of the order would be negated.

An investor who enters a limit order knows that if the order is executed, the stock will be bought or sold at the limit price 99.99 percent of the time. The danger is that the limit order will not be executed if the security's market price does not reach the limit price. For a buy limit order, the stock must trade down to at least the limit price. For a sell limit order, the stock must trade up to at least the limit price. Part of the skill in using a limit order is determining how far "away from the market" to set the limit price.

### Stop Order

**stop order:** an order that becomes a market order to buy (buy stop) or to sell (sell stop) when the stock trades at a specified price, known as the stop price. Also called a "stop-loss order."

Also called a stop-loss order, a *stop order* is used primarily to limit losses on profitable stock positions. As with a limit order, you enter a stop order at a price, called a "stop price," that is away from the stock's current market price. You expect the stock to rise or fall to the stop price within a reasonable period of time. The primary difference between a stop order and a limit order becomes clear in the execution of this order. When the stock's market price reaches the order's stop price, a stop order automatically becomes a market order and is then executed at the security's market price at that time. With a stop order, you know that if the market trades at or passes through the stop price, the order will be executed as a market order.

The risk is that the order may not be executed at the stop price. In reality, the stop price is only a "trigger," prompting the order to be entered as a market order. In fact, it may be executed at a price that is not advantageous—above or below the stop price. You do not learn the price at which a stop order has been executed until the confirmation is received. The examples and figures that follow demonstrate the effective use of both sell stop orders and buy stop orders. (Stop orders can be used only on stock exchanges. They are not accepted in the over-the-counter market.)

**Sell Stop Order.** A sell stop order is used to protect profits on a long stock position. Assume that you

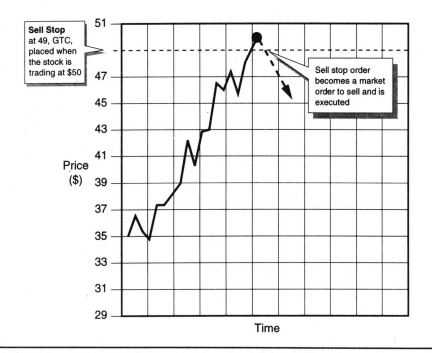

**Figure 3.7. Strategic placement of a sell stop order protecting the profits on a long stock position.** The line graph shows that ABC stock has risen from $35 to the current price of $50 per share, indicated by the bullet. You believe that a price decline may occur, indicated by the dotted line continuing from the current price on the graph, and wish to protect the $3000 profit you have made on the long stock position. You place a sell stop order at $49, below the current market price.

originally purchased 200 shares of ABC stock at $35. The price subsequently has risen to $50 per share, yielding a $3000 gross profit. However, you are concerned that the price may decline quickly and wipe out much of your gain. To protect the profits, you place a sell stop order below the stock's current market price, as shown in Figure 3.7.

If the stock price declines to $49 or lower, the sell stop order will become a sell market order and will be executed at the prevailing market price. If the stock is sold at $49 (the stop price), you have effectively limited the reduction of your gain to $200 ($1 × 200 shares), leaving a gross profit of $2800. To put it another way, you have protected approximately $2800 of the original $3000 profit on your long stock position. While the order can be executed at a price higher or lower than the stop price once the market reaches the specified price, in most cases a sell stop order is executed at the stop price.

You do not have to wait until the price reaches its peak before entering a protective sell stop order. You can place the order when you purchase the stock to limit your losses if an unanticipated downturn occurs. Or you can enter successively higher sell stop orders as the market price of the stock rises, canceling those that were entered when the stock was trading at a lower price. This strategy will provide you with continual protection.

**Buy Stop Order.** A buy stop order is used to protect profits on a short stock position. As illustrated in Figure 3.8, you have sold short 100 shares of ABC stock at $50 per share and the price has declined to $34, yielding a $1600 profit. Concerned that a price rise might cause you to lose the gain, you place a buy stop order at $35, above the current market price of the stock. If the market price of ABC stock rises from $34 to $35 per share, the buy stop order will become a market order to buy and will be executed at the stock's then-current market price. If the stock were bought in at $35, you would be left with a gross profit of $1500, having limited the losses to $100 ($1 per share).

Using the same strategies described for a sell stop order, you can enter a protective buy stock order when a short position is first established or enter them successively as the stock price declines to protect your position against an unexpected upturn.

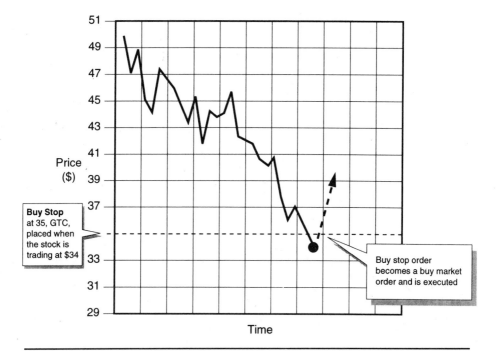

**Figure 3.8.** Strategic placement of a buy stop order protecting the profits on a short stock position. The graph shows that the 100 shares you sold short at $50 per share have declined to $34, indicated by the bullet. The dotted line indicates the anticipated price rise that would adversely affect your gains. In order to protect the profits (or limit the losses), you place a buy stop order at $35, above the current market price.

Stop orders have some of the same risks as limit orders. If the market does not reach the stop price, the order will never be executed. This is not a major concern, however. Because these orders are used largely to protect profits, they would remain unexecuted only if the stock were moving in a profitable direction for you.

A greater risk is that the order may be executed at a price significantly lower (in the case of a sell stop order) or higher (in the case of a buy stop order) than the stop price. Remember that unlike limit orders, stop orders become market orders when the stock reaches the specified price. If the stock price is moving quickly and many investors have entered stop orders at a given price, the market price at which the stop order may be executed can differ significantly from the stop price. This would be caused by the increased buying or selling that result from the execution of a large number of stop orders standing in the market at a specific price.

Perhaps the greatest risk in using a stop order is that the order may be executed on one of the small reversals that occur in the normal price movement of a stock. As all of the graphs have shown, a stock's price action is characterized by a series of small rises and falls. If an order's stop price is placed too close to the stock's current market price, the order may be executed during one of these small, insignificant reversals, thereby prematurely liquidating the position that you sought to protect. This could cost you profits as well as additional commissions if you choose to reestablish your original stock position.

In addition to protecting existing stock positions by liquidating them, stop orders can be used to establish new positions. Technical analysts enter buy and sell stop orders in anticipation of a significant short-term rise or decline in a stock value. A technician will place a buy stop order above a resistance level so that he or she can purchase the stock during the early phase of a significant price rise. He or she enters a sell short stop order below a support level in order to sell short at the beginning of a short-term decline. (This subject is discussed in Chapter 6.)

Figure 3.9 summarizes how limit orders and stop orders are placed in relation to a stock's current market price or trading range.

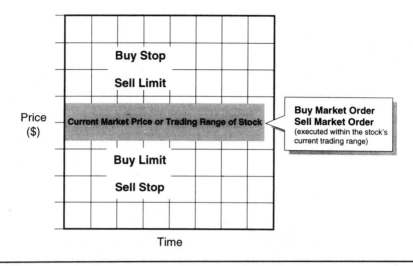

**Figure 3.9. Summary of a strategic placement of market, limit, and stop orders.** The figure shows the strategic placement of market, limit, and stop orders. Market orders to buy or sell are executed within the market's trading range. Sell limit and buy stop orders are placed above the current market. Buy limit and sell stop orders are placed below the current market price.

In conclusion, when you enter stop or limit orders, which will be executed only if and when the stock trades at the specified price, keep the following four points in mind:

1. Unless a time notation is specified for these orders, they are considered day orders and will be canceled at the end of the trading day if they are not executed.
2. No execution will occur unless the stock trades at or through the limit price or the stop price.
3. The stop or limit prices should be chosen with care so that they are not executed prematurely.
4. If the market is moving quickly, these orders may be executed at prices that are different from the specified limit price or stop price.

# CHAPTER 4

# Investment Strategies

"**W**hat is the best way to invest in stock?" and "Do I really have to read *The Wall Street Journal* every day?" These are two of the questions asked most frequently by beginning investors. The answers, especially to the first question, often surprise many people interested in the stock market. There is no perfect or best investment strategy for everyone. Even among the strategies used most frequently by beginning investors, some are only more or less speculative than others. And the frequency with which a person must follow the market—that is, read the financial news—is a function of the speculative characteristics and time frame of an investment. Usually the more speculative and short term the strategy is, the more closely it must be followed.

This chapter presents the most common beginning investment strategies, starting with those considered least speculative (and uncomplicated) and then proceeding to the most speculative:

1. Buy and hold, with dividend reinvestment
2. Dollar-cost averaging
3. Constant-dollar plan
4. Constant-ratio plan
5. Buying on margin
6. Short selling

The strategy that you choose should be in keeping with your investment objectives, financial means, and risk tolerance. Additionally, consider how often you want to read or monitor the financial news.

## BUY AND HOLD

The merits of buying high-quality stocks and holding them for the long term are rarely addressed. Yet this strategy can produce substantial returns, without your having to read the financial press every day or even every month. In fact, it is the passive management aspect of this investment strategy that is attractive to many people. It also minimizes timing risk—deciding when to buy or sell an investment. The success of the buy-and-hold strategy depends on three key elements: (1) the long-term trend of the stock market, (2) the characteristics of the stocks chosen, and (3) dividend reinvestment.

Historically, the stock market has moved upward, continually increasing in value over time. Clearly there have been market crashes (1929), market breaks (1987), and market corrections (1989) when the prices of all securities plummeted precipitously. Following each decline, however, the market recovered and moved still higher. Anyone who owned shares or a portfolio of stocks that reflected the broad movement of the market has seen their value steadily increase through the highs and lows of the market. By simply being in the market during a period of sustained growth, such as the 1980s, an investor would have seen his or her net worth increase. The buy-and-hold strategy puts you in a position to profit from this long-term upward trend of the stock market.

Selecting the stocks to buy and hold is somewhat more tricky. Look for stock of companies that have a high degree of financial strength (including good profit margins), are industry leaders or pacesetters in product sales and development, and are taking steps to improve their current market share and ensure long-term growth. The stocks that meet this description are generally blue chip stocks (except those that have lost their luster, like IBM), income stocks (particularly shares of public utilities and telephone companies), and established growth stocks. A typical conservative, income-oriented investor might place more money in income stocks, while a slightly more aggressive, although still conservative, investor might invest more in established growth stocks. The key factor is that the stocks in these categories have the potential to increase in price and pay higher dividends over the long term. For an investor who buys and holds, these features certainly increase the likelihood that the strategy will be successful.

One particularly beneficial aspect of the buy-and-hold strategy is the compounding effect that a *dividend reinvestment plan* can have on your return. Commonly referred to by the acronym DRP (pronounced "drip"), the plan is offered to existing stockholders by about 1000 companies, such as Procter & Gamble, American Express, Exxon, NationsBank, William Wrigley Jr. Company, Kemper, SmithKline Beechman, and British Petroleum. Instead of receiving dividends in cash, you can direct the company to use the money to buy additional common shares for you. Shortly after you buy a company's stock, you will receive a package of information from the shareholders' relations service department of the corporation. This correspondence welcomes you as a shareholder and invites you to participate in the company's dividend reinvestment plan.

Through the plan, you can buy whole or frac-

**dividend reinvestment plan:** a plan whereby a company's existing shareholders choose to have their cash dividend payments automatically reinvested in additional shares of the company's stock.

tional shares. A bank, acting as trustee for the company, holds the shares on your behalf. Every quarter the company sends you a statement showing the number of shares you hold that were purchased through a brokerage firm and the number of shares held in the plan on your behalf. At any time, you can request that certificates for the shares in the plan be issued in your name.

Most companies charge no brokerage fees for dividend reinvestment transactions; many, however, do assess a nominal handling fee. Usually you elect to participate in a dividend reinvestment plan when you first buy the company's stock, but you can elect to participate in the plan at any time while holding the shares. Over the long term, this essentially passive investment feature can increase your holdings in a company and thereby result in increased returns if the value of the stock appreciates.

The example that follows demonstrates the benefits of a dividend reinvestment plan for the small investor. In 1981, a friend bought 50 shares of du Pont common stock at a market price of $30 per share. His total original investment was $1500 (excluding commissions). At the time of this purchase, he elected to participate in the company's dividend reinvestment plan. He did not invest any "outside" monies in the stock; he simply bought and held the original 50 shares and through the plan used his dividends to buy additional shares. In 1986, he decided to sell all of the stock, when its price had risen to $98 per share. As a result of dividend reinvestment, his equity ownership had increased to 96 shares. The gross proceeds from the sale were $9408 (96 shares × $98).

What was the investor's percentage return on his investment? Most investors would simply divide the profit made on the transaction by the amount of the original investment. As the following calculation shows, he made a 527 percent profit on the original $1500 investment.

$$\frac{\$9408 - \$1500}{\$1500} = \frac{\$7908}{\$1500} = 527\%$$

This calculation does give a sense of the gross return on the original investment, but it is not an accurate measure of return. The technically correct way to measure the return would be to compute the year-by-year return, taking into account both the compounding effect of the dividend reinvestment and any taxes that the investor must pay. (This is a complex formula that can be found in many advanced texts on yield or portfolio analysis.) Applied to our example, this formula shows that the combined dividend payment and capital appreciation on the stock provided a total return (exclusive of any tax considerations) of approximately 44 percent per year.

Not all companies offer dividend reinvestment plans. You can find out which companies have such plans by referring to Standard & Poor's *Directory of Dividend Reinvestment Plans*, Moody's *Annual Dividend Record*, or Evergreen Enterprises' *Directory of Companies Offering Dividend Reinvestment Plans*, among other publications. The terms of reinvestment plans vary from company to company, although the following provisions are typical:

1. The company (the issuer) pays or absorbs all brokerage fees and other costs associated with reinvesting the dividend.
2. The additional common shares acquired through the plan may be purchased at a slight discount from the stock's current market price.
3. Participants in the plan may "round up" frac-

tional shares to full shares by depositing additional funds in the plan when the dividend is reinvested.

4.  Participants may be permitted to invest additional money in the plan beyond the amount of the dividend. (Typically, this additional money can be added only at the time of the dividend reinvestment and the company sets minimum and maximum limits on the amount.)
5.  Occasionally dividends from a company's preferred stock may be reinvested in the same company's common stock.
6.  The shares that the investor acquires through dividend reinvestment can be sold through the plan without commissions, provided the individual has not taken physical delivery of the shares.

Dividend reinvestment offers small investors an easy way to build wealth. It works best when the company has a solid history of dividend payments and steady price appreciation.

Dividend reinvestment plans do have some disadvantages, particularly in the area of taxation. First, dividends are considered taxable income to the investor in the year in which they are paid out, even if they have been used to buy additional shares of a company's stock under a dividend reinvestment plan. The investor in the du Pont example was taxed on the dividends paid each year, although he reinvested the money. And he paid taxes on the gross profits when he sold all of the shares accumulated under the plan. Second, the investor must keep records of the market price at which each additional share is purchased. When the shares are eventually sold, the amount of the investor's gain will not be simply the difference between the purchase price of the original shares and the later sale price of the accumulated shares, as the example implied. The Internal Revenue Service requires investors to compute the average cost basis of the total number of shares purchased during the holding period. The gain or loss is then the difference between the average cost of all shares and their sale price. If a person sells only some of the shares acquired through dividend reinvestment, different tax rules apply. A tax specialist should be sought for advice in this and similar situations. Despite these complex tax implications, dividend reinvestment plans provide a convenient and easy way for investors, particularly small investors, to build ownership in a company over a long period of time.

Indeed the buy-and-hold strategy is largely passive, but it should not be thought of as a synonym for what some people jokingly call the "buy-and-neglect" strategy. Investing by neglect—buying small amounts of different stocks, throwing the certificates in a drawer, and forgetting that you own them—has been known to provide some investors (or, depending on the degree of negligence, their heirs) with surprising gains, but profits from this strategy are more the apocryphal exception than the rule.

From a practical point of view, all reporting corporations are required by the Securities and Exchange Commission (SEC) to send quarterly reports to their stockholders. Thus, an investor has (and should use) the opportunity to review a company's performance, financial stability, dividends, the objectives of the management, and prospects for future growth every quarter. If a company has a number of bad quarters in a row, sell and switch to another company. There is, after all, no reason to stay on the *Titanic* just because you bought a first-class ticket.

The buy-and-hold strategy is not a glamorous

approach to investing. It will provide no great cocktail party stories about one-day killings in the market. In fact, some people might call it boring. Nonetheless, it has proved to be one of the most convenient ways for small investors to get started in stocks. Investors using this strategy must maintain a long-term view of the market and stay the course through the usual declines or reversals of the market. In a real sense, you are on autopilot after making the initial decision. You do not have to follow the financial news daily, weekly, or even monthly. Minimum vigilance is required—just enough to monitor any changes in the long-term prospects of the company that may warrant selling the stock and investing in shares of a more suitable company.

## DOLLAR-COST AVERAGING

*Dollar-cost averaging* is a long-term strategy whereby you invest the same amount of money in a stock or mutual fund at regular intervals—monthly, quarterly, or semiannually. You buy the security without consideration of its market price at the time of each purchase. Consistency in the amount invested and the regularity of the payments is essential to the success of dollar-cost averaging in order to minimize pricing and timing risk.

Dollar-cost averaging works on the following simple principles. When the price of the security declines, the fixed investment amount buys more shares. Hence, your purchasing power expands. When the price of the security rises, the fixed investment amount buys fewer shares. Consequently, your purchasing power contracts. Over the long term, you will discover that the cost of each share is lower than the average price per share during the investment period.

**dollar-cost averaging:** a strategy whereby a person invests the same amount of money at regular intervals in a stock or a mutual fund without regard for the price fluctuations of the security.

| Month | Dollars Invested | Price Per Share | Number of Shares Bought |
|---|---|---|---|
| 1 | $200 | $25.00 | 8.00 |
| 2 | 200 | 22.00 | 9.09 |
| 3 | 200 | 20.00 | 10.00 |
| 4 | 200 | 26.00 | 7.69 |
| 5 | 200 | 19.00 | 10.50 |
| 6 | 200 | 18.00 | 11.11 |
| 7 | 200 | 24.00 | 8.33 |
| 8 | 200 | 28.00 | 7.14 |
| 9 | 200 | 31.00 | 6.45 |
| 10 | 200 | 35.00 | 5.71 |
| 11 | 200 | 30.00 | 6.67 |
| 12 | 200 | 32.00 | 6.25 |
| **Total # of Payments** | **Total $ Invested** | **Average Price Per Share** | **Total # of Shares Bought** |
| **12** | **$2,400** | **$25.83** ($310 ÷ 12) | **97** |

**Figure 4.1.   12-Month investment period using dollar-cost averaging.**

At first reading, this explanation of dollar-cost averaging sounds like a form of investment alchemy. After all, how can securities bought over a period of time cost less than their average price? The simple example that follows illustrates the mechanics and benefits of dollar-cost averaging.

You invest $200 on the first of each month, purchasing odd lot units of a particular stock or shares of a mutual fund. As is characteristic of the market, the price fluctuates and is therefore different each time you buy the stock. Figure 4.1 shows the security's price per share on the first of each month and the number of shares purchased at that time. The investment period is 12 months.

You can see the benefit of this strategy by comparing the average cost per share over the period of investment with the average price per share over the same period. Over 12 months, you invested $2400 ($200 × 12) and purchased 97 shares. The average price per share of the stock during this period was $25.83. This value is computed by adding the price per share for each month and dividing the total by the number of periodic investments made:

$$\$310 \div 12 = \$25.83$$

The average cost per share for this period was $24.74. This is computed by taking the total amount invested regularly during the 12-month period and dividing it by the number of shares purchased:

$$\$2400 \div 97 = \$24.74$$

Each share cost $1.09 less than the average price per share during the same period. Given that the price of a security always fluctuates, dollar-cost averaging guarantees that your cost basis will always be lower than the average price per share.

The fact that the average cost is lower than the average price does not mean that you have a guaranteed gain. Such a guarantee would indeed be investment alchemy. If a stock's price trend is downward, for example, the average cost will still be lower than the average price; however, you would have an overall loss on the price of the stock. An examination of the first six months of the period illustrated in Figure 4.1 illustrates this point. The market price at the beginning of this period is $25.00 per share. In the sixth month, it is $18.00, a decrease of $7.00 per share. The average price per share during the six months is $21.67 ($130 ÷ 6). The average cost per share, however, is $21.28 ($1200 ÷ 56.38), $.39 lower than the average price. Dollar-cost averaging works in both a declining market and a rising market, and its benefits are enhanced when it is combined with a dividend reinvestment plan. However, the strategy offers no guarantees that you will make a profit on the investment or be protected against a loss.

There are several disadvantages to this method of investing. First, dollar-cost averaging can limit your profits during a rising market. If the price of a stock increases sharply with only small reversals or declines, then the average cost per share will most likely be higher than the market price of the stock when the strategy was started. In this case, dollar-cost averaging limits your gain. You would have had a greater profit by purchasing all of the shares at the outset.

This disadvantage is of minimal concern to most investors, however, for two reasons. First, dollar-cost averaging is primarily a means for a person with modest capital to begin investing regularly in the market. Typically, this person is able to buy only a few shares at one time. Wealth building is usually the long-term objective. Second, the relationship between the initial cost and the average cost varies according to the market price fluctuation during the investment period. In Figure 4.1, the average cost ($24.70) is lower than the market price of the stock when the plan was initiated ($25.00). For each investor, the specific benefits of dollar-cost averaging will be somewhat different, depending on the length of the investment period, the fluctuations in the security's price during this time, and the amount of money invested.

Taxation is the second potential problem facing an investor who uses dollar-cost averaging. As with the buy-and-hold strategy, the taxable gain or loss is based on the average cost of the shares over the period of the investment, which could be five years, ten years, or more. If this strategy is combined with dividend reinvestment, then calculating the cost basis for tax purposes becomes even more complicated. Investors should keep all year-end statements that they receive from their brokerage houses or mutual funds. These statements usually show the average cost of the stock purchased over the 12-month period.

Like the buy-and-hold strategy, dollar-cost averaging starts from the basic premise that the price or value of stocks has tended to increase over the long term. The success of this strategy depends on your discipline in adhering to the following principles:

1. Invest over a long period of time. Dollar-cost averaging should be continued for 7½ to 10 years. This recommendation is based on the cyclical history of the market. Over the past 100 years, there have been about 40 recessions—that is, severe market corrections—or a downturn about every 2½ years. If you continue to invest through about three of these corrections, the benefits of dollar-cost averaging tend to be maximized.
2. Invest at regular intervals; monthly or quarterly is preferable.
3. Invest regardless of the price of the stock.
4. Choose high-quality stocks or mutual funds. A company or fund with a history of regular dividend payments and the potential for capital appreciation is a good choice. Dividend reinvestment can enhance the benefits of dollar-cost averaging.

In addition, you should have sufficient fortitude so that you can stick to the plan through highs and lows, and sell out at the peak. Thus, the money allocated for dollar-cost averaging should be wealth-building funds, not committed funds.

Periodically, review the financial statements and other information of the relevant company to ascertain whether it is still in keeping with your stated investment objectives.

## CONSTANT-DOLLAR PLAN

**constant-dollar plan:** an investment method in which a person maintains a fixed-dollar amount of a portfolio in stocks, buying and selling shares periodically to maintain the fixed-dollar amount.

Under the *constant-dollar plan,* you invest a fixed-dollar amount of a portfolio in stock. You then maintain the same level of investment in stock regardless of the extent of the increase or decrease in the price of the stock. If the price of the stock rises, you sell enough to reduce the total value of your shares to the constant-dollar amount and invest the sale proceeds in fixed-income securities. Traditionally, the fixed-income securities in which the money would be invested is bonds, but this narrow interpretation is no longer true. Depending on the economic climate, you may choose to put your money in certificates of deposit (CDs) or in cash-equivalent securities or keep it as cash. If the price of the stock declines, you buy enough shares to return the total value of the stock to the constant-dollar amount. The funds used to buy these common shares do not come from the sale of the fixed-income securities. You must use money from other sources.

**averaging down:** a strategy in which an investor lowers the average price paid per share of stock by purchasing more shares when the price declines.

The benefit of this plan is that it forces you to take profits when a stock's price rises. Thus, most investors' tendency to buy more shares in response to a price rise, and therefore buy at the peak price, is mitigated. Conversely, when the price of a stock declines, this plan dictates that you buy more shares, thereby allowing you to take advantage of the expanded purchasing power of your money. You are also *averaging down*: lowering the overall

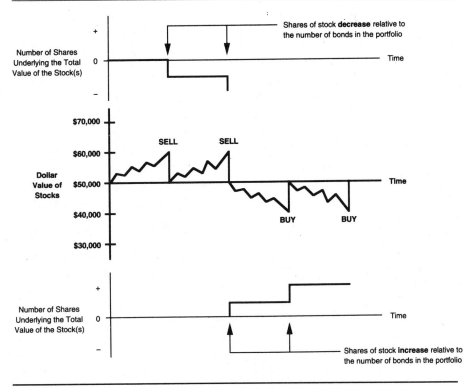

**Figure 4.2.   Constant-dollar plan.**

cost basis of the total shares in the portfolio. Throughout the term of this investment plan, the percentage of your portfolio invested in stocks and other investments will vary, as shown in Figure 4.2. When stock prices rise, prompting you to sell, the percentage of the portfolio invested in stock will decrease, and other investments will increase. When stock prices fall, prompting you to buy, the percentage invested in stock will increase, and other investments will decrease. The graphs at the top and bottom of the Figure illustrate these relationships.

Figure 4.2 illustrates how the constant-dollar plan works for an investor maintaining $50,000 of a portfolio in stocks and the remainder in bonds. At the time the portfolio is established, the individual determines that he will restore the portfolio to the constant-dollar amount when the price of the stock rises or falls by 20 percent of his original investment. Hence, when the value of the shares increases $10,000 (20 percent), he sells some of them, returning the total value of the stock position to $50,000. The proceeds of the sale are reinvested in bonds. When the stock's value declines $10,000 (20 percent) below $50,000, the investor buys enough shares to restore the total value of the position to $50,000.

The success of this plan is based on the observation that over the long term, the price of stocks rises. As this price appreciation occurs, the constant-dollar plan forces you to take profits from speculative investments (stocks) and transfer them to less speculative securities (bonds, preferred stocks, certificates of deposit).

The investor in Figure 4.2 establishes a $100,000 portfolio, in which $50,000 will be constantly maintained in stocks and $50,000 in bonds. Assume that the prices of the stocks steadily appreciate. Each time the price reaches the constant-dollar level and activates the sell signal, the customer transfers the equity that exceeds the constant-dollar amount into bonds, with interest rates that are probably lower than the total return he is making on the stocks. In a prolonged bull market, an investor using the constant-dollar plan does not maximize profits. In fact, the overall or total return from the investment portfolio will be lower than if the money were left in stocks. However, the transfer of profits made on speculative investments (stocks) into safer vehicles (bonds) is an overriding investment objective of the relatively cautious investor who relies on the constant-dollar plan.

Selecting the stock or mutual fund that will enable this plan to work most effectively is not easy. Stocks with relatively stable prices are not the optimum choices for the constant-dollar plan. Instead, look for companies whose stock has good potential for long-term appreciation and whose market price tends to fluctuate.

Determining the constant-dollar value of the portfolio to maintain in stocks depends as usual on the degree of risk that you are willing to accept. If you are conservative and averse to risk, invest more money in fixed-income and cash-equivalent securities than in stocks. If your objective is focused more on growth, maintain a larger dollar amount of the portfolio in stocks. Additionally, your decision will be influenced by market conditions. If interest rates are low, stocks are a preferable investment because they offer an opportunity for growth.

Unlike the situation prevailing under the buy-and-hold and dollar-cost averaging strategies, price risk and timing risk become significant factors in the constant-dollar plan. For example, should you sell stocks after only a small price rise or wait for a bigger rise and more profits? Should you buy more shares after a brief decline or wait for a bigger price dip? This dilemma can be handled in two ways, both of them totally arbitrary. You can set percentages (e.g., 20 percent, 25 percent, 30 percent) or dollar values (e.g., $2500, $5000, $7000) of price increases and decreases that will serve, respectively, as automatic sell and buy signals. For example, if the price of a stock declines 20 percent, purchase enough shares to restore the stock's value to the constant-dollar amount. Or, instead of using percentage of gain or loss as signals, set intervals of time (e.g., quarterly, semiannually). At the beginning or end of each period, review the status of your investments in the portfolio and take the appropriate buy or sell action. Usually an investor selects one parameter—dollar value, percentages, or time—to prompt a review of the investment portfolio.

Setting the parameters discussed above reduces, or at least mitigates, price and timing risk. You no longer have to figure out whether the stock's price is going higher or lower or what is the best time to buy or sell. The review and reinvestment decisions are automatically made when the stock reaches the designated percentage or at a designated period of time. These parameters also mitigate emotional risk—the risk that you might react inappropriately to a temporary sharp decline or rise in the market between review periods.

The most significant risk that remains is reinvestment risk. When, at the predetermined level, you sell the appreciating stock and buy fixed-income securities, you could be investing in a security that will provide a lower return than the stock. On the other hand, when the price declines, you could be buying more shares of a company or mutual fund whose suitability in view of your investment objectives has changed. Stock selection and a periodic review of the holdings are as essential to the success of this strategy as is the price fluctuation of the shares.

**constant-ratio plan:** an investment method in which a person maintains a fixed ratio between stocks and bonds throughout the investment period, with regular adjustments made to compensate for different levels of price increases and decreases.

## CONSTANT-RATIO PLAN

The *constant-ratio plan* is similar to the constant-dollar plan except that you maintain a fixed percentage of the portfolio invested in stocks and a fixed percentage invested in bonds—for example, 50 percent of the value of a portfolio in stocks and 50 percent in fixed-income securities. Another investor, following the recommended static asset allocation mix, would maintain 55 percent of the portfolio's value in stocks, 35 percent in bonds, and

10 percent in cash equivalents. The percentages chosen for each class of investment depend on each investor's objectives and risk tolerance and the climate for various investments at that time. A conservative investor allocates a larger percentage to fixed-income securities; an aggressive individual invests a higher percentage of dollars in stocks.

The ratio that is established must be maintained notwithstanding both the appreciation and depreciation of the securities. In the example in Figure 4.3, an investor has allocated 50 percent of her $60,000 portfolio to stock and 50 percent to bonds. She reviews the ratio of stocks to bonds at the beginning of each quarter and then buys and sells as appropriate to restore the ratio. During the first quarter, the value of the stocks rises to $40,000, and the bonds decrease in value to $26,000. The total value of the portfolio is now $66,000; however, the ratio of stocks to bonds is no longer 50:50. It is now 61 percent ($40,000 ÷ $66,000) stocks and 39 percent bonds ($26,000 ÷ $66,000). In order to restore the portfolio's value to the 50:50 constant ratio, she sells $7000 of the stocks, reducing the total value of the stock position to $33,000. She uses the proceeds to buy $7000 of bonds, raising their total value to $33,000. Thus, the 50:50 ratio of stocks to bonds is reestablished.

If the bonds had appreciated in value and the stocks had declined, as illustrated during the third quarter of Figure 4.3, the investor would sell the bonds and use the proceeds to buy enough stock to restore the constant ratio.

As with the constant-dollar plan, price risk and time risk are significant factors under the constant-ratio plan. However, the effect of these factors can be minimized by using the same strategy recommended before: setting arbitrary points—dollar values, percentages, or time periods—that trigger

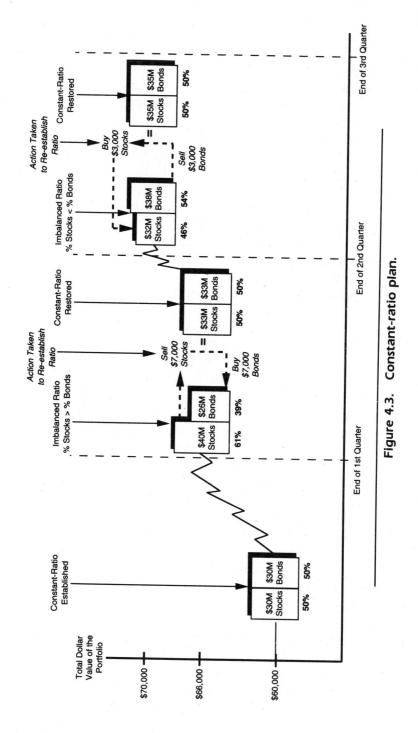

**Figure 4.3. Constant-ratio plan.**

buying and selling. Also, prudent investors sell stocks or bonds that do not meet performance expectations over an established period of time.

Significant reinvestment risk is associated with this investment plan. You must carefully select the stocks and bonds that will comprise the portfolio. Short-term fluctuations in the price of the securities during a general upward trend enhance the results that you will obtain using this strategy.

Keep in mind that the constant-ratio plan, like the constant-dollar plan, is a long-term strategy. The two basic premises are that the prices of stocks and bonds tend to fluctuate and that the values of stocks tend to increase over time. This strategy does not guarantee a gain or maximize your profit, but it does enable you to take profits on an appreciating class of securities and then to reinvest them in another class in which the buying power of the profits is greater. Over the long term, you increase the number of stocks and bonds in the portfolio and thereby expand the gains that can be made from the rise in the value of the securities.

At least annually, investors using the constant-ratio plan should review the percentages allocated to each class of security and to the securities in each class. They need to make certain that the individual securities and the percentages allocated among investments are suitable, given any changes in their objectives as well as the anticipated long-term trend of the stock market.

Many brokerage firms suggest an asset allocation plan suitable to the state of the market at the time. For example, at the writing of this book, Merrill Lynch recommends the following allocation for conservative growth-oriented investors with $100,000 or more: 55 percent stock, 40 percent bonds, and 5 percent cash and equivalents. Other investment advisers have a similar matrix of asset allocation.

# BUYING STOCK ON MARGIN

**initial margin requirement:** the percentage of a stock's market price that must be deposited when initially buying or selling short stock on margin. Set by the FRB under Regulation T.

In general, buying on margin is a suitable strategy for only experienced investors. It is a way for these investors, especially those with conservative, growth-oriented goals, to allocate some funds (**never** more than 10 percent) to high risk–high growth investments.

Buying stock on margin is buying stock by making a partial payment of its market value. You use your own money to make a "down payment," called the *initial margin requirement*. Currently set at 50 percent of a stock's purchase price, the initial margin requirement is controlled by the Federal Reserve Board under *Regulation T*. The brokerage firm loans you the remaining 50 percent of the stock's value. This loan is called the margin account's *debit balance* and is secured by the stock that you purchase.

**Regulation T:** the Federal Reserve's regulation that gives it the power to set the initial margin requirement on most corporate stocks and bonds.

**debit balance:** the balance owed to the brokerage firm by a customer who purchases securities on margin.

As long as you hold the shares, you are charged interest on the debit balance. As with a credit card balance, the interest charge is computed daily and added to the amount of the outstanding loan. Hence, the debit balance increases over your holding period. The rate of interest charged is usually a few percentage points above the *call loan rate*. Also referred to as the "broker loan rate," this is the rate that banks charge brokerage firms for loans collateralized by marketable securities. The firm earns the difference between the rate it pays to the bank and the rate it charges investors who trade on margin. Like all other short-term interest rates, the call loan rate changes frequently. Figure 4.4 shows the relationship of the broker call loan rate to other interest rates during a period when short-term interest rates were low. Usually the call loan rate is less than the bank's *prime rate*.

**call loan rate:** the interest rate that banks charge brokerage firms for loans collateralized by marginable securities.

**prime rate:** the short-term interest rate that commercial banks

Because shares bought on margin are not fully paid, they are never held in customer name. They

| | |
|---|---|
| **Treasury Bills** <br> Discount rate on T-Bills trading in the secondary market | **5.48%** |
| **Discount Rate** <br> Interest rate the Federal Reserve charges member banks for loans | **5.50%** |
| **Commercial Paper** <br> Discount rate on unsecured high-quality, short-term debt issued by a corporation | **5.75%** |
| **Certificate of Deposit** <br> Average yield on negotiable CDs with one month to maturity and in amounts of $1 million or more | **5.75%** |
| **Federal Funds** <br> Interest rate for overnight loans among commercial banks | **5.79%** |
| **Broker Call Loans** <br> Rate banks charge brokerage firms for loans collateralized by securities | **7.25-8.00%** |
| **Prime Rate** <br> Rate banks charge their most creditworthy business customers | **8.50%** |

**Figure 4.4.   Short-term interest rates (during a period when rates were considered moderate to low).**

are always held in street name. As we shall see later, this situation provides the brokerage firm with some protection should the investor fail to repay the loan.

The advantage of buying stocks on margin is leverage. You use a relatively small amount of money to control securities that have a much greater value. Any increase in a stock's value results in a greater percentage gain on each dollar invested than would be made if the securities were fully paid. Suppose that two investors buy 100 shares of the same stock that has a market price of

$40 per share. Investor A pays in full for the shares, depositing $4000 in his account. Investor B buys the stock on margin, depositing $2000, the 50 percent Regulation T initial margin requirement, in her account. The shares appreciate by $5 each. For investor A, the $500 total price increase ($5 × 100 shares) is a 12.5 percent return ($500 ÷ $4000) on the money invested. For investor B, who bought her shares on margin, the $5 per share increase provides a 25 percent return ($500 ÷ $2000) on each dollar invested. Thus, under the current 50 percent initial margin requirement, buying stock on margin doubles an investor's potential gross return on each dollar invested. Of course, commissions, interest on the margin loan, and taxes must be paid from the gain.

Buying on margin also doubles an investor's price risk. Using the same example, let's examine what would happen if the price of the stock were to fall $5 per share. Investor A, who paid in full for the 100 shares, would lose $500 of his $4000 investment—a 12.5 percent loss ($500 ÷ $4000). Investor B, who purchased the shares on margin, would also lose $500. However, since she put up only $2000—50 percent of the stock's value—her percentage loss would be 25 percent ($500 ÷ $2000), **double** the percentage loss incurred if the stock had been purchased fully paid. Clearly, leverage can provide investors with a higher percentage gain if a stock's price rises—but it also increases the percentage loss if a stock declines in value. This increased risk makes buying stock on margin more speculative than buying stock fully paid.

When you buy stock on margin, you must deposit the initial margin requirement promptly—within five business days of the trade (regular way settlement). If you do not meet the terms of regular way settlement, Regulation T states that the brokerage firm must either liquidate (sell) your position and freeze the account for 90 days or, if warranted, obtain an extension. You are liable for any loss that occurs during the settlement period.

The benefits and risks of buying stock on margin will become clear by following the price fluctuations of a simulated trade using Home Depot, Inc. (HD) common stock. Assume that HD's current price per share is $40. You buy 100 shares of HD on margin and deposit $2000 in your margin account. The brokerage firm lends you the remaining $2000 of the value of the securities. In the firm's *margin department*, your account looks as follows after this transaction:

| | |
|---|---|
| **Current market value (100 at $40)** | **$4000** |
| **− Debit balance** | **2000** |
| **= Equity in the account** | **$2000** |

**margin department:** *a division of a brokerage firm that computes an investor's equity in a margin account daily and sends out margin or maintenance calls, as appropriate.*

The margin percentage, computed by dividing the equity in the account by the stock's current market value ($2000/$4000), is 50 percent. Thus, you have met the Regulation T initial margin requirement.

The value of the shares in a margin account is *marked to market* daily. This means that the firm's margin department recomputes the equity in the account every day based on the stock's closing price in the market. At the same time, interest on the debit balance accrues daily. Hence, the equity in an investor's margin account changes continuously.

**marked to market:** *the process by which a brokerage firm computes the value of the shares in an investor's account based on the daily closing price.*

Let's examine what happens in the margin account when the market price of HD shares rises by $10 to $50. Your account would look as follows:

| | |
|---|---|
| **Current market value (100 at $50)** | **$5000** |
| **− Debit balance** | **2000** |
| **= Equity in the account** | **$3000** |

Notice that the debit balance does not change, except for interest added. An increase or decrease in a stock market price does not affect the amount of the loan that you obtained when you initially purchased the stock.

As a result of the price increase from $40 to $50 per share, you have a $1000 *unrealized gain* on the 100 shares of HD. This is a 50 percent gross return ($1000/$2000) on the money invested—twice as much as it would have been if you had bought the securities fully paid. If you are satisfied with this gain, you can now take your profits, turning them into a *realized gain* by selling long the 100 shares. Part of the proceeds is used to pay off the debit balance and the remainder is released to you.

When you purchase stock on margin, you do not have to sell the securities in order to be able to use the unrealized gains. This feature is one of the benefits of buying stock on margin. The process by which unrealized gains are made usable is simple, although the explanation sounds complex. Careful attention is required to understand how this feature of a margin account works.

As a stock's price rises, a portion of the unrealized gain, called "excess equity," is made available to you as a line of credit—similar to the line of credit that some banks provide to home owners against the appreciated equity of a house. This "credit" account is called a *special memorandum account*; hence the "excess equity" is commonly referred to by the letters in abbreviation for the account—SMA. The amount of the unrealized profits that is released as excess equity or SMA into the special memorandum account is that portion of the account's equity that exceeds **what would be** the initial margin requirement on the stock at its current market price.

The following example clarifies this point. After the price rise, the current total market value of HD is $5000, and the equity in the margin account is

**unrealized gain:** the profit resulting from an increase in the value of a security position that is still being held.

**realized gain:** the cash profit resulting from the liquidation of a stock position.

**special memorandum account:** an account used to show the excess equity or line of credit that an investor has in a margin account.

is $5000, and the equity in the margin account is $3000. If you were to purchase 100 shares of HD at the current market value, the initial margin requirement would be $2500. The current equity ($3000) exceeds this requirement ($2500) by $500. The SMA or credit available to you is thus $500. The formula for computing SMA when buying stock on margin is:

$$\text{SMA} = \text{Equity} - \left( \begin{array}{c} \textbf{Stock's current market value} \\ \times \textbf{ Reg T margin requirement} \end{array} \right)$$

How can you use this excess equity or SMA? There are basically two choices, both of which require the broker's approval:

1. **Withdraw part or all of the SMA as cash.** In the HD example, you can withdraw the $500 of SMA as cash. This is the equivalent of getting a cash advance on a credit card. Your debit balance increases, and additional interest begins to accrue from the first day of withdrawal.
2. **Buy shares of other marginable stocks.** With $500 of SMA, you can purchase shares with a total market value of $1000—two times the amount of SMA. You pay for half of the value of the stock using the SMA or "credit line," and the firm provides a loan for the remaining value. The account's debit balance therefore increases twice as much as the amount of the SMA used—a good deal for the firm.

Keep in mind that SMA is nothing more than a credit line backed by the unrealized profits on a customer's long stock position in a margin account. And like a credit line on a credit card, every time you use the SMA, your indebtedness increases.

Therefore, you cannot use SMA to pay off or reduce your debit balance. The debit is reduced only when you sell stock out of the margin account or deposit cash into the account.

When the price of stock purchased in a margin account declines, recall that your loss on each dollar invested mounts more quickly. In order to protect both the customer and the brokerage firm, the New York Stock Exchange (NYSE) and the National Association of Securities Dealers (NASD) set a *minimum maintenance margin*. This is the lowest percentage to which the equity in the account can fall in relation to the stock's current market value before the firm sends the customer a *maintenance call*. Currently, the NYSE and the NASD set the minimum maintenance margin at 25 percent of a stock's current market value. Individual firms often have more stringent requirements, such as 30 percent or 35 percent.

A maintenance call is sent when an account's margin percentage falls below the minimum maintenance margin. In response, the investor usually deposits enough additional cash in the account to return the margin percentage to the minimum. An investor must satisfy this call within five business days; otherwise, the firm liquidates a portion of the person's position. The individual is liable for all losses incurred on the trade during this time.

When the margin percentage in the account is between the initial amount and the minimum, no maintenance call is sent out on existing positions. At this point, you can still buy stock on margin by depositing the required 50 percent initial margin requirement in the account. However, restrictions are placed on the amount of proceeds that can be withdrawn from the account when shares are sold.

Using the HD example, I will illustrate how a price decrease prompts a brokerage firm to send a

**minimum maintenance margin:** set by the NYSE and the NASD, the minimum equity that a customer must maintain in a margin account. Below this percentage or amount, the customer gets a maintenance call.

**maintenance call:** a demand from a brokerage firm that an investor deposit enough cash in a margin account to restore the account to the minimum maintenance margin following an adverse price move.

maintenance call to an investor. When you bought HD on margin, the price of the stock was $40 per share; your margin account looked as follows:

| | |
|---|---|
| **Current market value (100 at $40)** | **$4000** |
| − **Debit balance** | 2000 |
| = **Equity in the account** | $2000 |

The price of HD subsequently drops from $40 to $25 per share; now your margin account looks as follows:

| | |
|---|---|
| **Current market value (100 at $25)** | **$2500** |
| − **Debit balance** | 2000 |
| = **Equity in the account** | $ 500 |

The margin percentage in the account is now 20 percent ($500/$2500), which is below the 25 percent minimum margin requirement. The brokerage firm immediately sends a maintenance call to you, requesting that you deposit enough cash to restore the account to the required minimum maintenance level of 25 percent. Using the current market value of $25 per share, the margin department would compute the equity necessary to meet the 25 percent minimum. That amount is $625 ($2500 × 25 percent). The current equity in the account is $500. Thus, the amount of the maintenance call sent to you would be $125 ($625 − $500).

At the end of the section explaining the effect of a price increase on a margin account, I noted that all cash deposits in the account are used to reduce the debit balance. Once you meet the $125 margin call, your account would look as follows:

| | |
|---|---|
| **Current market value (100 at $25)** | **$2500** |
| − **Debit balance (reduced by $125)** | 1875 |
| = **Equity in the account** | $ 625 |

The margin percentage is now 25 percent ($625/$2500). Your deposit in response to the maintenance call reduced the debit balance, thereby increasing your equity to 25 percent of the current market value.

Those who tend to buy stock on margin are speculators and traders whose investment objectives are usually short term. They make margin purchases in anticipation of a price increase in order to get a bigger bang for each buck. For long-term investors, buying on margin is not nearly as attractive. One reason is the interest charged on the debit balance. It compounds during the holding period. If the dividends do not cover the interest cost, the investor's potential return is steadily reduced by the increasing indebtedness. A second reason that buying on margin is less attractive to long-term investors is the constant risk that a steep price decline could prompt a large maintenance call, and the investor might be forced to sell part or all of his or her stocks in order to meet the call.

For an investor who has previously paid in full for stocks that could have been purchased on margin, a steep price decline can be beneficial. In theory, such a decline is generally interpreted to mean that the price of the stock is at a low point. By now placing the fully paid securities in a margin account, the customer can use additional buying power created by the SMA (special memorandum account) to "double up" on the number of shares owned. When the subsequent price rise occurs, the investor's doubled holdings yield double the profits.

The calculations were presented in this section as a means of clarifying the workings of a margin account and enabling you to understand better the rewards and risks associated with margin purchases. Figure 4.5 shows the various margin re-

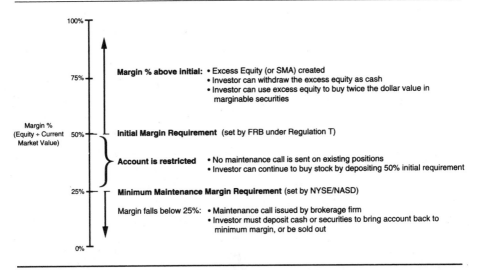

100% ⊤

75% ╪ — **Margin % above initial:** • Excess Equity (or SMA) created
• Investor can withdraw the excess equity as cash
• Investor can use excess equity to buy twice the dollar value in
  marginable securities

Margin %
(Equity ÷ Current   50% ╪ — **Initial Margin Requirement**  (set by FRB under Regulation T)
Market Value)

**Account is restricted**   • No maintenance call is sent on existing positions
• Investor can continue to buy stock by depositing 50% initial requirement

25% ╪ — **Minimum Maintenance Margin Requirement** (set by NYSE/NASD)

Margin falls below 25%:  • Maintenance call issued by brokerage firm
• Investor must deposit cash or securities to bring account back to
  minimum margin, or be sold out

0% ⊥

**Figure 4.5.   Effects of fluctuation in margin percentage of a margin account.**

quirements and summarizes the effect that the rise and fall of a stock's price has on investment activities that you can perform in a margin account.

Margin accounts are available through both full-service and discount brokerage firms. Be aware, however, that a firm's in-house margin requirements, especially the minimum maintenance requirement, may be more restrictive (higher) than those set forth by the New York Stock Exchange and the National Association of Securities Dealers.

## SELLING SHORT

Selling short is a strategy investors use to profit during a price decline. Its underlying principle is an inversion of the old "buy low, sell high" axiom. In anticipation of a price rise, you first buy a stock at a low price and later sell it at a higher price— you hope. In anticipation of a price decline, however, you first sell stock at a high price and later buy it back at a lower price.

For most people, this strategy seems to go against the natural order of investing. The difficulty in understanding short selling is captured in an often-asked question: "How can I first sell a stock when I don't own it?" The answer is that you borrow the shares from a brokerage firm or another investor who has authorized such a loan, and then you sell the shares in the market. Later you repurchase the same number of shares that you borrowed and return them to the lender's account. Although the lender has given permission for such a loan, he or she is unaware of when the loan has been made. The lender continues to receive all the benefits of owning the stock, including dividend payments, voting rights, and preemptive rights.

As Figure 4.6 illustrates, the process of borrowing the shares for a short sale is handled totally by the brokerage firm's back office and is therefore invisible to you. You simply place the order to sell short stock with the broker, and it is executed. Short sales can be performed only in a margin account, appropriately called a *short margin account*. Furthermore, like an investor who buys stock on margin, a short seller must deposit the 50 percent initial margin required by the Federal Reserve.

**short margin account:** a margin account in which a customer sells stock short.

Short sellers hope that a stock's price will decline. If it does, they will profit from the difference between the proceeds from the initial sale and the later cost of repurchasing the shares. Short sellers make their maximum profit if the price of the stock drops to zero.

If the price of the stock rises, however, short sellers lose. They can then repurchase the stock only at a cost that is higher than the proceeds received from the original sale. Also, since short sales are performed only in a margin account, an adverse price move can prompt a maintenance call if the margin percentage falls below the 30 percent mini-

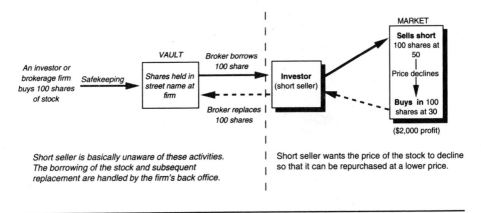

**Figure 4.6.   The mechanics of a successful short sale.**

mum maintenance margin set by the New York Stock Exchange (NYSE) and the National Association of Securities Dealers (NASD) for most short positions. (The minimum maintenance margin for an account in which an investor sells short—30 percent—is different from that in which a customer buys securities on margin—25 percent. The greater risk associated with selling short is the reason for its higher minimum maintenance.)

Because the price of a stock can rise an unlimited amount, at least in theory, an investor who sells short faces an unlimited potential loss. In contrast, the most an outright purchaser of stock can lose is the total value of the investment, which would occur only if the price of the stock drops to zero. This potential for unlimited loss makes short selling far riskier than any of the other purchasing strategies that already have been presented.

Because of its highly speculative characteristics, short selling is considered unsuitable for beginning investors. In fact, this strategy is rarely used by the public. It is used primarily by professional traders to hedge existing long stock positions against a price decline or as a tax strategy. (See selling short against the box in Chapter 6.) Investors interested in this strategy should read *Short Selling* by Joseph Walker (Wiley, 1991) for an explanation of the risks and rewards of this strategy.

## HOW MOST PEOPLE INVEST

Most people buy stocks by paying in full, and they usually make their first purchase based on the recommendation of a relative or friend. This first trade usually is for a small amount of stock. If it is successful, the person typically follows the friend's or relative's next recommendation and buys more shares than before. Eventually this cycle comes to an abrupt end when the person loses a substantial portion, if not all, of the money invested. From these types of experiences arise many of the horror stories about investing in stock.

The discipline and research required to develop a rational, long-term investment plan is often undermined by the desire for quick profits. Indeed, investing in stocks is usually less exciting than speculating in them. For the average investor, a long-term view will usually involve less anxiety and less need to follow the investment daily.

"Paper investing" is one good way for those who are deeply skeptical about investing in stock to get started. Select an investment strategy and, using a mock investment portfolio that is in keeping with your financial means, choose stock suitable to your stated objectives. Researching your selections is an essential part of this exercise; there must be a logical basis for making your selections. Follow the investments over a period of time to see how the strategy works and how your choices perform. This is a safe way for beginners to develop the confidence to invest in stocks.

# CHAPTER 5

# Fundamental Analysis

undamental analysis is the largely quantitative evaluation of a company's financial condition. It is used to determine the company's intrinsic value and to predict any changes in its anticipated earnings. Fundamentalists hold that any changes in earnings will be reflected in the dividend the company pays to its shareholders and in the market price of the stock. If earnings fall short of expectations and the decline is thought to be long term or permanent, investors will sell the stock because they anticipate that the company will announce lower dividends at the next dividend declaration date. Thus, the sell-off causes the price of the company's stock to fall. If earnings rise above expectations, more investors will want to buy the stock. They believe that the value of the company and its dividend payments will increase. As a result, the price of the stock rises.

Predicting whether a company will meet its sales, earnings, and growth targets and how this will affect the price of its stock is the job of professional analysts. They examine many of the company's reports that are filed with the Securities and Exchange Commission (SEC), including the quarterly reports (10Qs) and the annual reports (10Ks), paying careful attention to the audited *balance sheet*, audited *income statement*, and *cash flow statement* and

**balance sheet:** a constantly changing snapshot of the company's financial condition that shows all of its assets, liabilities, and stockholders' equity.

**income statement:** a summary of all of the income and expenses of a business for a period of time, usually one year. Also called a "profit-and-loss statement."

**cash flow statement:** a statement of the sources and uses of cash by a business for a period of time.

121

their accompanying footnotes. These statements summarize a company's current financial status. These hard data are analyzed in tandem with more qualitative information, such as the effectiveness of the company's management, the company's market share, its research and development (R&D) plans, its marketing efforts and the economic outlook for that particular industry. The analyst's objective is to predict the long-term growth prospects of the company—its sales, earnings, and dividend payments as well as its assets and liquidation values—and thereby predict the price movement of its stock.

When most beginning investors hear this explanation of fundamental analysis, their almost uniform consensus is that a person needs to know accounting or have a master's in business administration (M.B.A) in order to perform fundamental analysis. This is true only if the individual works as a professional securities analyst. Much of the information that these analysts evaluate, as well as their conclusions, are widely available to the public through such information services as Value Line and Standard & Poor's.

When a beginning investor first looks at the information published and distributed by these companies (Figures 5.1 and 5.2), it seems overwhelming because of the small, dense type. However, keep in mind that this information is published for individuals with various levels of investment experience. Beginning investors should not feel compelled to perform fundamental analysis *per se*. Instead, they should learn which information is most essential and attempt to understand the implications of that information on the decision to buy or sell a stock.

# Coca-Cola

# 562

NYSE Symbol KO Options on CBOE (Feb-May-Aug-Nov)  In S&P 500

| Price | Range | P–E Ratio | Dividend | Yield | S&P Ranking | Beta |
|-------|-------|-----------|----------|-------|-------------|------|
| Dec. 16'93 | 1993 | | | | | |
| 43⅜ | 44¾–37½ | 27 | 0.68 | 1.6% | A+ | 1.13 |

## Summary

Coca-Cola is the world's largest soft-drink company and has a sizable fruit juice business. Its bottling interests include 44% ownership of NYSE-listed Coca-Cola Enterprises. About 81% of 1992 operating profits came from international operations. Earnings are expected to continue in a strong uptrend through 1994, led by further aggressive worldwide expansion.

## Current Outlook

Earnings for 1994 are projected to rise to $2.00 a share, from 1993's estimated $1.68.

The $0.17 quarterly dividend is expected to be increased by approximately 18% in early 1994.

Revenues should remain in a strong uptrend through 1994, led by projected 5% to 7% annual growth in international unit case volume, and a 4% to 5% increase in the U.S. Profit margins are expected to continue to widen, aided by soft raw material costs, modest selling price increases, and an improving geographic profit mix. Equity income should benefit from the greater volumes. Ongoing stock buybacks will also contribute to share earnings progress.

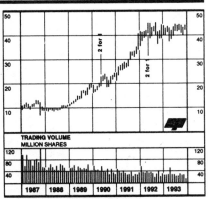

TRADING VOLUME
MILLION SHARES

1987 | 1988 | 1989 | 1990 | 1991 | 1992 | 1993

## Revenues (Billion $)

| Quarter: | 1993 | 1992 | 1991 | 1990 |
|----------|------|------|------|------|
| Mar. | 3.06 | 2.77 | 2.48 | 2.15 |
| Jun. | 3.90 | 3.55 | 3.04 | 2.74 |
| Sep. | 3.63 | 3.51 | 3.17 | 2.79 |
| Dec. | --- | 3.24 | 2.88 | 2.56 |
| | --- | 13.07 | 11.57 | 10.24 |

Revenues in the nine months ended September 30, 1993, advanced 7.7%, year to year. Margins widened, and with a substantial increase in equity income, pretax profits gained 15%. After taxes at 31.3%, versus 31.4%, income also advanced 15%, to $1.32 a share (on 1.2% fewer shares), from $1.13 (before charges of $0.17 for accounting changes).

## Common Share Earnings ($)

| Quarter: | 1993 | 1992 | 1991 | 1990 |
|----------|------|------|------|------|
| Mar. | 0.35 | 0.29 | 0.24 | 0.21 |
| Jun. | 0.52 | 0.43 | 0.36 | 0.31 |
| Sep. | 0.45 | 0.41 | 0.34 | 0.29 |
| Dec. | E0.36 | 0.30 | 0.27 | 0.22 |
| | E1.68 | 1.43 | 1.21 | 1.02 |

## Important Developments

Oct. '93— KO reported that in the first nine months of 1993, worldwide gallon shipments of soft drink concentrates and syrups increased 5%, year to year, with 5% gains for both U.S. and international shipments. Worldwide unit case volume was also up 5%, as were both U.S. and International shipments. Coca-Cola Foods operating income climbed strongly in 1993's first nine months, benefiting from lower costs and 23% higher unit volume.

Sep. '93— The company said that recently enacted changes in U.S. tax law would modestly raise its consolidated tax rate in 1993, to an annualized rate of 31.3%, from 30.8% reported for the first half. KO expects its 1994 tax rate to be approximately 32.5%.

Next earnings report expected in late January.

## Per Share Data ($)

| Yr. End Dec. 31 | 1992 | 1991 | 1990 | ¹1989 | 1988 | ²1987 | .²1986 | 1985 | 1984 | 1983 |
|-----------------|------|------|------|-------|------|-------|--------|------|------|------|
| Tangible Bk. Val. | 2.68 | 3.10 | 2.62 | 2.19 | 2.11 | 2.12 | 1.86 | 1.50 | 1.38 | 1.42 |
| Cash Flow | 1.67 | 1.41 | 1.20 | 0.98 | 0.83 | 0.71 | 0.88 | 0.65 | 0.51 | 0.44 |
| Earnings³ | 1.43 | 1.21 | 1.02 | 0.85 | 0.72 | 0.61 | 0.61 | 0.43 | 0.40 | 0.35 |
| Dividends | 0.560 | 0.480 | 0.400 | 0.340 | 0.300 | 0.280 | 0.260 | 0.247 | 0.230 | 0.223 |
| Payout Ratio | 39% | 39% | 39% | 39% | 41% | 46% | 43% | 56% | 57% | 65% |
| Prices—High | 45⅜ | 40⅞ | 24½ | 20¼ | 11⁹⁄₁₆ | 13¼ | 11³⁄₁₆ | 7⅜ | 5½ | 4¹³⁄₁₆ |
| Low | 35⁹⁄₁₆ | 21⅜ | 16⅝ | 10¹³⁄₁₆ | 8¾ | 7 | 6⅜ | 4¹⁵⁄₁₆ | 4¹⁄₁₆ | 3¹³⁄₁₆ |
| P/E Ratio— | 32–25 | 34–18 | 24–16 | 24–13 | 16–12 | 22–12 | 19–11 | 17–12 | 14–10 | 14–11 |

Data as orig. reptd. Adj. for stk. divs. of 100% May 1992, 100% May 1990, 200% Jul. 1986. 1. Refl. merger or acq. 2. Refl. acctg. change. 3. Bef. results of disc. ops. of +0.38 in 1989, +0.03 in 1985, and spec. item(s) of -0.17 in 1992. E-Estimated.

Standard NYSE Stock Reports
Vol. 60/No. 246/Sec. 9

**December 23, 1993**
Copyright © 1993 McGraw-Hill, Inc. All Rights Reserved

Standard & Poor's
25 Broadway, NY, NY 10004

---

Figure 5.1.  Standard & Poor's tear sheet. Reproduced with permission of Standard & Poor's Corporation. All rights reserved.

## Income Data (Million $)

| Year Ended Dec. 31 | Revs. | Oper. Inc. | % Oper. Inc. of Revs. | Cap. Exp. | Depr. | Int. Exp. | [4]Net Bef. Taxes | Eff. Tax Rate | [5]Net Inc. | % Net Inc. of Revs. | Cash Flow |
|---|---|---|---|---|---|---|---|---|---|---|---|
| 1992 | 13,074 | 3,080 | 23.6 | 1,083 | 310 | 171 | 2,746 | 31.4% | 1,884 | 14.4 | 2,194 |
| 1991 | 11,572 | 2,586 | 22.3 | 792 | 254 | 185 | 2,383 | 32.1% | 1,618 | 14.0 | 1,872 |
| 1990 | 10,236 | 2,237 | 21.9 | 642 | 236 | 231 | 2,014 | 31.4% | 1,382 | 13.5 | 1,600 |
| [1,2]1989 | 8,966 | 1,910 | 21.3 | 462 | 184 | 315 | 1,764 | 32.4% | 1,193 | 13.3 | 1,355 |
| 1988 | 8,338 | 1,768 | 21.2 | 387 | 170 | 239 | 1,582 | 34.0% | 1,045 | 12.5 | 1,208 |
| [3]1987 | 7,658 | 1,514 | 19.8 | 300 | 153 | 285 | 1,410 | 35.0% | [4]916 | 12.0 | 1,069 |
| [3]1986 | 8,669 | 1,755 | 20.2 | 373 | 430 | 208 | 1,511 | 38.2% | 934 | 10.8 | 1,364 |
| [1]1985 | 7,904 | 1,380 | 17.5 | 497 | 335 | 203 | 1,093 | 38.0% | 678 | 8.6 | 1,012 |
| 1984 | 7,364 | 1,227 | 16.7 | 396 | 170 | 150 | 1,068 | 41.1% | 629 | 8.5 | 798 |
| [1]1983 | 6,829 | 1,149 | 16.8 | 389 | 156 | 91 | 1,000 | 44.2% | 558 | 8.2 | 714 |

## Balance Sheet Data (Million $)

| Dec. 31 | Cash | Assets | Curr. Liab. | Ratio | Total Assets | % Ret. on Assets | Long Term Debt | Common Equity | Total Cap. | % LT Debt of Cap. | % Ret. on Equity |
|---|---|---|---|---|---|---|---|---|---|---|---|
| 1992 | 1,063 | 4,248 | 5,303 | 0.8 | 11,052 | 17.9 | 1,120 | 3,888 | 5,090 | 22.0 | 45.7 |
| 1991 | 1,117 | 4,144 | 4,118 | 1.0 | 10,222 | 16.6 | 985 | 4,426 | 5,611 | 17.6 | 39.6 |
| 1990 | 1,492 | 4,143 | 4,296 | 1.0 | 9,278 | 15.8 | 536 | 3,774 | 4,650 | 11.5 | 39.3 |
| 1989 | 1,182 | 3,604 | 3,658 | 1.0 | 8,283 | 15.5 | 549 | 3,185 | 4,330 | 12.7 | 38.5 |
| 1988 | 1,231 | 3,245 | 2,869 | 1.1 | 7,451 | 13.6 | 761 | 3,045 | 4,376 | 17.4 | 33.9 |
| 1987 | 1,468 | 4,136 | 4,119 | 1.0 | 8,356 | 11.1 | 803 | 3,224 | 4,237 | 19.0 | 27.7 |
| 1986 | 888 | 3,739 | 2,755 | 1.4 | 8,373 | 12.3 | 1,011 | 3,515 | 4,908 | 20.6 | 28.8 |
| 1985 | 865 | 2,970 | 2,004 | 1.5 | 6,898 | 10.6 | 889 | 2,979 | 4,189 | 21.2 | 23.7 |
| 1984 | 782 | 2,636 | 2,023 | 1.3 | 5,958 | 11.5 | 740 | 2,778 | 3,760 | 19.7 | 22.5 |
| 1983 | 611 | 2,330 | 1,391 | 1.7 | 5,228 | 11.0 | 513 | 2,921 | 3,611 | 14.2 | 19.5 |

Data as orig. reptd.; finance subs. consol. after 1987. **1.** Excl. disc. ops. **2.** Refl. merger or acq. **3.** Refl. acctg. change. **4.** Incl. equity in earns. of nonconsol. subs. **5.** Bef. spec. items.

## Business Summary

Coca-Cola is the world's largest soft-drink company and a major producer of orange juice. The company holds a 44% interest in Coca-Cola Enterprises, its largest bottler. Segment contributions in 1992 (excluding Coca-Cola Enterprises) were:

| | Revs. | Profits |
|---|---|---|
| Soft drinks | 87% | 96% |
| Foods | 13% | 4% |

The company makes soft-drink syrups and concentrates, which are sold to independent (and company-owned) bottlers and fountain wholesalers. Brand Coca-Cola (best-selling soft drink in the world, including Coca-Cola classic) and diet Coke currently rank number one and three, respectively, in domestic unit volume. Other brands include Tab, Sprite, Diet Sprite, Fanta, Fresca, Cherry Coke and Minute Maid soda.

The food segment includes fruit juices, beverages, mixers and snacks sold under the Minute Maid, Hi-C and Bacardi labels.

International operations in 1992 accounted for 67% of net operating revenues (31% European Community; 19% Pacific & Canada; 11% Latin America; 6% Northeast Europe/Africa) and 81% of

operating profits (29% Pacific & Canada; 28% European Community; 16% Latin America; and 8% Northeast Europe/Africa).

During 1992, KO's acquisition and investment activity, which includes investments in bottling operations in the Netherlands, the U.S. and Brazil, totaled $717 million. Acquisition and investment activity amounted to $399 million and $301 million in 1991 and 1990, respectively.

### Dividend Data

Dividends have been paid since 1893. A dividend reinvestment plan is available.

| Amt. of Divd. $ | Date Decl. | Ex–divd. Date | Stock of Record | Payment Date |
|---|---|---|---|---|
| 0.17 | Feb. 18 | Mar. 9 | Mar. 15 | Apr. 1'93 |
| 0.17 | Apr. 15 | Jun. 9 | Jun. 15 | Jul. 1'93 |
| 0.17 | Jul. 15 | Sep. 9 | Sep. 15 | Oct. 1'93 |
| 0.17 | Oct. 21 | Oct. 24 | Dec. 1 | Dec. 15'93 |

### Capitalization

**Long Term Debt:** $1,479,000,000 (9/93).

**Common Stock:** 1,298,830,144 shs. ($0.25 par).
Berkshire Hathaway Inc. controls 7.1%.
Institutions hold 53%.
Shareholders of record: 163,817.

**Office**—1 Coca-Cola Plaza, N.W., Atlanta, GA 30313. **Tel**—(404) 676-2121. **Chrmn & CEO**—R. C. Goizueta. **SVP & CFO**—J. L. Stahl. **Secy**—Susan E. Shaw. **Investor Contact**—Juan D. Johnson. **Dirs**—H. A. Allen, R. W. Allen, W. E. Buffett, C. W. Duncan, Jr., R. C. Goizueta, S. B. King, J. T. Laney, D. F. McHenry, P. F. Oreffice, J. D. Robinson III, W. B. Turner, P. V. Ueberroth, J. B. Williams. **Transfer Agent & Registrar**—First Chicago Trust Co. of New York, NYC. **Incorporated** in Delaware in 1919. **Empl**—31,000.

Information has been obtained from sources believed to be reliable, but its accuracy and completeness are not guaranteed. Kenneth A. Shea

**Figure 5.1.** *continued*

# COCA-COLA NYSE-KO

| RECENT PRICE | P/E RATIO | | RELATIVE P/E RATIO | DIV'D YLD | VALUE LINE |
|---|---|---|---|---|---|
| 41 | 24.1 (Trailing: 25.3 / Median: 17.0) | | 1.46 | 1.7% | 1535 |

U S
S E R V I C E

| TIMELINESS | 2 Above Average | High: | 4.5 | 4.8 | 5.5 | 7.4 | 11.2 | 13.3 | 11.3 | 20.3 | 24.5 | 40.9 | 45.4 | 44.8 | Target Price Range 1996 1997 1998 |
| (Relative Price Performance Next 12 Mos.) | | Low: | 2.5 | 3.8 | 4.1 | 5.0 | 6.4 | 7.3 | 8.8 | 10.8 | 16.3 | 21.3 | 35.6 | 37.5 | |

SAFETY **1** Highest
(Scale: 1 Highest to 5 Lowest)
BETA 1.15 (1.00 = Market)

**1996-98 PROJECTIONS**

| | Price | Gain | Ann'l Total Return |
| High | 65 | (+60%) | 14% |
| Low | 55 | (+35%) | 10% |

**Insider Decisions**

| | F | M | A | M | J | J | A | S | O |
| to Buy | 0 | 0 | 1 | 2 | 2 | 1 | 2 | 0 | 0 |
| Options | 0 | 2 | 1 | 1 | 0 | 2 | 2 | 0 | 1 |
| to Sell | 0 | 0 | 0 | 0 | 0 | 0 | 0 | 0 | 0 |

**Institutional Decisions**

| | 4Q'92 | 1Q'93 | 2Q'93 |
| to Buy | 153 | 179 | 189 |
| to Sell | 270 | 294 | 279 |
| Hld's(000) | 668689 | 677623 | 678014 |

Percent shares traded 9.0 / 6.0 / 3.0

16.5 x "Cash Flow" p sh
3-for-1 split
2-for-1 split
2-for-1 split

Relative Price Strength

Options: CBOE

Shaded areas indicate recessions

© VALUE LINE PUB., INC.

| 1977 | 1978 | 1979 | 1980 | 1981 | 1982 | 1983 | 1984 | 1985 | 1986 | 1987 | 1988 | 1989 | 1990 | 1991 | 1992 | 1993 | 1994 | | 96-98 |
|---|---|---|---|---|---|---|---|---|---|---|---|---|---|---|---|---|---|---|---|
| 2.43 | 2.93 | 3.35 | 3.99 | 3.97 | 3.84 | 4.17 | 4.69 | 5.12 | 5.63 | 5.14 | 5.88 | 6.65 | 7.66 | 8.71 | 10.00 | 10.95 | 12.20 | Sales per sh A | 18.60 |
| .28 | .32 | .36 | .37 | .40 | .41 | .44 | .51 | .55 | .63 | .72 | .85 | 1.01 | 1.20 | 1.41 | 1.69 | 1.95 | 2.25 | "Cash Flow" per sh | 3.40 |
| .22 | .25 | .28 | .29 | .30 | .33 | .34 | .40 | .43 | .52 | .61 | .71 | .85 | 1.02 | 1.22 | 1.43 | 1.65 | 1.95 | Earnings per sh B | 2.95 |
| .13 | .15 | .16 | .18 | .19 | .21 | .22 | .23 | .25 | .26 | .28 | .30 | .34 | .40 | .48 | .56 | .68 | .80 | Div'ds Decl'd per sh ■ C | 1.20 |
| .18 | .21 | .22 | .19 | .22 | .20 | .23 | .22 | .32 | .24 | .20 | .27 | .34 | .44 | .60 | .83 | .95 | 1.00 | Cap'l Spending per sh | 1.50 |
| 1.06 | 1.17 | 1.29 | 1.40 | 1.53 | 1.71 | 1.79 | 1.77 | 1.93 | 2.28 | 2.16 | 2.15 | 2.36 | 2.82 | 3.33 | 2.98 | 3.45 | 4.15 | Book Value per sh D | 7.00 |
| 1466.4 | 1482.3 | 1482.7 | 1483.1 | 1483.5 | 1628.9 | 1636.2 | 1569.9 | 1543.9 | 1540.0 | 1489.4 | 1419.2 | 1348.1 | 1336.5 | 1329.0 | 1306.9 | 1290.0 | 1270.0 | Common Shs Outst'g E | 1210.0 |
| 14.3 | 13.7 | 11.4 | 9.7 | 9.6 | 9.6 | 12.6 | 12.2 | 13.6 | 17.3 | 18.0 | 13.9 | 17.8 | 20.4 | 24.4 | 28.7 | Bold figures are | | Avg Ann'l P/E Ratio | 20.0 |
| 1.87 | 1.87 | 1.65 | 1.29 | 1.17 | 1.06 | 1.07 | 1.14 | 1.10 | 1.17 | 1.20 | 1.15 | 1.35 | 1.52 | 1.56 | 1.75 | Value Line estimates | | Relative P/E Ratio | 1.55 |
| 4.0% | 4.2% | 5.0% | 6.5% | 6.7% | 6.5% | 5.2% | 4.8% | 4.2% | 2.9% | 2.6% | 3.0% | 2.3% | 1.9% | 1.6% | 1.4% | | | Avg Ann'l Div'd Yield | 2.0% |

**CAPITAL STRUCTURE as of 6/30/93**
Total Debt $3486.0 mill.
LT Debt $1163.0 mill. LT Interest $76.0 mill.
(Total interest coverage: 17x)
(21% of Cap'l)

Pension Liability None

Pfd Stock None

Common Stock 1,300,447,559 shs.
as of July 30, 1993 (79% of Cap'l)

| | 6829.0 | 7364.0 | 7903.9 | 8668.6 | 7658.3 | 8337.8 | 8965.8 | 10236 | 11572 | 13074 | 14100 | 15500 | Sales ($mill) A | 22500 |
| | 16.8% | 16.6% | 15.5% | 17.2% | 19.8% | 21.2% | 21.3% | 21.4% | 22.3% | 23.7% | 24.0% | 24.5% | Operating Margin | 25.0% |
| | 153.7 | 166.1 | 178.1 | 166.8 | 153.5 | 169.8 | 183.8 | 243.9 | 261.4 | 321.9 | 360 | 380 | Depreciation ($mill) | 500 |
| | 558.3 | 628.8 | 677.6 | 800.3 | 916.1 | 1044.7 | 1192.8 | 1381.9 | 1618.0 | 1883.8 | 2140 | 2495 | Net Profit ($mill) | 3535 |
| | 44.2% | 41.1% | 38.0% | 39.2% | 35.0% | 34.0% | 32.4% | 31.4% | 32.1% | 31.4% | 31.5% | 32.5% | Income Tax Rate | 32.5% |
| | 8.2% | 8.5% | 8.6% | 9.2% | 12.0% | 12.5% | 13.3% | 13.5% | 14.0% | 14.4% | 15.2% | 16.1% | Net Profit Margin | 15.7% |
| | 939.2 | 613.1 | 966.5 | 984.6 | 17.7 | 376.5 | d54.4 | d153.7 | 26.6 | d1056 | d1295 | d1560 | Working Cap'l ($mill) | d1600 |
| | 513.2 | 740.0 | 889.2 | 1011.2 | 803.4 | 761.1 | 548.7 | 535.9 | 985.3 | 1120.1 | 1320 | 1370 | Long-Term Debt ($mill) | 1520 |
| | 2920.8 | 2778.1 | 2979.1 | 3515.0 | 3223.8 | 3345.3 | 3485.5 | 3849.2 | 4425.8 | 3888.4 | 4480 | 5290 | Net Worth ($mill) | 8330 |
| | 17.1% | 18.9% | 18.7% | 18.8% | 23.8% | 28.2% | 30.2% | 32.2% | 30.6% | 38.4% | 37.5% | 38.0% | % Earned Total Cap'l | 36.5% |
| | 19.1% | 22.6% | 22.7% | 22.8% | 28.4% | 31.2% | 34.2% | 35.9% | 36.6% | 48.4% | 48.0% | 47.0% | % Earned Net Worth | 42.5% |
| | 6.6% | 9.5% | 9.7% | 11.3% | 15.3% | 19.8% | 22.0% | 22.0% | 22.1% | 29.5% | 28.0% | 28.0% | % Retained to Comm Eq | 25.0% |
| | 65% | 58% | 57% | 50% | 46% | 42% | 41% | 40% | 40% | 39% | 41% | 41% | % All Div'ds to Net Prof | 41% |

**CURRENT POSITION** ($MILL.)

| | 1991 | 1992 | 6/30/93 |
|---|---|---|---|
| Cash Assets | 1117.2 | 1063.0 | 1080.0 |
| Receivables | 933.4 | 1055.2 | 1383.0 |
| Inventory (Avg Cst) | 987.8 | 1018.6 | 1115.0 |
| Other | 1105.8 | 1110.9 | 1298.0 |
| Current Assets | 4144.2 | 4247.7 | 4876.0 |
| Accts Payable | 1914.4 | 2253.0 | 2219.0 |
| Debt Due | 1302.3 | 2087.3 | 2323.0 |
| Other | 900.9 | 962.9 | 1169.0 |
| Current Liab. | 4117.6 | 5303.2 | 5711.0 |

**ANNUAL RATES**

| of change (per sh) | Past 10 Yrs. | Past 5 Yrs. | Est'd '90-'92 to '96-'98 |
|---|---|---|---|
| Sales | 8.5% | 10.5% | 13.5% |
| "Cash Flow" | 14.0% | 18.0% | 15.0% |
| Earnings | 15.0% | 18.5% | 15.5% |
| Dividends | 9.5% | 13.0% | 16.5% |
| Book Value | 7.0% | 7.5% | 14.5% |

| Cal- endar | QUARTERLY SALES ($ mill.) | | | | Full Year |
|---|---|---|---|---|---|
| | Mar.31 | Jun.30 | Sep.30 | Dec.31 | |
| 1990 | 2148 | 2739 | 2793 | 2556 | 10236 |
| 1991 | 2481 | 3039 | 3173 | 2879 | 11572 |
| 1992 | 2772 | 3550 | 3508 | 3244 | 13074 |
| 1993 | 3056 | 3899 | 3629 | 3516 | 14100 |
| 1994 | 3350 | 4300 | 4000 | 3850 | 15500 |

| Cal- endar | EARNINGS PER SHARE B | | | | Full Year |
|---|---|---|---|---|---|
| | Mar.31 | Jun.30 | Sep.30 | Dec.31 | |
| 1990 | .21 | .31 | .29 | .21 | 1.02 |
| 1991 | .24 | .37 | .35 | .26 | 1.22 |
| 1992 | .29 | .43 | .41 | .30 | 1.43 |
| 1993 | .35 | .52 | .45 | .33 | 1.65 |
| 1994 | .40 | .60 | .55 | .40 | 1.95 |

| Cal- endar | QUARTERLY DIVIDENDS PAID C ■ | | | | Full Year |
|---|---|---|---|---|---|
| | Mar.31 | Jun.30 | Sep.30 | Dec.31 | |
| 1989 | -- | .085 | .085 | .17 | .34 |
| 1990 | -- | .10 | .10 | .20 | .40 |
| 1991 | -- | .12 | .12 | .24 | .48 |
| 1992 | -- | .14 | .14 | .28 | .56 |
| 1993 | -- | .17 | .17 | .34 | |

**BUSINESS:** The Coca-Cola Company is the world's largest soft drink company. Distributes major brands (Coca-Cola, Sprite, Fanta, TAB, etc.) through bottlers throughout the world. Foreign operations accounted for about 67% of net sales and 81% of profits in 1992. Food division, world's largest distributor of juice products (Minute Maid, Five Alive, Hi-C, etc.). Coca-Cola Enterprises, 44%-owned soft drink bottler. Advertising costs, 8.5% of sales. Has approximately 31,300 employees; 110,000 stockholders. Berkshire Hathaway owns 7.1% (1993 Proxy). 1992 depreciation rate: 6.1%. Estimated plant age: 5 years. Chairman and Chief Executive Officer: Roberto C. Goizueta. Incorporated: Delaware. Address: One Coca-Cola Plaza, Atlanta, Georgia 30313. Tel.: 404-676-2121.

**Coca-Cola continues to sparkle.** Once again, in the third quarter, the benefits of geographical diversification were clearly demonstrated. While unit case sales were actually down in a number of major markets, including the European Community and Japan, where the economy and the weather caused problems, growing business elsewhere more than made up for the shortfall. Demand was particularly brisk in much of Latin America, East Central Europe, and Australia. Volume also grew rapidly in China, albeit from a small base. And after being in something of a slump for several years, the U.S. market finally picked up this summer, with case volume up 6%. All in all, worldwide case volume was up 4% in the quarter, and gallon shipments of concentrate rose 5%. Third-quarter share profits were 45¢, and would have been 4¢ higher if not for the negative effect of the new tax law.

**We're forecasting share earnings gains of 15% this year and 18% in 1994.** The latter assumes some improvement in the economies of continental Europe and Japan, but as shown above, Coke is likely to report solid growth even without higher

sales in these areas. Many of the markets in Eastern Europe, Latin America and Asia should see double-digit volume gains both this year and next. With selective price increases, profits should grow faster than sales.

**We expect solid earnings growth through 1996-98.** Coke has the advantage of building on one of the strongest franchises in the world—the Coke name is well known worldwide, and the product is liked virtually everywhere. And many of the markets are still largely untapped, with per capita consumption of soft drinks far less than they are in North America. The biggest challenge is to build and develop the infrastructure necessary to produce and deliver the product, and management has clearly demonstrated that it can do that. The company also has the financial resources to do it.

**Shares of financially strong Coke are timely.** The price-earnings ratio is somewhat higher than we would like, but the stock should still appeal to investors seeking dependable, above-average earnings growth.

Stephen Sanborn, CFA November 19, 1993

(A) Includes Columbia Pictures: 7/82-12/86.
(B) Based on average shares outstanding. Next earnings report due late Jan. Excludes special gains: '81, 4¢; '86, 17¢; disc. op. gain

(loss) '83, (1¢); '85, 5¢; '89, 3¢; nonrec. gain (loss): '89, 73¢; '92, (17¢). (C) Next div'd meeting about Feb. 15. Goes ex about Mar. 9. Div'd payment dates: April 1, July 1, Oct. 1, Dec. 15.

■Div'd reinvestment plan available. (D) Incl. intangibles. In '92: $383.3 mill., 29¢/sh. (E) In millions, adjusted for stock splits.

Company's Financial Strength A++
Stock's Price Stability 85
Price Growth Persistence 95
Earnings Predictability 100

---

**Figure 5.2.** Value Line Investment Survey analysis sheet. Copyright © 1993. By Value Line Publishing, Inc. Reprinted by permission. All rights reserved.

Here are six fundamental measures you as a beginning investor should examine closely:

1. Price-earnings ratio
2. Current yield
3. Earnings per share and earnings growth pattern
4. Current ratio
5. Debt ratio
   (The current ratio and debt ratio are, respectively, measurements of corporate liquidity and indebtedness or risk of financial failure. They will be discussed together.)
6. Book value

In explaining how this information is derived and the possible ways of interpreting it, this chapter will try to avoid much of the "number crunching" that most people dread. Only those simple, basic ratios and calculations that are most pertinent to the information that beginning investors need to evaluate are included in this chapter.

Keep in mind at all times that all of the measures cited require interpretations that are relative. There is no totally correct interpretation of their meaning, whether evaluated individually or as a group. As an old saying on Wall Street goes, "If you give 10 different analysts the same information and ask them to interpret it, you'll end up with an argument, not a consensus."

**price-earnings (P-E) ratio:** measures how many times greater a stock's current price is relative to its current earnings per share.

## PRICE-EARNINGS RATIO

Perhaps the most important ratio to understand is the *price-earnings (P-E) ratio*. The formula is:

$$\text{P-E ratio} = \frac{\textbf{Current market price of the stock}}{\textbf{Annual earnings per share}}$$

This ratio, published daily in the financial press, tells how many times greater a stock's current price is relative to its current earnings per share. For example, using the earning figures shown in the section labeled "Common Share Earnings ($)" in Figure 5.1, The Coca-Cola Company (a.k.a. Coca-Cola) reported total earnings per share for the previous 12 months of $1.62. This comprises the last quarter of 1992 ($0.30) and the first three quarters of 1993 ($0.35, $0.52, and $0.45). Given that the market price of Coca-Cola common stock on the day this information was compiled was $43.375 per share, the company's P-E ratio is 27.

$$\text{P-E ratio} = \$43.375 \div \$1.62 = 27$$

This means that Coca-Cola is currently trading at "27 times earnings." Stated another way, the stock's market price is trading at a multiple of 27 times the company's annual earnings.

In the financial press, the annual earnings per share used in the calculation is that which the company reported for the previous year. When computed in this way, the ratio is called the trailing P-E. Information services companies like Value Line and Standard & Poor's use more up-to-date earning figures. Their annual earnings figure may be the total of the reported earnings from the two most recent quarters and the estimated earnings for the next two quarters. This is called the forward P-E. Or as I just demonstrated in the Coca-Cola example, the annual earnings may be the total reported earnings from the most recent 12 months. This explains why the P-E ratios that appear in the newspaper are different from those that appear on the tear sheets. Also, the P-E ratio is a dynamic measure, changing with the market price of the stock.

It is easiest to think of the P-E ratio as a measure

of a stock's relative expensiveness compared to its earnings. A "high" P-E ratio means that the price of the stock is expensive relative to the earnings it provides. A "low" P-E ratio means that the price of the stock is thought to be inexpensive relative to the company's earnings. The adjectives "high" and "low" are relative terms. The standard or "normal" P-E ratios against which a stock is compared varies over time depending on investor sentiment as well as the economic outlook for the company and its industry. Historically, for example, the long-term P-E ratio for the S&P 500 stocks has been approximately 15 to 1. However, when investors are bullish on the overall market, the prices of stock tend to rise. Thus, the ratios tend to be higher. When interest rates are high, investors might leave the stock market and invest their money in bonds. As a result, stock prices fall, and P-E ratios tend to be low.

Fundamentalists interpret P-E ratios in various ways. The most common of these are summarized next.

### High P-E Ratio

A P-E ratio is considered high when it is above 20 to 1 (although this is more a rule of thumb than an absolute rule). Such ratios are characteristic of growth companies. Established growth companies like Coca-Cola, McDonald's and Apple Computer may have ratios that are only slightly below or above 20. This generally reflects investors' belief that new product development or marketing effort show a strong likelihood of increasing sales and returns to investors. On the other hand, an emerging growth company (such as Amgen) or a penny-stock company may have a P-E ratio that is 40 to 1, 90 to 1, or higher.

Some analysts believe a high P-E ratio means that investors are bullish on the long-term growth prospects of the company. Hence, they are willing to pay a relatively high price for the stock today in order to benefit from its growth tomorrow. Others see a high P-E ratio as a contrary indicator. To them it means that the company's stock is overvalued and that the price will soon decline to relatively correct values.

These contradictory interpretations should lead beginning investors to one safe conclusion: high P-E ratios usually indicate greater risk, and greater risk means a greater opportunity for profit. If the company's earnings improve as expected or, even better, exceed expectations, then you have a reasonable chance of making substantial capital gains on the appreciation of the company's stock. Expectations of growth, however, do not always turn into real growth. When a company fails to meet its earnings target, investors tend to abandon the stock like proverbial rats from a sinking ship. The rush to sell causes the price to fall sharply and quickly. Greater volatility is usually characteristic of stocks with high P-E ratios.

## Low P-E Ratios

A P-E ratio is considered low when it is under 10 to 1. Low P-E ratios are characteristic of mature companies with low growth potential (e.g., food companies), blue chip companies, and companies that are in trouble or heading toward it. Thus, a low ratio could indicate a solid investment that is undervalued due to temporary market conditions, such as low sales, a slow economy, or investors' bearish sentiments. Or the low ratio could be the first sign of a Chapter 11 bankruptcy filing. Look at how the information services rank the company's safety and financial stability before deciding to buy stock with a low ratio.

Contrarians, on the other hand, believe that if overall P-E ratios are low, the market as a whole has bottomed out and a moderate- to long-term rally is about to occur. To these analysts, a low P-E ratio for the overall market indicates that it is time to buy stocks.

Ultimately, P-E ratios are used to get a relative measure of the price of a company's stock. Do not interpret this measure in isolation. Instead, compare it with the average P-E ratio of companies in the same business sector or industry, as well as with the average ratio of one of the standard measures of the market, such as the Dow Jones Industrial Average, the S&P 500, or the Value Line Index. Much of this information can be found in various publications available at many public libraries.

## CURRENT YIELD (DIVIDEND YIELD)

**current yield:** a stock's annual per share dividend (in dollars) divided by its current market price.

*Current yield* is the percentage of return that a stock's annual dividend payments represent relative to the stock's current market price. In simple terms, it tells you the return you are making on a stock today. The formula for current yield is:

$$\text{Current yield} = \frac{\textbf{Annual per share dividend in \$}}{\textbf{Stock's current market price}}$$

The importance of the current yield depends on the importance that you place on receiving dividend payments. Many investors believe that current and increasing future dividend payments are an indication of a company's financial strength. Logically, steadily increasing dividends should follow increased profits and earnings for a company. This reasoning is not necessarily true. The amount of dividend payments is a reflection of the dividend policy, which is determined by a company's board of directors. Even when a corporation's profits and earnings are down, the board may choose to maintain a relatively steady dividend amount in order to support the company's image as a solid investment. The board may also decide to maintain the same dividend, although the company's profits and earnings have increased. Therefore, like the P-E ratio, there is no absolute correlation between the amount of the dividend payment and the quality of the investment. Nevertheless, there are some generalizations that beginning investors can use.

## High Current Yield

A high current yield tends to be characteristic of a mature blue chip company, an income stock, a company in a slow growth industry (e.g., food companies), and regulated industries (e.g., utilities). Such companies usually have substantial earnings and distribute a large portion of them to the shareholders. They pay high dividends because they offer little or no opportunity to reinvest in the growth of a mature business. Their market prices will remain relatively stable or will fluctuate in accordance with the general market trend. If you are looking for good, steady current income, buy stock with high current yields.

Some fundamentalists track the aggregate current yield of all stocks as an indication of the future direction of the market. They believe that when the market's aggregate current yield is high (again, a relative term), it indicates the bottom of a market downtrend. If stock prices relative to dividend payments have reached a low point, this foretells an uptrend. Investors begin buying stocks because they believe the stocks are undervalued relative to the returns they are now providing.

## Low Current Yield

Low (or no) current yield is characteristic of growth stocks. As both Figures 5.1 and 5.2 show, Coca-Cola has a current yield or dividend yield of 1.6 percent. Clearly it is considered a growth company. Instead of paying a large part of its earnings as dividends to its shareholders, the company retains most of the earnings and reinvests them in the company. These earnings are usually allocated for research and development, and marketing, in order to build the overall worth of the company. Investors profit from the capital appreciation of these securities.

To contrarians, a low current yield in the overall market is a sign that the price of stock is about to reach or has already reached a high point. Investors will become dissatisfied with the price they are paying for a stock relative to the dividend they are receiving and consequently will sell their holdings. Low current yield is therefore a bearish indicator.

The weight you give to current yield, and therefore to dividend payments, when deciding to invest in a company's stock depends very much on your need for current income or long-term appreciation. To be sure, it is riskier to bet on the future growth of a company than to take your returns as cash dividends today. The choice, however, is hardly ever totally black or white. In almost all investments in stock, you must choose the point along the spectrum of dividend income versus capital gains that is most suitable for your situation.

In making such decisions, also consider total return. A simplified version of the formula for calculating total return follows:

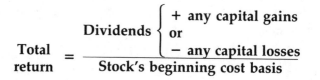

$$\frac{\text{Total}}{\text{return}} = \frac{\text{Dividends} \begin{cases} + \text{ any capital gains} \\ \text{or} \\ - \text{ any capital losses} \end{cases}}{\text{Stock's beginning cost basis}}$$

Although historic total yield information should be consulted as a reference, the total annual dividends and the annual capital gain amounts used in the formula are estimates, made when deciding what stock to buy or sell. In relying too heavily on current yield as a reason for all investment decisions, you may be shortchanging yourself on the total return.

## EARNINGS PER SHARE AND EARNINGS GROWTH PATTERN

*Earnings per share (EPS)* is perhaps the most widely used and publicized measure of a company's current and future growth. EPS is the amount of the company's net earnings that is allocated to each share of outstanding common stock. Net earnings are those profits that remain after the company has paid, in this order, all interest payments on any outstanding bonds, all taxes, and all dividends on outstanding preferred stock. The formula used for calculating earnings per share (EPS) is:

**earnings per share:** the amount of a company's net earnings allocated to each share of outstanding common stock.

$$\text{EPS} = \frac{\textbf{Net earnings form common}}{\textbf{Number of outstanding common shares}}$$

The number of outstanding common shares equals the total amount of authorized, issued common stock minus any shares repurchased by the issuer as treasury stock. Additionally, if the company has any common-stock equivalents outstanding—convertible bonds, convertible preferred stock, rights, warrants, and stock options issued to employees—whose conversion could increase the number of common shares outstanding and therefore dilute (lessen) the earnings per share, these must also be included in the calculation. When the conversion of the stock equivalents is included, the resulting earnings figure is called the *fully diluted earnings per share*. When reading any report of a

**fully diluted earnings per share:** the amount of a company's net earnings allocated to already outstanding plus any additional shares that could result from the conversion or exercise of any outstanding stock equivalents.

company's earnings, be careful to understand how the number of outstanding shares is calculated.

Determining if there is a trend or pattern in the company's EPS over a period of time is an important consideration when making an investment decision. Traditional thought holds that the longer a trend has lasted, the greater is the likelihood that it will continue. For example, Figure 5.2 (in the table immediately below the graph depicting the price movement of the stock) shows that Coca-Cola's actual earnings from 1977 through 1992 increased steadily from $0.22 to $1.65 per share. Indeed, there were a few years (in the late 1970s and early 1980s) when the earnings were relatively flat; still, the trend has been consistently upward. [**Note:** Figure 5.1 shows the same information from 1983 through 1992 in the sections labeled "Common Share Earnings ($)" and "Per Share Data ($)" on the first page of the figure.] Based on the information presented in the financial statements filed with the SEC, fundamental analysts at S&P and Value Line predicted that earnings would increase in 1994 to $2.00 per share, and $1.95 per share. (On the S&P tearsheet, the projected earnings are presented in the section labeled "Current Outlook.")

The Coca-Cola example implies that the correlation between increases or decreases in the earnings per share and the company's growth potential is direct. However, some other information must be considered when interpreting the significance and implications of the EPS.

## Increasing EPS

Steadily increasing earnings per share usually mean that a company is growing or that its financial condition is improving. If the increase is due to a corresponding improvement in sales and profits, then the company is growing. By logical extension, you can expect the market value of the shares that you own to increase accordingly.

Better sales, however, are not the only factor that can cause a rise in EPS. The company may be buying back its stock—turning it into treasury stock. In this case, the number of outstanding shares will decline. Depending on the number of shares repurchased, the net effect could be an increase in EPS even when sales (and earnings) are declining. In short, a company's stock repurchase plan can mask the fact that the sales (and earnings) are **not** improving. Thus, while earnings improve, investors may lose confidence in the company's ability to generate continually increasing sales and begin selling their holdings. Thus, the market value of the company's shares will decline.

## Decreasing EPS

A decrease in the earnings per share is generally not a good sign. Lower earnings are the result of lower sales or higher costs, and thus lower profits. However, investors are wise to try to determine if the decline is due to internal or external factors.

Internal factors may include a stock split, a stock dividend, the issuance and exercise of rights or warrants, or the forced conversion of outstanding bonds or preferred stock. In each of these cases, the EPS would decline because there are more shares outstanding. Depending on the circumstances, analysts may see this as only a short-term decline, eventually leading to an increase. In the case of a forced conversion, the company would be eliminating the interest payments on the bonds or dividends on the preferred. This should eventually lead to higher earnings for the common shareholders. Stock dividends are also interpreted as a positive sign. To be sure, the company has more shares outstanding, but typically the earnings (and dividends paid) increase. In the case of a stock split or stock dividend, the company and the information services adjust their historical data to reflect the change. In Figure 5.1, the footnotes in the section labeled "Per Share Data ($)" highlight these adjustments.

External factors in general refer to business conditions or the state of the overall economy. Perhaps the business sector in which the company is currently involved is in a temporary slump but will gradually improve, or the overall economy is in a recession and all businesses are experiencing lower earnings. In the latter case, the decrease in EPS may be part of the cyclical character of the business or industry.

In summary, when evaluating earnings per share, also look at the company's sales per share to see if they confirm the trend seen in the earnings. If they do not, determine why. A decrease in earnings that results from a stock split is usually taken as a bullish sign, especially if the company's sales and earnings show no decline.

## CURRENT RATIO AND DEBT RATIO

Respectively, these ratios measure a company's liquidity and indebtedness—its ability to meet its current obligations. A company may have respectable levels of income but may be "cash poor" and unable to pay its current liabilities. The *current ratio* measures a company's ability to pay its current obligations—wages, taxes, accounts receivable, interest on debt, and so forth—from its current assets. The formula for the calculation is:

**current ratio:** a measure of a company's ability to pay its current expenses and obligations from its current assets.

$$\text{Current ratio} = \frac{\text{Current assets}}{\text{Current liabilities}}$$

The "Balance Sheet Data" section on the second page of Figure 5.1 and the small box labeled "Current Position" in the middle of the left side of Figure 5.2 show that as of December 31, 1992, Coca-Cola had a current ratio of 0.8 to 1.

$$\text{Current ratio} = \frac{\$4248}{\$5303} = \frac{.80}{1}$$

In simple terms, this means that The Coca-Cola Company has $0.80 of assets for every $1.00 of liabilities. In previous years (from 1983 to 1992) its current ratio has ranged from 1.7:1 to 1:1.

Clearly, the higher the current ratio is, the better. However, like all other measures, the terms "high" and "low" are extremely relative—even more than the ratios that we have already examined. While a ratio of 2 to 1 used to be thought of as the widely accepted benchmark, in reality the adequacy of the ratio very much depends on the business sector in which the company is involved. Companies like utilities, telephones, and other essential services have low current ratios because of their short billing cycles and the relative steadiness of the payments from these billings. Manufacturing firms, on the other hand, need a much higher current ratio because of the amount of time that can exist from acquiring the raw material, manufacturing the item, and then selling it. When analyzing current ratio, look at the current ratio for the entire business sector to see whether the company's ratio is high or low compared to similar companies within that sector.

The *debt ratio* answers the question, "How much of this company's total capitalization is made up of long-term debt?" Stated another way, "How leveraged is this company?" The formula for this ratio is:

**debt ratio:** a measure of the percentage of bonds that comprise a company's total capitalization.

$$\frac{\text{Debt}}{\text{ratio}} = \frac{\text{Total \$ amount of outstanding bonds}}{\text{Company's total capitalization}}$$

The S&P tear sheet (Figure 5.1, in the section on the second page labeled "Balance Sheet Data (Million $)") and the Value Line report (Figure 5.2, in the box on the left middle labeled "Capital Structure") show Coca-Cola's debt ratio to be .22 to 1 (22%) and .21 to 1 (21%), respectively. The percentages differ because the information service companies computed the ratio at times when the price of the outstanding stock was different. This is a moderate-to-slightly-high debt ratio. Traditionally a debt ratio above .30 to 1 (or 30 percent) classifies a company as being highly leveraged. (Imagine if your credit card bills ate up 30 percent of your take-home pay!) During the 1980s, many companies exceeded this percentage in what became known as leveraged buy-outs. The company would issue bonds, usually junk bonds with a high rate of interest, in order to acquire another company. Such high debt makes a company highly susceptible to downturns in the economy. If sales drop and the company is unable to pay interest on the bonds, it will be in default and could be forced into bankruptcy. This risk could be compounded if the bonds had an adjustable rate feature. This would mean that the company would have to increase interest rates as its business worsened. Although the degree of bankruptcy risk associated with the debt ratio varies from industry to industry, it nonetheless gives a sense of how much debt the company is carrying and whether the percentage is too high.

**book value:** the amount of a company's assets backing each common share after intangibles have been deducted and all outstanding liabilities paid.

## BOOK VALUE

In simple terms, *book value* is the amount of money each common shareholder might reasonably expect to receive if a company's assets (not including intangibles such as copyrights, patents, and goodwill) were sold at the value at which they are carried on the balance sheet and all liabilities were paid. An improvement in a company's book value, while not directly related to earnings, could indicate asset growth or a decrease in the company's liabilities.

A company's market price is often compared to its book value to determine how much above its "real" value the company is selling. There are average book values for each business sector. For example, banks typically have a market-to-book value ratio of 1.5 to 1. Other industries may be higher.

Sometimes a company's market price may be below its book value. Fundamental analysts interpret this as a buy signal. In such a case, analysts believe, the company is trading for less than the net value of its assets. By purchasing the stock and holding it, an investor will eventually profit when the price moves up to the industry standard.

Companies that grow through leverage (borrowing), such as utilities, tend to have relatively stable book values. Such companies have a stable cash flow (e.g., from bill payments) and use it to borrow heavily. For the most part, the steady influx of cash offsets the increased liability associated with the debt outstanding.

Growth companies tend to have higher market-to-book values. Without the stable cash flow of a larger corporation or a long credit history, borrowing is difficult, so these companies reinvest their net earnings in the company instead of paying them as dividends to investors. Therefore, an investor can usually interpret an increase in book value to mean a growth in the company's assets.

## KNOW THE COMPANY AND KNOW ITS PRODUCTS

In addition to checking all of the ratios about earnings, growth, book value, and other items, there is another essential bit of advice that applies to any beginning investor who is using fundamental analysis to decide whether to invest in a company: know the company and know its products. Later in this book, I give an example of a beginning investor who owns a word processing business and decides to invest part of his earnings in the stock of computer companies. He makes this decision based on the fact that he works with different companies' products every day. He therefore had a sense of:

- Which companies were not keeping their products current
- Which companies were creating new and innovative products
- Which companies' products were facing increasing competition
- Which companies were diversifying into new areas that would help to offset the losses due to increased competition
- With what products the users were increasingly satisfied (or dissatisfied)

Many people think that "fundamental analysis" is just another term for "financial statement analysis." While it is important to check the ratios, it is equally important to know the company and know its products.

## ANALYZING PREFERRED STOCK

Because the majority of preferred stock is purchased by large corporations (due to preferential tax rules), in-depth analysis is inappropriate for this

| Moody's | S&P | Meaning |
|---|---|---|
| aaa | AAA | Superior quality preferred stock with excellent asset protection and the least risk of dividend nonpayment. |
| aa | AA | Excellent quality preferred stock with good earnings and asset protection and little risk of dividend nonpayment. |
| a | A | Very good quality preferred stock with adequate levels of earnings and asset protection. Dividend nonpayment risk is somewhat greater than the preceding rating. |
| baa | BBB | Adequate quality preferred stock with sufficient earnings and asset protection for the short term. Long-term prospects of dividend payment involve some risk. |
| ba | BB | First speculative rating for preferred stock. Asset protection for stock may be sufficient at present, but insufficient to withstand long-term adversity. |
| b | B | This rating (and those that follow)denote an undesirable issue of preferred stock. |
| caa | CCC | Preferred stock may have defaulted on dividend payments. |
| ca | CC | Very risky and likely to be in default and in arrears on dividend payments. Little likelihood that back payments will be made up. |
| c | C | Lowest rated and most risky preferred stock. Issue has extremely poor prospects of achieving higher investment rating. |

**Figure 5.3.   Ratings of preferred stock by Moody's and Standard & Poor's.**

book. Selecting preferred stock is somewhat easier for investors because both Moody's and Standard & Poor's rate preferred issues according to the amount of asset protection each issue has and their relative risk of default. The ratings and their meanings are shown in Figure 5.3.

Like a bond, the first four ratings of preferred stock are considered investment grade. Below BB (S&P) and ba (Moody's), the stock is considered speculative. While the investment grade ratings will invariably pay the lower dividend, as the interpretations indicate, there is reasonable certainty that the stock will continue to pay its preferred dividend for the long term. The speculative ratings offer a higher stated return; however, there is some doubt as to the company's ability to pay over the long or short term.

# CHAPTER 6

# Technical Analysis

**technical analysis:** research that seeks to predict the future price movement of a stock or the overall market by using price and volume as indicators of changes in the supply and demand for a stock. Best used to predict short- and intermediate-term price movements.

**price:** in technical terms, the point at which supply (sellers) and demand (buyers) meet and a trade occurs.

**volume:** the total number of shares

*Technical analysis* is the study of the market's or a stock's past movement as a means of predicting its future price movement. Three premises form the foundation of this approach. First, all information necessary to forecast the movement of the market is contained in the market itself. Outside information—usually meaning such fundamental factors as a company's earnings, its sales, and the demand for its products—is discounted by the market. Second, price movements in the market tend to repeat themselves. And, third, investors tend to have the same reactions to the changes each time they occur. A good analyst has charted or studied charts of the market's past movement and has been able to determine consistencies in the supply and demand for securities during certain periods. When he or she sees similar circumstances in the present, the analyst uses this information as a basis for predicting the market's future movement. Not only will the analyst be able to forecast the direction of the market, he or she can also predict the strength and duration of the price movement. Often, but not always, the predictions of a knowledgeable analyst are accurate.

The market indicators with which analysts are most concerned are *price* and *volume*. Price is the

| Price | Volume | Indication |
|:---:|:---:|---|
| ↑ | ↑ | **Bullish.** Price will continue to rise. The increasing trading volume reflects growing demand to buy the security, which adds momentum to or supports the upward direction of the market. |
| ↓ | ↑ | **Bearish.** Price will continue to decline. Increasing volume indicates more and more investors are selling, leading to greater downward momentum. |
| ↑ | ↓ | **Moderately Bearish.** The price increase is losing momentum, as indicated by the decline in trading volume. The price rise is unsupported ad will soon reverse itself, becoming a decline. |
| ↓ | ↓ | **Moderately Bullish.** The decreasing trading volume indicates that the price decline is losing some of its steam. Demand is still relatively low. Soon, however, the market will reach its bottom, the price will again be attractive to new investors, and the resulting increased demand will cause the price to rally. |

↑ = Rising    ↓ = Falling

---

**Figure 6.1.   Four basic interactions of price and volume.**

---

point at which a trade occurs—the point at which a buyer, seeking the lowest price, and a seller, seeking the highest price, agree to conduct a transaction. Volume is the number of shares traded in a given period of time. The interaction of these forces in the market provides the clues to the current or future supply of and demand for the security. Analysts base their predictions and time their buying and selling on these indications. The four basic interactions between price and volume and their indications are summarized in Figure 6.1.

Technical analysts' primary tool is *charting;* hence, they are sometimes called *chartists.* For most investors, the terms "technical analysis" and "charting" are virtually synonymous. Charting is used to create a picture of the market's movement, which the analyst then interprets. Charts, however, are only one of the factors a technician consid-

traded in a given period of time.

**charting:** capturing the patterns of a stock's price and volume movements on a line, bar, point and figure, or moving average graph.

**chartist:** a technical analyst who uses charts to capture a stock's price and volume movement and then analyzes this

**sentiment indicators:**
statistics used to measure the bullish or bearish mood of the market and its investors.

**flow of funds indicators:**
statistics that enable analysts to determine in which markets—money markets, stock, bonds, savings accounts—individual and institutional investors are most likely to invest their money during given economic conditions or periods of time.

**investment advisory services:**
companies or individuals registered with the Securities and Exchange Commission who, for a fee, provide

information as a basis for making buy and sell recommendations.

ers when seeking to forecast the direction of the market. Others are *sentiment indicators* and *flow of funds indicators*. Sentiment indicators measure whether investors and their advisers feel bullish or bearish about the market. These measurements are usually determined by monitoring the recommendations made in newsletters published by various *investment advisory services*. Importantly, sentiment indicators are usually interpreted as *contrary indicators*. When investors feel very bullish, technicians interpret this as a signal that the market is about to decline. Conversely, a strongly bearish sentiment prefigures an upturn in the market.

The flow of fund indicators show where both individual and institutional investors are investing their money. In short, these indicators measure the demand for securities. Depending on market conditions, investors may decide to invest in stocks or fixed-rate securities or to maintain a high degree of liquidity by leaving cash in money market accounts.

Given all the factors that a chartist considers, it is easy to understand why technical analysis is best suited for forecasting the short-term or intermediate movement of stock prices. Technicians are not interested in the dividend income to be made from an investment in an equity security. They are most interested in the capital gains that can be made from short-term price moves. Long-term price forecasting is better served by fundamental analysis, although some people use technical analysis for this purpose.

Since charting is the primary tool of the technical analyst, this chapter will look at some of the information that an analyst charts, the theories about market movement, the ways a chartist may depict this information, and how a chartist interprets some of the basic formations that the market's movement creates.

# STOCK MARKET AVERAGES AND INDEXES

The charts that most people are familiar with are the market *averages* or *indexes*: the Dow Jones Industrial Average, the Standard & Poor's 500 Index, the New York Stock Exchange Composite Index, the NASDAQ Index, the Russell 2000 Index, and others (Figure 6.2). These indicators chart the broad movement of the overall market. Each average or index is structured and calculated differently, using different numbers of stocks, different divisors, and different *weightings*. As a result, the price movements of different groups of stock have a greater or lesser influence on the index. These averages move in the same direction about 90 percent of the time but occasionally move in opposite directions because of the mix of securities and their weightings. Technical analysts are aware of these differences and take them into consideration when using a specific index to forecast the market's movements.

Like the market they seek to represent, these indexes are not static. Their compositions, divisors, and weightings are affected by corporate mergers, business failures, stock splits, stock dividends, and other changes in a company's capitalization or financial status. The companies that calculate the indexes and averages must be constantly watchful and adjust their measurements to incorporate these effects.

Let's examine the most widely used averages and indexes.

## Dow Jones Industrial Average

On any given day anyone listening to an evening news program will hear a report of the level at which "the Dow" closed and the number of points that day's close is up or down over the previous day's— for example, "The Dow Jones Industrial Average

---

investment advice or money management, usually in specific types of investments.

**contrary indicators:** information used to establish the bullish or bearish sentiment of the market to which an investor responds by taking the opposite position (e.g., if a contrary indicator is bullish, this is a sign for an investor to sell).

**average:** a composite measure of the movement of the overall market or of a particular industry that consists of a small number of stocks and is usually not weighted.

**index:** a composite measure of the movement of the overall market or of a particular industry that consists of a large number of

## STOCK MARKET DATA BANK 1/10/94

### MAJOR INDEXES

| HIGH | LOW (↑365 DAY) | | CLOSE | NET CHG | % CHG | ↑365 DAY CHG | % CHG | FROM 12/31 | % CHG |
|---|---|---|---|---|---|---|---|---|---|
| **DOW JONES AVERAGES** | | | | | | | | | |
| 3865.51 | 3241.95 | 30 Industrials | 3865.51 | + 44.74 | + 1.17 | + 602.76 | + 18.47 | + 111.42 | + 2.97 |
| 1819.58 | 1466.93 | 20 Transportation | 1819.58 | + 20.37 | + 1.13 | + 329.88 | + 22.14 | + 57.26 | + 3.25 |
| 256.46 | 218.39 | 15 Utilities | x224.23 | + 1.25 | + 0.56 | + 5.59 | + 2.56 | − 5.07 | − 2.21 |
| 1413.37 | 1201.66 | 65 Composite | x1413.37 | + 15.06 | + 1.08 | + 207.72 | + 17.23 | + 32.34 | + 2.34 |
| 449.67 | 408.81 | Equity Mkt. Index | 449.67 | + 4.81 | + 1.08 | + 40.86 | + 9.99 | + 7.48 | + 1.69 |
| **NEW YORK STOCK EXCHANGE** | | | | | | | | | |
| 262.76 | 237.09 | Composite | 262.76 | + 2.42 | + 0.93 | + 25.67 | + 10.83 | + 3.68 | + 1.42 |
| 321.94 | 287.65 | Industrials | 321.94 | + 3.31 | + 1.04 | + 32.07 | + 11.06 | + 6.68 | + 2.12 |
| 246.95 | 207.88 | Utilities | 225.71 | + 1.29 | + 0.57 | + 17.83 | + 8.58 | − 4.21 | − 1.83 |
| 279.58 | 219.87 | Transportation | 279.58 | + 3.01 | + 1.09 | + 58.18 | + 26.28 | + 9.10 | + 3.36 |
| 233.33 | 198.50 | Finance | 218.54 | + 1.53 | + 0.71 | + 20.04 | + 10.10 | + 1.72 | + 0.79 |
| **STANDARD & POOR'S INDEXES** | | | | | | | | | |
| 475.27 | 430.95 | 500 Index | 475.27 | + 5.37 | + 1.14 | + 44.32 | + 10.28 | + 8.82 | + 1.89 |
| 553.49 | 496.48 | Industrials | 553.49 | + 6.47 | + 1.18 | + 52.09 | + 10.39 | + 13.30 | + 2.46 |
| 443.28 | 364.15 | Transportation | 443.28 | + 5.69 | + 1.30 | + 67.61 | + 18.00 | + 17.68 | + 4.15 |
| 189.49 | 157.46 | Utilities | 169.62 | + 1.50 | + 0.89 | + 12.16 | + 7.72 | − 2.96 | − 1.72 |
| 48.40 | 40.21 | Financials | 44.86 | + 0.48 | + 1.08 | + 4.65 | + 11.56 | + 0.59 | + 1.33 |
| 179.47 | 155.71 | 400 MidCap | 179.47 | + 0.67 | + 0.37 | + 21.23 | + 13.42 | + 0.09 | + 0.05 |
| **NASDAQ** | | | | | | | | | |
| 787.42 | 645.87 | Composite | 786.69 | + 3.75 | + 0.48 | + 104.29 | + 15.28 | + 9.89 | + 1.27 |
| 822.98 | 660.17 | Industrials | 822.98 | + 4.19 | + 0.51 | + 88.42 | + 12.04 | + 17.14 | + 2.13 |
| 956.01 | 788.28 | Insurance | 910.86 | + 12.20 | + 1.36 | + 122.58 | + 15.55 | − 9.73 | − 1.06 |
| 725.65 | 534.66 | Banks | 689.74 | + 0.10 | + 0.01 | + 155.08 | + 29.01 | + 0.31 | + 0.04 |
| 348.25 | 285.44 | Nat. Mkt. Comp. | 348.25 | + 1.76 | + 0.51 | + 45.51 | + 15.03 | + 4.64 | + 1.35 |
| 330.05 | 263.79 | Nat. Mkt. Indus. | 330.05 | + 1.82 | + 0.55 | + 35.01 | + 11.87 | + 7.29 | + 2.26 |
| **OTHERS** | | | | | | | | | |
| 484.28 | 396.41 | Amex | 478.78 | − 0.71 | − 0.15 | + 81.54 | + 20.53 | + 1.63 | + 0.34 |
| 298.83 | 265.36 | Value-Line(geom.) | 298.83 | + 1.38 | + 0.46 | + 33.20 | + 12.50 | + 3.55 | + 1.20 |
| 260.17 | 217.55 | Russell 2000 | 259.75 | + 0.57 | + 0.22 | + 38.59 | + 17.45 | + 1.16 | + 0.45 |
| 4717.19 | 4242.36 | Wilshire 5000 | 4717.19 | + 39.91 | + 0.85 | + 471.39 | + 11.10 | + 59.36 | + 1.27 |

†-Based on comparable trading day in preceding year.

**Figure 6.2. Stock Market Data Bank showing major indexes. Reprinted by permission of *The Wall Street Journal*, © 1994 Dow Jones & Company, Inc. All rights reserved worldwide.**

stocks and is usually weighted by other factors, such as capitalization.

**weighting:** the method for determining the worth of each company's stock relative to the value of the overall index.

closed at 3865.51 today, up 44.74 points." The Dow Jones Industrial Average (DJIA) is the oldest, most popular, and most widely reported indicator of the stock market's performance. It was developed by Charles Dow, founder of the Dow Jones Company, which publishes *The Wall Street Journal*. The industrial average is actually one segment of a larger composite measure known as the Dow Jones Average, comprising 65 companies' stocks: 30 industrial companies, 20 transportation companies, and 15 utilities. As Figure 6.2 shows, there is an average for each of the three business segments.

The Dow Jones Industrial Average consists of 30 blue chip industrial companies whose stocks trade on the New York Stock Exchange. These companies are thought to represent the broad spectrum and character of industry in America. Their collective price movement is one of the most accurate leading indicators of the state of the economy. Currently, the following 30 companies are contained in the DJIA:

1. Allied-Signal
2. Alcoa
3. American Express
4. AT&T
5. Bethlehem Steel
6. Boeing
7. Caterpillar
8. Chevron
9. Coca-Cola
10. Disney
11. du Pont
12. Eastman Kodak
13. Exxon
14. General Electric
15. General Motors
16. Goodyear
17. IBM
18. International Paper
19. J. P. Morgan
20. McDonald's
21. Merck and Co.
22. 3M (Minnesota Mining)
23. Philip Morris

**24.** Procter & Gamble

**25.** Sears

**26.** Texaco

**27.** Union Carbide

**28.** United
   Technologies

**29.** Westinghouse

**30.** Woolworth

As you can see from the list, not all of the companies in the average are strictly industrials. Some are services companies (American Express), some are retail companies (Sears, Woolworth), and others are communications companies (AT&T).

Because the DJIA consists of only 30 blue chip stocks that trade on the New York Stock Exchange, it has been criticized as being too narrow—not truly representative of the broad spectrum of business in the United States, especially smaller, entrepreneurial businesses—and as being too influenced by high-priced stocks. Additionally, its critics believe that the stability of the companies included in the Dow causes the average itself to be too stable. It does not, they assert, reflect the volatile price movements that sometimes characterize the stocks of growth companies, for example. The first criticism leads to a second: that the stability of the DJIA causes its movements to lag behind the overall trend in the market. Changes in the economy tend to affect smaller companies and their stock prices first. Many of these criticisms are logical and valid. Nonetheless, they have not reduced the popularity of the Dow Jones Industrial Average as the most widely followed market indicator.

## New York Stock Exchange Composite Index

This index measures the movement of the nearly 2271 common stocks that trade on the New York Stock Exchange. The other types of securities that trade on the exchange are not included in this index. Unlike the DJIA, the movement of this index is not quoted in points; it is quoted in dollars and cents. Using an example from Figure 6.2, we would say that the NYSE Composite Index closed at $262.76, up $2.42 from the previous day's close.

## Standard & Poor's Composite Index of 500 Stocks

The S&P 500, as it is more popularly known, is composed of 500 of the largest companies that trade on the New York Stock Exchange and in the over-the-counter market. Like the Dow Jones Average, the 500 stocks that comprise the S&P index are grouped into business segments: 400 industrials, 40 utilities, 40 financial companies, and 20 transportations. Each segment has its own index. (See Figure 6.2.) Also like the NYSE Composite Index, the S&P is quoted in dollars.

The S&P 500 Index is very popular with institutional investors (mutual funds, banks, insurance companies) and technical analysts. Over the years, it has become the standard against which these investors measure the performance of their portfolios. The reason is that the stocks that make up this composite index are selected because of their impact on the economy. This is not the basis for selecting the stocks in the NYSE or American Stock Exchange indexes, which are composed of the stocks that trade on the exchanges. The result of the more focused selection is that the S&P 500 is a great leading index. Today many investment managers index their portfolios to match the S&P 500; that is, they construct their portfolios of securities so that they reflect or match the composition and weighting of the S&P. In this way, the total investment returns from their portfolios will keep pace with the performance of the index.

## NASDAQ Composite Index

This is an index of all the common stocks of domestic companies that trade on the NASDAQ System (National Association of Securities Dealers Automated Quotation System). Stocks from six sub-indexes representing different business segments make up the composite index: industrial (the broadest), banking, insurance, other finance, transportation, and utilities.

## American Stock Exchange Index

This index is composed of common stock, warrants, and American Depositary Receipts (ADRs) listed on the American Stock Exchange (AMEX).

## Value Line Index

The Value Line Index is composed of more than 1700 stocks that trade on the exchanges and in the over-the-counter market. It is structured as if an equal amount of money were invested in each of the 1700 companies. The result is that the same dollar amount buys more shares of lower-priced stock than of higher-priced stock. The movement of the Value Line Index is therefore strongly influenced by changes in the value of the lower-priced stocks, a characteristic that makes it more volatile than either the Dow Jones Industrial Average or the S&P 500 Index.

## Russell 2000 Index

Created by Frank Russell Company in Tacoma, Washington, this is the principal index of the small capitalization stocks. The company compiles a list of the 3000 largest capitalized stocks across all securities markets. The top 1000 are used in the Russell 1000 Index. The remaining 2000 "small cap" stock are used in the Russell 2000 Index. "Small cap" is defined as a company whose market capitalization is approximately $380 million or less. As this explanation suggests, this index is weighted by capitalization.

## Wilshire 5000 Index

Constructed like the S&P 500 Index and the NYSE Composite Index, the Wilshire 5000 Index is the broadest measure of the market. It consists of more than 5000 common stocks that trade on the NYSE, the AMEX, and the over-the-counter market. It also represents that largest dollar amount of all actively traded securities in the United States. Because it is so broad, this index tends to be less influenced by the stability of the blue chip stocks. It is therefore, like the Value Line Index, somewhat more volatile than the indicators weighted by large capitalization stocks.

Many more averages and indexes exist than the few discussed here, which were selected to represent those that are most widely used in technical analysis. Still, all indexes serve basically the same purpose: to portray current market activity and provide a basis for predicting future price movements. Investors interested in technical analysis must research the various indexes to find which one or two best fits with individual theories about price movement in the marketplace.

## MARKET THEORIES

### The Dow Theory

The Dow theory was the first technical theory developed. It divides the movement of the stock market into three groups: primary movement, secondary movement, and daily movement. Figure 6.3 illustrates the difference between primary movement and secondary movement.

The primary movement is the long-term direction of the market. In Figure 6.3, the primary movement shown between points A and B is bullish. The movement from point B to point C is bearish.

The secondary movement is a series of brief reversals that occur during the primary movement, represented by the smaller letters *a–g* in Figure 6.3. These reversals are normal during any trend in the market. After all, the market moves not straight up or straight down but in a jagged series of rises and falls. The frequency and percentage of the reversals serve to indicate a possible change in the direction of primary market movement. The small letters *a–d* indicate the secondary market moves during a bull market. Notice that each subsequent secondary decline is never lower than the previous reversal. During a bear market, each subsequent secondary price rise—letters *e–g*—is never higher than the previous one.

The market's daily movements are no more than emotional reactions, "Dow-ists" believe, and are not worth considering. They have no effect on either the primary or the secondary movement of the market.

Additionally, the Dow theory states that in or-

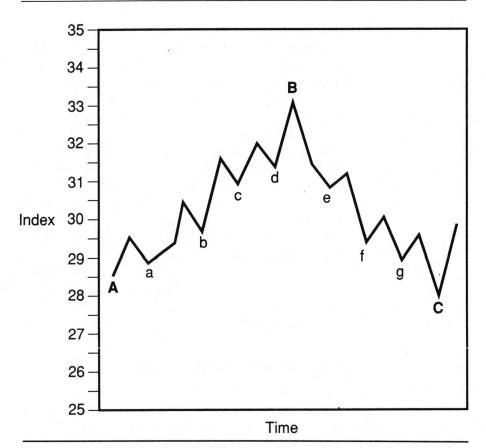

**Figure 6.3.   The Dow theory: Primary and secondary market movements.**

der for the direction of the primary movement to
be valid, it has to occur in both the industrial average and the transportation average; that is, the
movements of the industrial average and the transportation average must confirm each other. Around
1900, when this theory was developed by Charles
Dow, S. A. Nelson, and William P. Hamilton, this
qualifier made quite good sense. The country's primary industrial production was durable goods. As
the demand for these goods rose or was anticipated
to rise, there was an increased need for transporta-

tion—primarily trains in those days—to deliver the products to the marketplace. Conversely, decreased demand for durable goods meant a decreased need for transportation. The movement of the industrial sector was therefore validated by the same movement in the transportation sector.

The Dow theory was not designed to help investors "beat the market" by improving their return from investing in the stocks during the primary movements. Nor was it able to estimate the duration of a trend. Its purpose was to predict any change in the market's primary movement, thereby permitting investors to take appropriate actions to protect the value of their holdings.

Today, virtually no one advocates the Dow theory. Historically, it has produced mixed results and has been criticized for being superficial, imprecise, and slow to confirm market direction.

## The Advance-Decline Theory

This theory looks at the total number of issues traded during a session and compares the number of stocks whose prices advanced with those whose prices declined. The total number of issues traded, called the *breadth of the market*, varies from market to market. The greater the number of issues traded compared to the number of issues listed, then the greater the breadth of the market.

**breadth of the market:** the number of individual stocks traded out of the number of stocks listed.

In Figure 6.4, of all the common and preferred shares listed on the New York Stock Exchange, 2660 issues traded on Friday; of the total issues traded, 1200 advanced in price, 856 declined, and 604 were unchanged. Of the total number of stocks in the NASDAQ system, 4620 issues traded. On the American Stock Exchange, 850 issues traded.

Advance-decline theorists use these data to compute a positive or negative percentage figure that represents the strength of the advance or the

| DIARIES | | | |
| --- | --- | --- | --- |
| **NYSE** | FRI | THUR | 11/12 WK |
| Issues traded | 2,660 | 2,661 | 2,806 |
| Advances | 1,200 | 934 | 1,561 |
| Declines | 856 | 1,115 | 891 |
| Unchanged | 604 | 612 | 354 |
| New highs | 71 | 65 | 163 |
| New lows | 43 | 23 | 114 |
| zAdv vol (000) | 214,146 | 137,720 | 763,179 |
| zDecl vol (000) | 81,940 | 112,857 | 469,565 |
| zTotal vol (000) | 322,317 | 283,824 | 1,396,587 |
| Closing tick¹ | +204 | −210 | .... |
| Closing Arms² (trin) | .54 | .66 | .... |
| zBlock trades | 7,006 | 6,470 | 31,148 |
| **NASDAQ** | | | |
| Issues traded | 4,620 | 4,611 | 4,899 |
| Advances | 1,498 | 1,571 | 2,336 |
| Declines | 1,465 | 1,352 | 1,757 |
| Unchanged | 1,657 | 1,688 | 806 |
| New highs | 105 | 130 | 389 |
| New lows | 40 | 38 | 178 |
| Adv vol (000) | 155,025 | 183,417 | 841,585 |
| Decl vol (000) | 114,062 | 102,385 | 481,765 |
| Total vol (000) | 307,747 | 318,740 | 1,510,752 |
| Block trades | 5,468 | 5,768 | 26,446 |
| **AMEX** | | | |
| Issues traded | 820 | 825 | 959 |
| Advances | 308 | 337 | 469 |
| Declines | 298 | 260 | 353 |
| Unchanged | 214 | 228 | 137 |
| New highs | 28 | 35 | 72 |
| New lows | 11 | 7 | 33 |
| zAdv vol (000) | 7,835 | 10,483 | 44,355 |
| zDecl vol (000) | 7,776 | 4,761 | 31,566 |
| zTotal vol (000) | 19,195 | 17,956 | 91,060 |
| Comp vol (000) | 23,240 | 21,292 | 110,275 |
| zBlock trades | n.a. | 318 | y1,220 |

**Figure 6.4.  Diary of advancing and declining issues. Reprinted by permission of *The Wall Street Journal*, ©️ 1993 Dow Jones & Company, Inc. All rights reserved worldwide.**

decline, respectively. Using the New York Stock Exchange data an analyst would calculate the percentage of the advance or the decline by subtracting the number of declining issues from the number of advancing issues and then dividing the net difference by the total number of issues traded:

$$\frac{+1200 - 856}{2660} = \frac{+344}{2660} = +13\%$$

Continued positive and high net percentages indicate a technically strong bullish market. Increasing negative percentages indicate a technically weak market and are a bearish indicator. During either of these market trends, if the net percentage begins to show a continued and increasing shift in the opposite direction, the analyst interprets the movement as an indication that the market is about to change direction and responds by initiating new positions to take advantage of the change or liquidating existing positions to take profits. Additionally, an increase in the breadth of the market during a bullish market is thought to be a positive sign; conversely, an expansion in negative breadth portends a weak market.

Because of its focus on the breadth of the market instead of just selected issues (as with the Dow theory), the advance-decline theory has been widely used as the basis for developing more complex technical measures and theories about the market's movement, such as the ARMS Index.

Named after its creator, Richard Arms, the ARMS index is a slightly more complex and accurate application of the advance-decline theory. Popularly called TRIN (Trading Index), it factors into the calculation the volumes associated with both advancing and declining issues, in addition to the number of issues advancing and declining.

## The Short Interest Theory

**short interest:** the total amount of a company's outstanding shares that have been sold short and have not been covered or bought in.

*Short interest* is the number of shares investors have sold short that are still standing open in the market—in other words, the short sellers have not repurchased the borrowed stock and returned it to the lenders. Technical analysts view short selling as a sentiment indicator. As we discussed in Chapter 4, investors sell short when they expect the market price of a security to decline. It would seem logical that large outstanding short interest is a bearish indicator. Indeed, this is true for the short term; however, technical analysts take a different view for the long term. Recall that every short seller borrows the stock that he or she sold short in the market. Eventually this individual must repurchase the stock and return it to the lender. When the short sellers begin to cover their positions—they "buy in" the borrowed stock—because of a reversal in the downward price movement of the stock, the increased demand for the security will cause the price to rise even higher. Large outstanding short interest is therefore considered to be a long-term bullish indicator. Small or moderate amounts of short interest are considered to have little potential impact on a stock's price.

Short interest data are published in *The Wall Street Journal*, usually around the twentieth of the month; this information is compiled around the fifteenth of the month. The information contained in Figure 6.5 shows all the stocks with substantial short interest and those whose short interest changed significantly during the month. By the time this information is available to the public, it is already somewhat out of date; for many analysts, the delay limits the usefulness of the information.

The short interest theory is not thought to be reliable because less than 1 percent of all investors sell short. Hence, the number of short sellers does not represent a sufficient breadth of the market. The lower percentage is largely due to two factors: selling short is not popular, and an investor who uses this strategy is subject to unlimited loss. Also, many investors sell short only for tax reasons—specifically to defer paying taxes on a capital gain. This strategy is known as *selling short against the box*. The following example illustrates this strategy.

An investor owns 100 shares of a stock that she purchased early in 1993 at $15 a share. By December

**selling short against the box:** a strategy used to lock in a gain on securities that an investor owns and defer taxes to the next year. The investor sells short the same security that he or she owns and later uses the long position to cover the short sale.

## SHORT INTEREST HIGHLIGHTS
### NASDAQ ISSUES

### Largest Short Positions

| Rank | Nov. 15 | Oct. 15 | Change |
|---|---|---|---|
| 1 Amer Pwr Convers | 13,718,410 | 14,536,663 | −818,253 |
| 2 Snapple Beverage | 10,247,541 | 10,137,888 | 109,653 |
| 3 Tele-Comm Inc A | 9,255,607 | 12,178,793 | −2,923,186 |
| 4 Comcast Cl A Spcl | 9,111,597 | 6,349,968 | 2,761,629 |
| 5 MCI Comm | 8,834,282 | 8,340,435 | 493,847 |
| 6 Mobile Tele Tech | 8,774,788 | 8,039,081 | 735,707 |
| 7 Comcast Cl A | 7,615,929 | 5,193,776 | 2,422,153 |
| 8 Dell Computer | 7,603,875 | 8,025,916 | −422,041 |
| 9 Checkers Drive-In | 6,732,353 | 5,927,202 | 805,151 |
| 10 Synoptics Commun | 5,487,515 | 4,821,668 | 665,847 |
| 11 Casino Magic | 5,246,571 | 5,135,454 | 111,117 |
| 12 Noble Drilling | 5,138,116 | 5,111,986 | 26,130 |
| 13 Grand Casinos | 4,769,901 | 3,489,936 | 1,279,965 |
| 14 TPI Enterprises | 4,668,158 | 4,080,322 | 587,836 |
| 15 Food Lion Cl A | 4,542,141 | 4,329,162 | 212,979 |

### Largest Changes

| Rank | Nov. 15 | Oct. 15 | Change |
|---|---|---|---|
| 1 Comcast Cl A Spcl | 9,111,597 | 6,349,968 | 2,761,629 |
| 2 Comcast Cl A | 7,615,929 | 5,193,776 | 2,422,153 |
| 3 Price/Costco | 3,592,395 | 2,185,659 | 1,406,736 |
| 4 U.S. Healthcare | 4,246,952 | 2,946,719 | 1,300,233 |
| 5 Grand Casinos | 4,769,901 | 3,489,936 | 1,279,965 |
| 6 Geotek Inds | 1,574,132 | 688,686 | 885,446 |
| 7 Checkers Drive-In | 6,732,353 | 5,927,202 | 805,151 |
| 1 Apple Computer | 2,803,342 | 7,623,179 | −4,819,837 |
| 2 Spectrum Info Tech | 3,152,512 | 6,308,189 | −3,155,677 |
| 3 Tele-Comm Inc A | 9,255,607 | 12,178,793 | −2,923,186 |
| 4 Gen Nutrition Cos | 464,884 | 2,583,082 | −2,118,198 |
| 5 Intel | 3,849,319 | 5,850,805 | −2,001,486 |
| 6 Oracle Systems | 2,255,363 | 3,943,180 | −1,687,817 |
| 7 Sun Microsystems | 3,612,864 | 5,133,352 | −1,520,488 |

### Largest Short Interest Ratios

The short interest ratio is the number of days it would take to cover the short interest if trading continued at the average daily volume for the month.

| | Nov. 15 Short Int | Avg Dly Vol-a | Days to Cover |
|---|---|---|---|
| 1 Dibrell Brothers | 2,556,585 | 41,311 | 62 |
| 2 Summit Tech | 3,201,962 | 75,772 | 42 |
| 3 Mail Boxes Etc | 832,866 | 21,276 | 39 |
| 4 Smithfield Foods | 1,340,847 | 36,622 | 37 |
| 5 Circon | 1,786,112 | 53,235 | 34 |
| 6 Amtech | 3,565,331 | 107,006 | 33 |
| 7 Healthinfusion | 744,078 | 27,722 | 27 |
| 8 Diamond Entertain | 594,986 | 22,677 | 26 |
| 9 Healthcare Svcs | 1,142,919 | 43,889 | 26 |
| 10 Starbucks | 4,118,733 | 164,400 | 25 |
| 11 Farm & Home Fin | 573,129 | 24,776 | 23 |
| 12 Medical Marketing | 756,811 | 33,168 | 23 |
| 13 Puritan Bennett | 1,417,461 | 62,461 | 23 |
| 14 Littelfuse | 1,095,037 | 48,969 | 22 |
| 15 Biochem Pharm | 553,686 | 26,643 | 21 |
| 16 Fastenal | 1,755,635 | 85,318 | 21 |
| 17 Schuler Homes | 1,407,270 | 70,194 | 20 |
| 18 CellCm Puerto Rico | 755,497 | 38,116 | 20 |
| 19 Cabot Medical | 425,332 | 21,489 | 20 |
| 20 Amer Pwr Convers | 13,718,410 | 712,273 | 19 |
| 21 Fortune Bancorp | 854,660 | 45,764 | 19 |
| 22 Thomas Nelson Inc. | 419,571 | 23,381 | 18 |
| 23 Presstek | 604,404 | 34,136 | 18 |
| 24 Rochester Cmm Sav | 1,127,478 | 65,559 | 17 |
| 25 Bindley Wstn Ind | 564,077 | 32,811 | 17 |
| 26 Idexx Labs | 986,185 | 57,440 | 17 |
| 27 Tseng Labs | 3,520,274 | 210,418 | 17 |

a-Includes securities with average daily volume of 20,000 shares or more.
r-Revised. The largest percentage increase and decrease sections are limited to issues with previously established short positions in both months.

### Largest % Increases

| Rank | Nov. 15 | Oct. 15 | % |
|---|---|---|---|
| 1 AER Enry Res | 78,903 | 76 | 103,719.7 |
| 2 Amrion | 293,251 | 1,166 | 25,050.2 |
| 3 Bankatlantic Fsb | 288,552 | 3,247 | 8,786.7 |
| 4 Liberty Natl Bncp | 190,864 | 2,292 | 8,227.4 |
| 5 Pharmos Cop New | 181,057 | 4,250 | 4,160.2 |
| 6 Dual Drilling | 103,000 | 3,000 | 3,333.3 |
| 7 Intertel | 59,054 | 2,082 | 2,736.4 |
| 8 Surgical Tech | 190,117 | 7,414 | 2,464.3 |
| 9 Microprbe Cp Wts 98 | 200,700 | 8,000 | 2,408.8 |
| 10 Stant Cp | 52,416 | 2,183 | 2,301.1 |
| 11 VSI Enterprises | 110,747 | 4,697 | 2,257.8 |
| 12 Koll Real Est Cl A | 202,721 | 8,953 | 2,164.3 |
| 13 Zale | 762,341 | 43,257 | 1,662.4 |
| 14 WRT Energy | 153,848 | 9,420 | 1,533.2 |
| 15 Northrim Bank | 90,036 | 5,880 | 1,431.2 |

### Largest % Decreases

| Rank | Nov. 15 | Oct. 15 | % |
|---|---|---|---|
| 1 Out-Takes B Wts | 0 | 91,000 | −100.0 |
| 2 Trans Gbl Res adr | 0 | 98,184 | −100.0 |
| 3 Ceco Envir | 81 | 87,980 | −99.9 |
| 4 PDK Labs A pfd | 500 | 85,411 | −99.4 |
| 5 Hansen Natural | 700 | 90,939 | −99.2 |
| 6 Osmonics | 1,215 | 89,718 | −98.6 |
| 7 GTS Duratek | 1,506 | 54,304 | −97.2 |
| 8 Armanino Foods | 1,761 | 60,891 | −97.1 |
| 9 Ross Systems | 8,858 | 280,031 | −96.8 |
| 10 MDL Inform Systems | 5,770 | 128,641 | −95.5 |
| 11 Siskon Gold Cp A | 5,037 | 106,682 | −95.3 |
| 12 Intercargo Cp | 4,601 | 94,396 | −95.1 |
| 13 Amer Colloid | 5,951 | 111,732 | −94.7 |
| 14 Brunos | 76,637 | 864,953 | −91.1 |
| 15 Gamma Intl Ltd | 12,042 | 130,788 | −90.8 |

**Figure 6.5.** Short interest data. Reprinted by permission of *The Wall Street Journal*, © 1993 Dow Jones & Company, Inc. All rights reserved worldwide.

1993, the price of the stock has appreciated to $55 per share. The investor wishes to take profits ($4000), but she also wants to defer paying taxes on the gain until 1994. In order to accomplish this, she establishes a second but **opposite** position in the same stock by selling short 100 shares of the stock at the current market price of $55. She now has two positions in the stock: she is long 100 shares at $15 and short 100 shares at $55. In effect, she has locked in the $40 per share gain. If the stock's price appreciates, every dollar she makes on the long position will be lost on the short. If the stock's price declines, every dollar made on the short position will be lost on the long position. With the gain protected, the investor holds both positions open until the new tax year begins. She then uses the stock held in the "box"—the long position—to replace the stock she borrowed for the short sale. Now that the positions have been liquidated in the new tax year, the investor pays taxes on the gain in that year. This strategy gets its name from the time when a customer's securities were held in a safety deposit box or in the firm's vault (referred to as the "box"), and the customer would sell short against those securities.

The short sales involved in shorting against the box are included in the short interest reported in *The Wall Street Journal*. Also included in this report are the short sales that are part of an arbitrage. These make up an even larger portion of the short interest data than do the short-against-the-box sales. However, these sales do not always represent any eventual demand for the security because the investors and arbitrageurs can or will use the securities that they own to cover their short positions. Again, given the small number of investors who sell short and the purposes for which they do it, tracking the increases and decreases in open short positions may not provide analysts with much useful information.

Technical analysts consider the *short interest ratio* to be a more useful measure of the market's potential movement:

$$\text{Short interest ratio} = \frac{\textbf{Short interest position}}{\textbf{Average daily trading volume}}$$

**short interest ratio:** a calculation (a stock's short interest divided by its average daily trading volume) used to determine the number of days it would take to cover or buy in the number of shares that investors have sold short.

The ratio obtained by dividing a stock's short interest position by the average daily trading volume indicates the number of days it would take to cover the outstanding short positions. Using an example from Figure 6.5, the short ratio for Mail Boxes, Etc. is 39.

The ratio does not represent a hard and fast

indicator of a bullish or bearish sentiment, but there are some rule-of-thumb norms against which the ratio is compared. Generally, the short interest ratio is considered to be high when it is greater than 2. This is a bullish indicator because there are a large number of investors in the market who eventually will have to buy back the shares that were sold short.

This section has explained some of the more widely applied and basic technical theories that are used to determine the movement of individual stocks, as well as the overall securities market. More in-depth information on technical analysis can be found in other authoritative texts. Keep in mind that few technical analysts use or follow just one theory. Most apply several theories at one time, using one to confirm the indications of another.

## THE BASICS OF CHARTING

The terms "technical analysis" and "charting" are virtual synonyms. All chartists hold to the basic theory that past patterns of price movements, properly analyzed, can be used to predict future price movement. In short, all the information necessary to predict reasonably the direction in which the market will move is contained in the chart patterns. Chartists do, however, differ as to which charting method they consider to be most effective. In this section, we will explore some of the three basic charting techniques.

### Line Charting

This is the type of chart that we first learned to construct in elementary school. Many securities analysts use line charts to plot the closing prices of

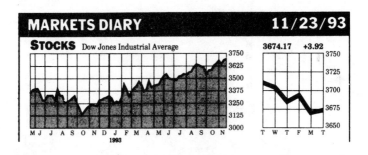

**Figure 6.6.    Line chart showing the movement of the Dow Jones Industrial Average. Reprinted by permission of *The Wall Street Journal*, © 1993 Dow Jones & Company, Inc. All rights reserved worldwide.**

the market over a period of days. These charts are also used to show the hourly or monthly price movement of a security. Figure 6.6 shows a line chart depicting the movement of the Dow Jones Industrial Average from mid-May 1992 to November 23, 1993. The line records the closing level on each day of this period. Many technicians who use line charts believe that much of the information necessary to judge the market is reflected in the succession of closing prices.

## Bar Charting

This is the simplest charting technique used by technical analysts. Price is indicated on the chart's vertical axis, and time is indicated on the horizontal axis. The market or price movement for a given session is represented on one line. The vertical part of the line shows the high and the low prices at which the stock traded or the market moved. A short horizontal tick on the vertical line indicates the price or level at which the stock or market closed.

In the example in Figure 6.7, the first bar shows that the stock represented traded at a high of 26⅝ and a low of 25¼ during the session; its closing

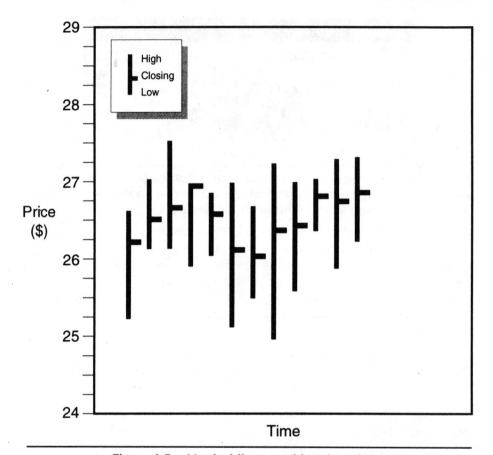

**Figure 6.7.   Vertical lines used in a bar chart.**

price was 26¼. Figure 6.8 is a bar chart showing the movement of the Dow Jones Industrial Average for the same period depicted as the line chart in Figure 6.6.

## Point and Figure Charting

This charting method uses the boxes on a graph to record the price movements of a stock. When the price rises up, the increase is depicted by a series of x's in a column of boxes. When the stock price reverses downward, the chartist moves over one

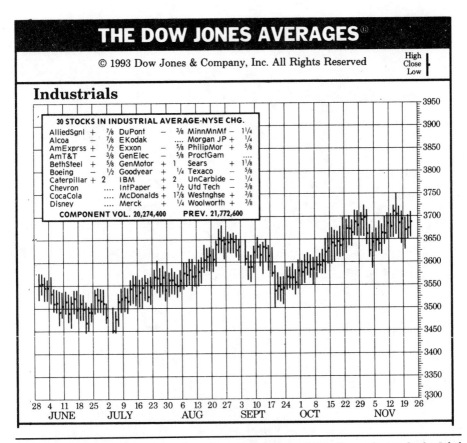

**Figure 6.8.   Bar chart showing the movement of the Dow Jones Industrial Average. Reprinted by permission of *The Wall Street Journal*, © 1993 Dow Jones & Company, Inc. All rights reserved worldwide.**

column and uses a series of o's to denote the decline. Figure 6.9 is an example of a point and figure chart.

This chart shows the price movement of the stock in units of one point ($1). (Smaller units may be used depending on the price sensitivity that the technician wishes to monitor.) In the example, the x's in the first column show that the price of the stock rose from $23 to $29. When the price fell by

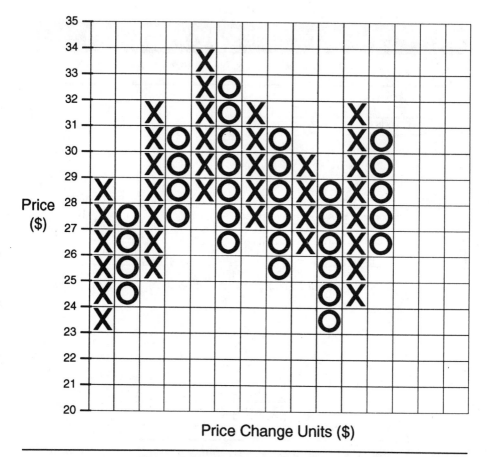

Price ($)

Price Change Units ($)

**Figure 6.9.   Point and figure chart.**

one point ($1), the chartist moved over one column and depicted the price decline from $28 to $24 using o's in the second column. Then it rose again from $25 to $32. Given the type of information this chart contains, an analyst interested in the daily price movement of a security can construct a point and figure chart from information contained in newspapers.

The time at which the price rises or falls is not recorded; nor is the volume recorded. Analysts who use point and figure charts are interested only in recording the fact that price changes occur. The degree or percentage of the change, as an indicator of continued movement in a direction or of a potential shift in direction, is more important than when it occurs. Buy and sell signals may be more easily discerned from a point and figure chart than from the other types.

Once you decide which charting method you prefer, you can create your own charts, buy them from a charting service, or get them from your broker at a full-service brokerage house. You must then learn to analyze the charts, looking for certain formations to emerge as the stock's price movement is recorded. Keep in mind that the formations occur as the market moves in its usually jagged pattern—a series of peaks (high points) and troughs (low points). (See Figures 6.6 and 6.8.) With bar charting, the most common formations are illustrated and interpreted below.

## Formations

A *trend* can be defined simply as the direction in which the market is moving. However, the market does not move straight up or straight down. Instead, it moves in a series of peaks and troughs that form a jagged pattern. If the succession of highs (peaks) and lows (troughs) occurs at increasingly higher prices, then the market is clearly in an *uptrend* (Figure 6.10). This trend is bullish, indicating a good time to buy securities. But if the peaks and troughs occur at successively lower prices, the market is in a *downtrend* (Figure 6.11). This trend is bearish, indicating a good time to sell securities.

Many investors think that the market moves only up or down. This is a misconception. At least a third of the time, according to technical analysts, the market moves sideways. A sideways trend is characterized by stock prices trading in a range

**trend:** in technical terms, the up, down, or sideways movement of the overall market (as reflected in an average or index) or a stock's price over a period of time, usually longer than six months.

**uptrend:** the upward movement of a stock's price or of the market as measured by an average or index over a period of time.

**downtrend:** the downward movement of a stock's price or of the market as measured by an average or index over a period of time.

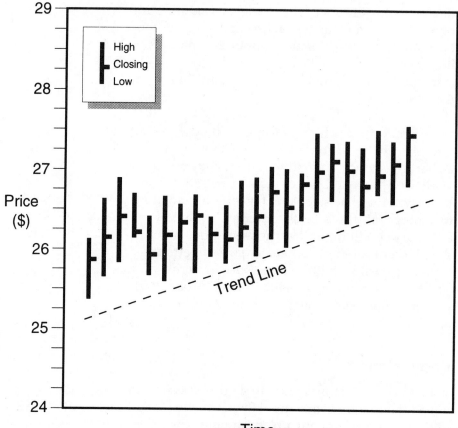

Figure 6.10. **Bar chart showing an uptrend.**

**resistance level:** a price level to which a stock or the market rises and then falls from repeatedly. Selling increases as the stock price approaches this level.

where successive peaks occur at the same level and successive troughs occur at the same level (Figure 6.12). The two levels create parallel horizontal trend lines. This trend often thwarts technical analysts because there are no clear buy or sell signals. During this time, many investors react cautiously and prudently. They sit on the sidelines and wait for more definite indicators of the market's future movement.

A *resistance level* occurs during an uptrend or a

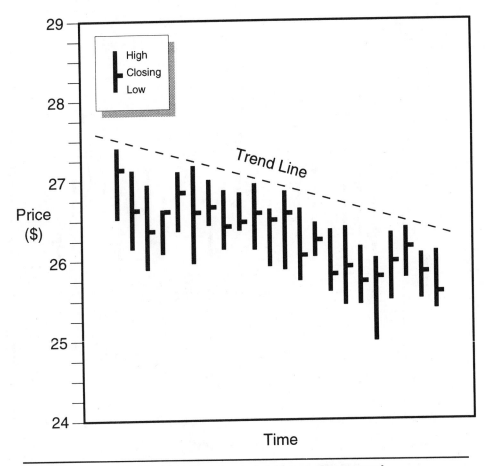

**Figure 6.11.   Bar chart showing a downtrend.**

sideways trend. It is a price point to which the market rallies repeatedly but cannot break through. Each time the stock approaches the identified price level, investors begin selling the stock, which causes the price to fall.

A *support level* occurs during a downtrend or a sideways trend. It is a price point to which the market declines repeatedly but cannot fall below. At the identified price level, the stock's downward movement is stopped because investors begin buy-

**support level:** *a price level to which a stock or the market falls or bottoms out repeatedly and then bounces up again. Demand for the security increases as the*

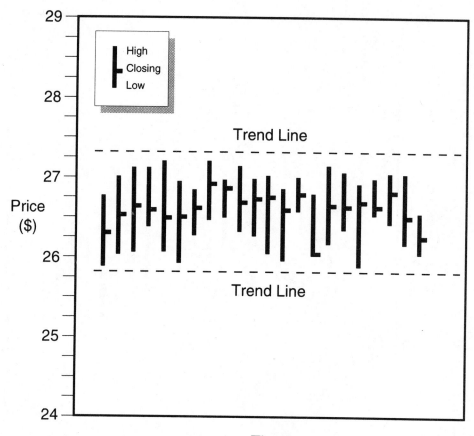

**Figure 6.12.   Bar chart showing a sideways trend.**

price approaches a support level.

ing the stock. This buying pressure or demand supports the price of the stock, preventing it from going lower. (See Figure 6.13.)

Technical analysts have two theories about resistance and support levels:

**1.** If the market breaks through a resistance level, the price will continue upward, reaching a new high.

**2.** If the market breaks through a support level,

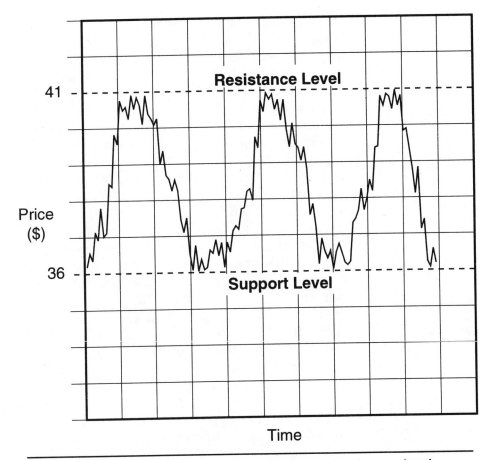

**Figure 6.13.** Line chart showing support and resistance levels.

the price will continue downward, falling to a new low.

Chartists therefore try to identify the *breakout*, the point at which the market penetrates a support or resistance level, indicating the beginning of a new short-term uptrend (in the case of resistance levels) or a downtrend (in the case of support levels). When the breakout occurs in an uptrend, the

**breakout:** a price rise above a resistance level that results in a substantial advance, or a price fall below a support level that results in a substantial price decline. Breakouts usually establish new support and resistance levels.

old resistance level often becomes the new support level. In a downtrend, the old support level sometimes becomes the new resistance level.

The head and shoulders pattern indicates the reversal of an uptrend. Figure 6.14 contains an example of this formation. The formation begins with a strong price advance (A), which is supported by a high volume of trading. (Volume changes are depicted at the bottom of the graph.) A pause or slight decline (B) follows. The price then advances to a higher level (C) but supported by a lighter trading volume. A price decline follows (D) but to a level no lower than the first price decline (B), forming what is called the "neckline" of the formation. This pause is then followed by a rally to a lower peak (E) than the previous one (C) but still on decreasing volume.

The head and shoulders bottom pattern, shown in Figure 6.15, is an inverted version of the head and shoulders top formation. It indicates the reversal of a downtrend.

Two other basic patterns also indicate the reversal of a trend. The double top (Figure 6.16), sometimes referred to as the "m" formation, occurs as an uptrend is about to reverse itself. In addition to indicating that a security's price has reached a peak, the second top is supported by substantially less volume than the first, indicating an upcoming price decline.

In the double bottom (Figure 6.17), sometimes called the "w" formation, the second decline is supported by substantially more volume, indicating that the price is about to rise.

The kinds of formations identified by chartists—rising bottoms, saucers, pennants, flags, and others—and their indications are as varied as the flag symbols seamen use. And they are also as confusing to beginning investors as the flags are to first-time sailors. Investors must study the logic of

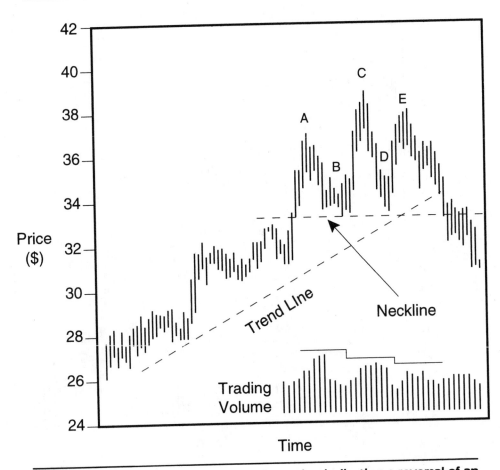

**Figure 6.14.   Head and shoulders top formation indicating a reversal of an uptrend.**

each formation carefully before they can successfully apply them in analyzing the market.

## CONCLUSION

The basic attraction of technical analysis is its belief
that all information necessary to forecast the movement of the market is in the market itself. This
information is contained in the interaction of price
and volume, which tends to repeat itself over time.

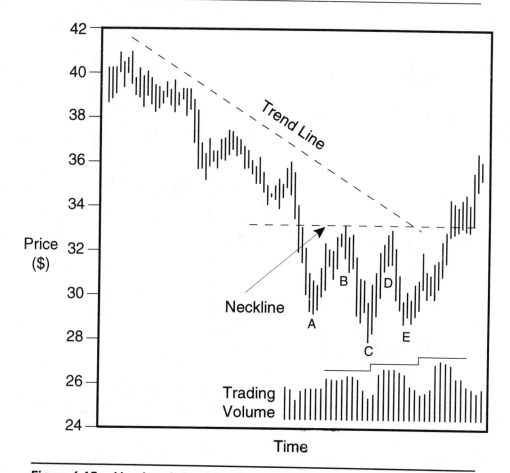

**Figure 6.15. Head and shoulders bottom formation indicating a reversal of a downtrend.**

Investors interested in technical analysis soon discover that there is no shortage of theories that have been developed from this simple premise. Some can be used by all investors; some are used only by traders; still others can be applied to only certain industries. The numerous variations and interpretations make using technical analysis difficult. Nonetheless, it remains popular among securities traders and of keen interest to serious students of the securities markets.

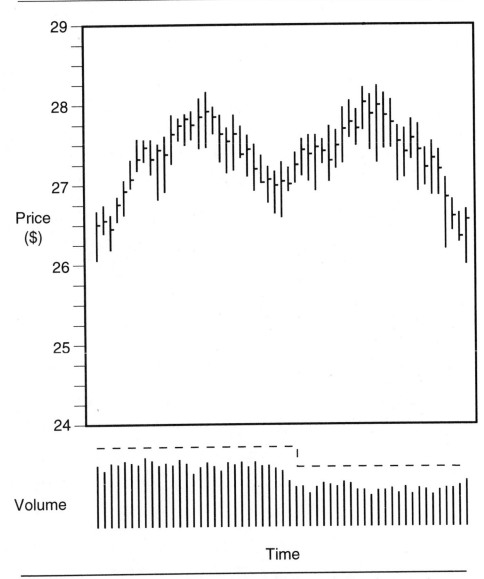

**Figure 6.16.   Double top formation indicating a reversal of uptrend.**

Technical analysis is not without its detractors. It has been compared to reading tea leaves and to the ancient Greek practice of reading goat entrails as a method of predicting the future. Other invest-

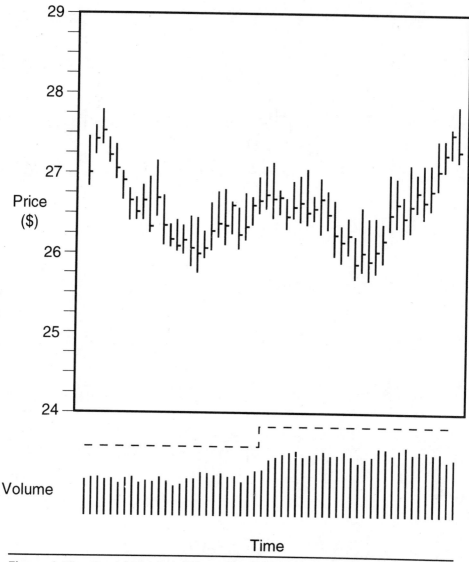

**Figure 6.17. Double bottom formation indicating a reversal of a down-trend.**

ors and traders view technical analysis as a self-fulfilling prophesy. They argue that there is only a fixed and limited amount of price information about each security that each analyst uses to make forecasts. Thus, the "group" actions of these analysts, not "real" supply and demand forces, cause the "technical rises" and "technical declines" in the markets.

Today, technical analysis is easier, more accurate, and more efficient than in the past because it is performed using computers. Analysts also use moving averages as a way of smoothing out the chart patterns. These enable analysts to keep the big picture of the market's movement in view without getting lost in the day-to-day movement. This has not necessarily brought about increased accuracy in the predictions made using these data. At the very least, the technical approach organizes information about the movement of price and volume, showing where the market is today. At its best, technical analysis offers clues that prefigure where the market will move tomorrow, becoming a useful tool for profiting from the short-term and intermediate-term movements of the stock market.

# CHAPTER 7

# Building Your Own Portfolio Versus Buying Mutual Fund Shares

S hould you build your own portfolio, buying shares of individual companies, or should you buy investment company shares, whose professional staff organizes and manages portfolios? The answer to this question can be found in the answer to another question: How actively do you want to become involved in stock selection and portfolio management?

## BUILDING AND MANAGING YOUR OWN PORTFOLIO

Recently a young businessman who owns a growing word processing and computer design firm told me proudly, "I've just opened a discount brokerage account and bought my first stock—200 shares of Dell Computer. I wish I had bought more." He added, "This is just the first step to building my own portfolio of investments. Good things are ahead as I learn to make money from stocks." This person works long days—12 to 14 hours—in order to keep his business growing. And his business is becoming successful; but when will he find the time to do the necessary research and devote his attention to building a portfolio?

Some investors, this businessman included, believe that the best way to learn about stocks and how to make money from them is to "try their hand," getting directly involved. They want to do the research, select the stocks, follow the fluctuations in the stock's price, and decide when to buy or sell. These individuals want to be fully responsible for the profits and losses that result from their trades. Another factor that may increase their desire to invest directly is the perceived financial sophistication associated with directing one's own account and broker at a brokerage firm.

For many small and beginning investors, however, selecting individual stocks and self-managing a portfolio can be risky. In addition to the time needed, two other factors—the lack of diversification (stock-specific risk) and high transaction costs—have direct effects on the risk these investors face and the investment return that the portfolio yields.

Given that most people begin by investing a modest amount of money in the stock market, it is difficult for small investors to acquire stocks in enough different business sectors to protect themselves against stock-specific risk—the risk of selecting individual stocks with varying business fortunes. As investors add different stocks to their portfolio, this risk decreases as the holdings become more diversified. How many stocks must they own before stock-specific risk is neutralized? Numerous studies have confirmed that a portfolio consisting of only 8 to 10 stocks in diverse industries from the Standard & Poor's 500 will achieve 90 percent of the benefits of a portfolio diversified across the entire market.

Diversification can be costly for investors who wish to establish a portfolio. If, for example, the average price of a stock in the S&P 500 is $50 per share and the customer buys one round lot of 8 to 10 different stocks as required for sufficient diversification, the total cost of establishing a portfolio would be $40,000 ($50 per share × 8 stocks × 100 shares). In order to lower the initial cost, the investor could buy the shares on margin. The initial out-of-pocket costs would be $20,000 (the 50 percent Regulation T initial margin requirement); however, interest would be charged on the broker's loan used to pay in full for the securities. The investor could also buy odd lots, but the commission cost per share is higher for these transactions than for round lot transactions. Hence, the percentage of an investor's overall costs increases. Even if the investor uses a discount brokerage firm, the total initial investment and associated costs are substantial. Furthermore, if the investor plans to trade actively in the account—or even change the stocks in the portfolio only occasionally—transaction costs increase even more. As a result, the price points at which the stock positions will become profitable are higher.

Time commitment, stock-specific selection risk, and high transaction costs are just a few of the adverse factors that investors must consider in establishing their own portfolio. Others (all discussed in Chapter 1) include knowledge of various investment instruments, asset allocation, diversification, timing risk, transaction costs, and, perhaps least often spoken of, expertise. Clearly the businessman cited at the beginning of this section has tried to lower his transaction costs by using a discount broker. Nonetheless, he still remains vulnerable to many other investment risks.

What can he do to lower the number of risks his investment is subject to and at the same time try his hand at direct investing in stock? He could allocate a certain percentage—say 10 percent, 20 percent, or 30 percent—of his investment dollars to direct investing and purchase a *mutual fund* with the remaining money. (Mutual funds and other types of investment companies are discussed in the next section of this chapter.) The advantage of this approach is that the larger portion of his capital is in an investment vehicle that, by definition, provides diversification, professional management, and relatively low fees. He can use the remainder for riskier investments.

**mutual fund:** common name for an open-end management company that establishes a diversified portfolio of investments. These companies issue new shares and redeem old shares representing ownership in the portfolio.

In what areas should he choose to invest? The old adage first written by Pliny comes to mind: "The cobbler should stick to his last." The businessman who owns the word processing firm decided to invest in computer stocks because he works with computers every day. For him, this is a sound decision: He is aware of innovations being made in hardware and software, and he assists companies in setting up word processing systems. His work experience has become the basis for his investment decision.

In choosing a specific computer company's stock to buy, he went through a rudimentary version of fundamental analysis. He observed that many of the companies for which he works are ordering Dell Computers and are pleased with the price relative to the quality of the machine. He concluded that demand would increase as more people became aware of the excellence of the company's product and its quite reasonable price. On a technical level, he noted that the company's quality control is good because there are few problems with the product when it is delivered. And finally, he believed that the firm's customer service department works hard to support the products it has sold. His conclusion was that a quality product sold at a reasonable price, combined with increased awareness will turn into increased sales, and good product support will enable the company to sustain its growth. His optimism is not without some concerns, however; he worries that the company may be unable to sustain its success if it expands too fast and that stiff price competition could result in lower profits.

The point of recounting this businessman's decision-making process is to illustrate and emphasize that he is choosing to invest in a product area or business sector in which he has some first-hand knowledge. Using your own work experience—in computers, medical research, building, printing, or some other field—is a good starting point for choosing your first investment in stocks. Other places from which to begin include your interests (e.g., motorcycles) and hobbies (e.g., electronics). You already have some knowledge of the reputations, products, services, and growth potential of the companies in these areas. Therefore, in making your investment decision, whether you use a full-service broker or a discount broker, you are not completely a novice.

Putting all of your investment dollars in only a few stocks is usually not a prudent decision for beginners. However, by using some of your money to purchase mutual funds and then allocating the remainder to invest directly in the market, you decrease the overall exposure without totally sacrificing the direct investment experience.

## MUTUAL FUNDS

Mutual funds are the means by which a large number of people invest in stocks. Today all of the stock in the market is worth about $3.6 trillion; 60 percent is held by individuals. Thus, over $2 trillion of stock is individually owned. In all of the mutual funds together (both equity and money markets), the public has invested over $1 trillion. Increasingly, financial newspapers are devoting more columns to articles about investing in and the performance of mutual funds. Bookstores are devoting more and more shelf space in the finance/business section to publications on the subject. And new types of funds are being created in response to the development of new financial instruments (*stock index funds*), new investment opportunities (*special situation funds*), world political events (the *country funds* of Eastern Europe), and social concerns (the *socially responsible funds*). In many ways, investing in a mutual fund **is** investing in the stock market for most small or beginning investors.

The reasons for the popularity of investing in mutual funds can be summarized in three phrases: convenience, perceived safety, and reasonable return. The first item, convenience, is an inherent feature of this type of investment. The second and third features are variables, although they are widely perceived by most investors as being built-in characteristics of mutual funds.

This section presents an overview of mutual fund investing and clarifies and explains many of the issues related to the convenience, perceived safety, and anticipated returns of mutual funds. While much of the information presented will apply to all mutual funds, emphasis will be placed on items to consider when choosing and investing in an *equity fund*.

## Overview

"Mutual fund" is the commonly used name for an *open-end management company*—a company that pools the money of many investors who have es-

**stock index fund:** a mutual fund that invests in a group of securities whose performance reflects the performance of a particular stock market index, such as the Standard & Poor's 500 or the New York Stock Exchange Composite.

**special situation fund:** a mutual fund that invests in companies that are candidates for takeover or those that are emerging from bankruptcy.

**country fund:** a mutual fund that invests in the equity securities of a particular foreign country.

**socially responsible fund:** mutual funds that do not invest in any company that has holdings in politically or environmentally incorrect sectors of the world.

**equity fund:** a mutual fund that invests primarily in common and/or preferred stocks. In practice, the term is used for both stock and bond funds and balanced funds.

**open-end management company:** an investment company that, after the initial public offering of shares to the public, continually issues new shares and redeems outstanding shares; legal name for a mutual fund.

**investment adviser:** the financial professional who manages the investment portfolio of a mutual fund and charges a management fee for these services. Often called a "portfolio manager."

sentially the same investment objective and uses it to establish a portfolio of securities, which is then managed by a financial professional, called an *investment adviser* or portfolio manager. In accordance with the fund's stated objective, the manager chooses the types of securities and the allocations of each that will constitute the portfolio. The manager also determines the best times to buy or sell securities in the portfolio in order to take advantage of investment opportunities.

Each share of a mutual fund represents an undivided interest in the investment portfolio. Unlike the common or preferred stock distributed by a corporation, there is not a fixed number of mutual fund shares issued and outstanding in the market. After the initial public offering, a mutual fund continually issues new shares and redeems already outstanding shares. (This is why mutual funds are described as "open end.") Hence, the fund's capitalization changes constantly depending on whether there are more purchases or redemptions.

Unlike equity securities, there is no secondary trading market for mutual fund shares. These shares are not listed on a stock exchange and they are not traded over NASDAQ. You can buy them only from the fund itself, from the fund's own in-house salespersons, or from a securities firm, bank, or insurance company that is an authorized sales agent. Each share that you buy is a **new** share of the fund, **not** a redeemed share that is being resold.

Since there is no secondary trading market for mutual fund shares, what determines the price at which each share can be bought or sold? It is not the supply and demand for the mutual fund shares. Rather, the price is determined by the supply and demand for the securities that make up the investment portfolio. Each day, based on the closing price of each individual security, the fund calculates the total value of the portfolio. After deducting its operating expenses (management fees, commissions, legal fees, etc.), the net amount is divided by the number of outstanding shares. This resulting dollar amount, called the *net asset value (NAV)*, is the unit value of one share of the mutual fund. (It is also called the fund's "bid price.") The NAV is the price at which you can redeem (i.e., sell) mutual fund shares. An additional *redemption fee* may or may not be charged when you cash in your shares.

When you want to buy mutual fund shares, you do so at the fund's *public offering price (POP)*—the asked price of the fund. The POP may be higher than the NAV, as illustrated by the Capstone Group of funds highlighted in Figure 7.1. In this case, a *sales charge* is included in the POP. If a sales charge is included in the asked price (the purchase price of the fund), the mutual fund is called a *front-end load fund*. To many investors, the sales charge or load is a commission. While this is conceptually correct, the use of the word "commission" is actually incorrect. By definition, a commission is a charge that is added to a securities' purchase price, not included in its market price.

The maximum total sales charge that a load fund can assess is 8.5 percent. The entire load, however, is not always charged up front. Some funds assess a *contingent deferred sales charge*, also called a "back-end load." This charge is assessed when you redeem shares within a relatively short period of time (four to five years) after purchasing them. In the listings in Figure 7.1, the letter "r" following the name of the fund denotes those with back-end loads.

Recently many funds have begun to offer investors Class A and Class B shares of the same mutual fund. Two examples are the GT Global Telecommunications A and B shares, and the Aim

**net asset value (NAV):** the market value of each share of a mutual fund, computed by subtracting the fund's liabilities from its total assets and dividing the remainder by the total number of outstanding shares.

**redemption fee:** a fee that some mutual funds sometimes charge investors when they liquidate their shares.

**public offering price (POP):** the price at which a mutual fund share is purchased. Also called the asked price, it may or may not contain a sales charge.

**sales charge:** a fee, included in a fund's public offering price, that an investor pays when buying a mutual fund share. Also called a "load."

## MUTUAL FUND QUOTATIONS

| | NAV | Offer Price | NAV Chg | | NAV | Offer Price | NAV Chg |
|---|---|---|---|---|---|---|---|
| AHA Bal | 11.55 | NL | + .04 | Fenimre | 14.71 | 15.48 | + .15 |
| AHA LtM | 10.27 | NL | + .02 | *Fidelity Invest:* | | | |
| **AIM Funds:** | | | | AgTF  r | 11.64 | 11.64 | + .02 |
| Chart  p | 8.24 | 8.72 | + .02 | CpInc  r | 7.10 | NL | + .01 |
| Const  p | 11.00 | 11.64 | + .07 | DisEq  r | 16.22 | NL | + .03 |
| CvYld  p | 11.92 | 12.51 | + .09 | EmGr  r | 14.73 | NL | + .11 |
| HiYld  p | 5.20 | 5.46 | + .01 | **Franklin Mgd Tr:** | | | |
| LimM  p | 10.01 | 10.19 | + .01 | CpQul p | 21.17 | 21.49 | + .08 |
| Sumit | 9.56 | ... | + .03 | InvGd p | 8.58 | 8.94 | + .02 |
| Weing  p | 15.68 | 16.59 | + .09 | RisDv p | 13.96 | 14.54 | + .04 |
| **Advance America** | | | | *Freedom Funds:* | | | |
| EqInc | 9.89 | 10.38 | ... | EqVal  t | 11.24 | 11.24 | + .04 |
| TF In  p | 9.95 | 10.45 | + .01 | Globl  t | 10.56 | 10.56 | + .03 |
| US Gv  p | 9.41 | 9.88 | + .03 | Gold  t | 14.92 | 14.92 | + .10 |
| **Capstone Group:** | | | | Gvtln  t | 10.13 | 10.13 | + .04 |
| CshFr | 9.75 | 10.24 | + .02 | MgTE  t | 11.00 | 11.00 | + .02 |
| Fd SW | 16.72 | 17.02 | + .04 | RgBk  t | 13.17 | 13.17 | + .14 |
| GvtInc | 4.70 | 4.70 | + .01 | GatwyGr | 13.46 | NL | + .03 |
| MedRs | 16.59 | 17.42 | + .10 | GatwyIn | 14.91 | NL | − .01 |
| PBHG | 11.62 | 12.20 | + .09 | **Gen Elec Inv:** | | | |
| Ray El | 6.74 | 7.08 | + .01 | ElfDiv | 12.66 | NL | + .04 |
| Trend | 14.45 | 15.17 | + .04 | ElfGl | 12.29 | NL | + .02 |
| CarilCa | 12.21 | 12.85 | + .03 | Elfmin | 11.33 | NL | + .05 |
| Cnt Shs | 19.30 | NL | ... | ElfnTr | 32.18 | NL | + .06 |

12-b-1 plans are denoted using the letter "p"

Mutual funds with a front-end load

Mutal funds with a contingent-deferred sales charge or back-end load. The letter "r" following the name of the fund denotes the charges

Mutual finds with both a back-end load and 12-b-1 charges. The letter "t" denotes these funds

No-load (NL) funds

**Figure 7.1. Mutual fund price quotations. A mutual fund quotation consists of a bid price (labeled "NAV") and an asked price (labeled "Offer Price"). The offer price is the price an investor pays when purchasing mutual fund shares. The NAV is the price an investor receives when the shares are redeemed. Load funds have an offering price that is higher than the NAV, thus indicating that a sales charge is included in the offering price. In the financial press, usually the POP listed includes the fund's maximum sales charge. For no-load funds, the offering price is listed as "NL," indicating that the NAV and the offering price are the same. No sales charge is assessed.**

**front-end load:** a sales charge that is applied when an investor buys a mutual fund share.

**contingent deferred sales charge:** a fee that

Value Fund A and B shares. Usually the A shares have a moderately high front-end sales load. The B shares, on the other hand, have no front-end sales load, but have a contingent deferred sales charge that declines to zero over a period of time, usually five or six years. If the shares are sold during the defined period, this deferred sales charge is computed based on the amount of the original purchase, not the mutual fund's appreciated value, if any. Mutual funds began offering these two types of shares in response to many investors' aversion to paying up-front sales charges. At first glance this would seem to be an ideal way for the long-term mutual fund investor who only invests in no-load funds to invest in many of the "hot" load funds. However, in reading the prospectus of many of these funds, you will discover that the management fees and other expenses for the B shares are usually higher than those for the A shares. Hence, over time, as is disclosed and illustrated in clear simple terms in the prospectus, the B shares produce a lower return than the A shares. The longer you remain in the fund, the larger the return differential will be between the A shares and the B shares.

Some funds are permitted to charge existing shareholders distribution fees and a portion of costs associated with attracting new shareholders. These funds are called *12-b-1 plans*, named after the rule of the Investment Company Act of 1940 that permits such charges. The fund's intention to deduct these charges must be registered with the Securities and Exchange Commission and disclosed to customers in the fund prospectus.

A pure *no-load fund* has neither a front-end load nor a back-end load. Such funds in Figure 7.1 are denoted by the abbreviation "NL" with no other notation. The POP and NAV of these funds are the same. When you buy a no-load fund, all of the money is used to buy shares of the investment portfolio.

All money market funds are no-load funds. Approximately 40 percent of equity funds in the market are no-load funds. The remaining 60 percent have either a front-end or back-end load.

A mutual fund's NAV and POP change daily as the values of the securities in the investment

is charged when an investor redeems shares within a relatively short period of time after purchasing them. Also called a "back-end load."

**12-b-1 plan:** a mutual fund that charges investors distribution fees and a portion of advertising costs. Normally these costs are borne by the fund.

**no-load fund:** a mutual fund that does not charge its purchasers a sales charge.

portfolio rise and fall. One way that you can profit from investing in a mutual fund is from an increase in the shares' net asset value. Like a stock, you can buy the share at a low POP and later redeem it at an NAV that is higher. You would have a capital gain on the investment. There are three other ways by which the net worth of the mutual fund shares can increase:

1. Dividend payments from the common and preferred stocks in the investment portfolio
2. Interest payments from the debt securities in the portfolio
3. Capital gains from the portfolio manager selling securities out of the fund's portfolio that have appreciated in value.

While we have discussed many of the differences between mutual funds and equity securities, there is one area in which they have much in common: shareholders' rights. Like most common stockholders, all mutual fund shareholders have the right to vote. They elect the board of directors of the fund, approve the fund's annual contract with the investment adviser or portfolio manager, and by a majority vote approve any changes in the investment objectives of the fund. Mutual fund shareholders can vote by proxy, voting *in absentia*, or give someone else the right to vote on their behalf. Mutual funds are required by law to send semiannual reports (including an audited financial statement) to shareholders in the same way that the Securities and Exchange Commission requires reporting corporations to provide reports to their shareholders.

## Conveniences of Investing in Mutual Funds

Professional management is one of the conveniences that a mutual fund provides individual investors. Because they are usually quite large, mutual funds try to hire the best investment advisers available. However, hiring the best people does not always result in the funds providing the best investment return. More than any other factor, the expertise of the portfolio manager is pivotal to the return that you receive from investing in a mutual fund. This is especially true for common stock funds, which have greater price fluctuation and greater potential for capital appreciation, just as the equity securities that make up the investment portfolio do.

In addition to professional management, a mutual fund provides small or beginning investors with other conveniences that could not be easily obtained if they chose to invest directly in individual stocks: diversification and low transaction costs. All of these are a result of the *economy of scale* that the large pool of investors' funds creates.

Diversification is an inherent feature of mutual funds. It also provides a relative amount of safety against the substantial losses that could result from having too much money in only a few stocks. Because the fund's portfolio is made up of a variety of different securities, the decline of a single company's stock will have less impact on the total value of the mutual fund's portfolio. Also, as some securities in the portfolio are declining in value, others are appreciating. Thus diversification provides some protection against stock-specific risk.

Additionally, you can sell part of your mutual fund holdings and the sale will not reduce the diversification of the remaining shares. Remember that each mutual fund share represents an undivided interest in an investment portfolio. Selling part of the shares reduces the percentage ownership in the overall portfolio but does not affect the remaining shares' diversification among the securities that make up the fund's portfolio.

**economy of scale:** a reduction in the ratio of expenses to assets as the size of a mutual fund increases.

A typical beginning investor who wants to invest in individual stocks will be able to buy only a small number of shares. Consequently, the commission cost per share will be high. However, when many small investors' funds are pooled, as they are in a mutual fund, the collective buying power increases. In effect, the fund manager is able to buy more shares at a substantially lower commission cost per share. Hence, diversifying the investment portfolio as well as making changes in it can cost each investor a fraction of a cent per share.

There are other conveniences that mutual funds offer purchasers that are designed to make investing relatively easy:

**1. Smaller amount of capital required for investment.** Whereas stock purchases are made for a given number of shares, mutual fund purchases are made for a given dollar amount. Also, you can purchase fractional shares of a mutual fund. This feature makes it easy (and effective) to use dollar-cost averaging as an investment strategy. Individuals can invest small amounts of money ($25, $50, or $100) on a regular basis. (See Figures 7.3 and 7.4.) Some funds set no minimum on the amount you can invest.

**2. Automatic reinvestment.** Most mutual funds permit shareholders to reinvest dividends and capital gains automatically at the fund's net asset value. Thus, the purchaser of a front-end load fund is able to reinvest without paying an additional sales charge. Over the long term, the compounding that results from automatic reinvestment will tend to benefit the shareholder—if the NAV does not fall.

**breakpoint:** a quantity discount on the sales charge an investor pays when buying mutual fund shares.

**3. Breakpoints.** A *breakpoint* is a reduction in a mutual fund's sales charge for large dollar purchases. Each load fund has its own breakpoint

| Amount of Purchase | Sales Charge (as a % of Offering Price) |
|---|---|
| Less than $10,000 | 5.50% |
| $20,000, but less than $25,000 | 4.80% |
| $25,000, but less than $50,000 | 4.20% |
| $50,000, but less than $100,000 | 3.50% |
| $100,000, but less than $250,000 | 3.00% |

**Figure 7.2.   An example of a mutual fund breakpoint schedule.**

schedule, an example of which is illustrated in Figure 7.2.

Load funds usually reduce their sales charges to investors under two situations: for lump-sum purchases and under the *right of accumulation*. Referring to the sample breakpoint scale, an investor who makes a lump-sum purchase of $40,000 of the fund's shares would be entitled to a reduced sales charge of 4.20 percent on the entire amount. Under the right of accumulation, when an investor's deposits or the total value of mutual fund share holdings reach a breakpoint, all subsequent purchases receive the lower sales charge. For example, the total value of an investor's current mutual fund holdings is $23,000. He is about to make a $5000 purchase. His sales charge for this purchase will be 4.20 percent because the total of both the market value and the purchase, $28,000, places him above the $25,000 breakpoint. Breakpoints encourage in-

**right of accumulation:** a reduction in the sales charge on all subsequent purchases when the value of an investor's shares and current purchases reaches a breakpoint.

dividuals to invest more in a mutual fund in order to reduce the sales charge.

**family of funds:** a group of different funds with portfolios made of different securities or having different investment objectives, all managed by the same investment adviser.

**4. Exchange feature.** Many mutual funds are grouped into a *family of funds*—different funds with different investment objectives but all managed by the same investment adviser or team of investment advisers. Investors in a given fund within a family can usually exchange their shares for an equal dollar amount of another fund within the same family. This feature gives investors the flexibility of switching their holdings to different funds should their investment objectives or their outlook on a particular segment of the market change. If, for example, you expect stock prices to be bullish over the long term, you might switch from a bond fund to an equity fund within the same family. Parents who have invested money in a bond fund to pay for their children's education may switch to a stock fund during periods of low interest rates in order to protect the value of the investment against inflation. An investor who is approaching retirement and wants a steady source of income may switch from a growth fund to an income fund within the same family. Usually you can switch from one fund to another at the new fund's net asset value with no additional charges or only a modest transfer fee.

**5. Liquidity.** You can buy mutual fund shares or redeem them with the same ease as buying and selling shares of a stock—in some cases, more easily. You can purchase mutual fund shares regularly through automatic deductions from your checking account, thereby relieving you of having to write a check. If you use dollar-cost averaging, this option makes investing even more passive. You can place buy orders for load funds with any securities firm that is authorized to offer them. You can place orders to redeem shares directly with the mutual fund or, in the case of a load fund, with the securities firm from which you bought the shares. Also, by law, a mutual fund must be ready to redeem its outstanding shares on any day the securities markets are open. Most mutual fund buyers hold their shares in street name in order to avoid the bother of safekeeping. As with stock transactions, this makes selling (i.e., redeeming) the shares easy.

**6. Withdrawal plans.** Once you have accumulated a certain amount of money in a mutual fund, you can begin making regular withdrawals. The terms of the withdrawal, including how dividend payments and capital gain distributions will be handled during this period, are detailed in the fund's prospectus. There are four withdrawal plans that a mutual fund can offer investors:

> **Fixed dollar.** You specify a fixed-dollar amount that you want to receive at each payment period, and the fund regularly liquidates as many shares as necessary to pay the stated amount.
> **Fixed shares.** You specify a fixed number of mutual fund shares that you want the fund to liquidate at each regular payment period. The proceeds, which will vary with the net asset value of the shares, are paid to you.
> **Fixed percentage.** You specify a fixed percentage of your total mutual fund holdings that will be liquidated at each payment period. The amount of each payment will vary with the net asset value of the shares at the time of liquidation.
> **Fixed time.** You specify the number of years over which your total holdings in the fund will be liquidated. This withdrawal method may be chosen for a fund set aside to pay for education.

If you choose one of the first three withdrawal plans, it is generally recommended that you withdraw no more than 6 percent of your entire holdings in the fund each year. Large withdrawals can reduce your holdings more rapidly than anticipated and result in the total depletion of your investment.

Once you have chosen a particular withdrawal plan, you are not locked into it for life. You can change the time (monthly, quarterly, annually) at which the payments are made; switch from one withdrawal plan to another; increase or decrease the number of shares, dollar amount, percentage, or time period that applies to the plan; or discontinue the withdrawal plan at any time.

**7. Simplified record keeping.** For record-keeping purposes, a mutual fund investment is treated as if it were an investment in a single security. At year end, the fund provides a detailed statement of all purchases, sales, dividends, and capital gain distributions, as well as all reinvestments. The fund provides a single tax statement early in the calendar year so that you can file your tax return simply and accurately. Thus, you are spared the bookkeeping problems that often face individual investors—tracking down the dividend distributions and realized capital gains from a number of different stocks.

Many mutual funds even have 24-hour toll-free telephone numbers assigned to their shareholder services departments. You can buy, sell, or switch funds at your leisure any time of day or night.

## Perceived Safety and Higher Return

A fund manager selects the securities for the mutual fund's portfolio in keeping with the stated investment objectives set forth in the prospectus. The risk associated with each fund corresponds to the collective character of the securities in the portfolio. Therefore, you can choose a portfolio whose objectives and risk are suitable for your investment goals.

A list of the most common fund objectives with brief descriptions follows this paragraph. They are noted in order of increasing risk. Those at the top of the list are considered the safest. They offer the highest potential for steady, current income—yet the lowest potential for capital appreciation. Those nearest the bottom of the list offer the greatest potential for capital appreciation but little, if any, opportunity for current steady income. They are considerably more speculative. Additionally, those at the bottom of the list tend to be less diversified than those at the top. For new investors, one of the funds in the middle of the list is probably an appropriate first selection.

**Money market mutual fund:** Invests in safe, short-term debt securities—such as treasury bills and high-rated commercial paper—and pays a yield that reflects short-term interest rates.

**U.S. government/agency bond fund:** Invests in long-term U.S. Government or agency debt securities such as T-bonds and Fannie Maes. Because many of these bonds are backed by the full faith, credit, and taxing power of the U.S. government, they are very safe—and offer a low yield.

**Municipal bond fund:** Invests in high-grade municipal bonds. Some funds are triple-tax exempt and therefore offer a lower yield than U.S. government/agency bond funds.

**Balanced fund:** Emphasizes preservation of capital as a main objective and invests in bonds, preferred stock, and common stock. In a typical balanced fund, 60% of the assets are invested in stocks and 40% in bonds.

**Income fund (debt and equity):** Conservative income funds invest in blue chip stocks that have high dividend payout ratios and bonds with modest interest rates; more speculative income funds have a mix of blue chip and speculative stocks and high-yield bonds in the investment portfolio.

**Income fund (equity):** Invests in common and preferred stocks that pay high dividends.

**Stock index fund:** Invests in a group of common stocks whose performance closely reflects that of one of the market indexes such as the Standard & Poor's 500 Index.

**Asset allocation fund:** A recent variation on the balanced fund that invests in stocks, bonds, and cash equivalents. However, unlike a balanced fund, whose percentages are usually fixed, an asset allocation fund adjusts the mix in response to changing market conditions. The advantage of this type of fund is diversification and flexibility. The disadvantage is that its success depends almost entirely upon the fund manager's skill.

**Income/growth fund:** A fund with two investment objectives that invests in a combination of high-yield common stocks (e.g., utilities) and established growth stocks.

**Growth/income fund:** A dual-purpose fund that, in emphasizing growth over income, invests in established growth companies that pay steady dividends.

**Growth fund:** Invests in the common stock of new companies in new industries that have the potential for greater capital appreciation and increasing dividend payments. In the short term, this fund typically provides no income, and its price tends to be quite volatile.

**Aggressive growth fund:** Invests in the common stock of very speculative companies in emerging industries; it may or may not be diversified.

**High-yield fund:** Also called a junk bond fund, it invests in high-yield bonds with lower than investment-grade ratings.

**International/global fund:** Invests in the common stock of foreign companies or in the common stock of foreign companies and U.S. companies with strong international presences.

**Specialty/sector fund:** Invests in one industry (e.g., gold and precious metals) or one geographical area (e.g., Korea, Hungary).

**Hedge fund:** Highly leveraged mutual fund that uses some of the most speculative trading strategies, such as trading on margin and short selling.

In reality, the distinction between certain types of funds tends to overlap somewhat. The actual makeup of the portfolio depends on the analysis and perspective of the fund's manager. One company's aggressive growth fund may look very much like another company's specialty fund. It is important to read the fund's prospectus before making the final investment decision.

## Selecting a Mutual Fund

As with individual stocks, your interest in investing in a mutual fund must first be determined by your investment objectives. Always keep in mind that, with the exception of money market funds, a mutual fund is a long-term investment. You must clearly decide the amount of risk that you are willing to accept in pursuit of the objective.

Once you have determined the objective, you must choose the fund in which to invest. Comparing funds with similar investment objectives is not easy. Recall that the skill of the investment adviser or portfolio manager is key to the returns that a fund provides its investors. Therefore, it is wise and prudent to examine the quality of the fund's management and its investment policies while at the same time examining the fund's past performance.

Some of the questions you may want answers to are:

- **What is the fund's track record in bull and bear markets over the 1-year, 5-year, and 10-year periods?**
  This historic information helps investors determine how the fund might continue to perform in the future; but is no guarantee of future performance. Today's hot, high-performing fund may be tomorrow's laggard.
- **What is the minimum amount required for the initial investment?**
  Many people who are considering investing for the first time think they need thousands of dollars to get started. This is not true. Minimums required for initial investment vary widely. The Fidelity Magellan Fund, for example, requires $2500 and Vanguard U.S. Growth Portfolio Fund requires $3000. Others, such as the Franklin Growth fund (see Figure 7.3 and 7.4) require as little as $100, and others such as the Twentieth Century Funds, have no minimum initial investment.
- **What is the minimum purchase amount the fund will accept after the initial investment?**
  In order to make mutual fund investing more attractive—and easier—for a broader range of individuals, funds permit shareholders to in-

vest as little as $25 per month. When the amount is this low, many funds require the contribution to be transferred automatically from your bank account, money-market fund, payroll, and social security checks. The restrictions and minimum amounts of the transfers vary from fund to fund. Automatic monthly investment plans have proved enormously popular, primarily for two reasons. For the investor, the money is invested before you can spend it and, as discussed earlier, you benefit from dollar-cost averaging. And second, for the fund, it reduces administrative and operations costs associated with check clearing.

- **Does the fund permit automatic reinvestment of dividends, interest, and capital gains at the net asset value?**
This is a common feature among funds. Automatic reinvestment enables compounding of investors' interest, dividends, and capital gains so they work more effectively for them.

- **What are the fund's annual expenses—management fees paid to the investment adviser, the cost of providing various services to the shareholders, audit fees, legal fees?**
Excessive expenses can substantially reduce any gain a fund yields. As a rule of thumb, a total expense ratio of 1 percent or less is reasonable. However, many companies, such as the Vanguard Group and the Franklin Group of Funds, specialize in offering mutual funds with substantially reduced expense ratios.

- **What other fees (front-end load, back-end load, 12-b-1 fees) does the fund charge?**
Multiple fee charges are becoming quite popular among funds. Keep in mind that the total charge for all of these fees together cannot exceed 8.50 percent. It is important to be aware of what addi-

tional fees you may be paying because fees reduce your overall return. Currently many funds, including Chase Manhattan's Vista Growth and Income Fund and GT Global's Telecommunication Fund, offer Class A shares, in which the customer pays a front-end sales charge and Class B shares in which the customer is assessed a declining back-end sales charge (usually declining from 5% to 0% over 5 or 6 years) if the shares are redeemed within a designated period after purchase date. This is an attractive option for those wishing to avoid an up-front sales fee. However, a cursory review of many of the fund's Class B shares reveals higher expenses than those of the Class A shares.

- **How varied are the offerings of your mutual fund family and do they have an exchange feature permitting you to buy and sell funds within the family without any additional sales charges?** Choosing a company with a large number of funds in the family benefits an investor. It allows an investor to apply the principles of asset allocation as investment goals and economic conditions change. This is especially useful if the investor is not charged additional fees to make the changes.

- **What are the most important things to know about redeeming shares of a mutual fund?** Some of the issues surrounding this question are timing, tax consequences, and fees depending on whether the fund has a back-end load and you are selling before the time limit.

Where can you find the information necessary to compare and select an appropriate mutual fund? Start with the fund's prospectus and its *Statement of Additional Information*. Both will show the performance record of the fund over at least 10 years.

**Statement of Additional Information:** an addendum to a mutual fund's prospectus that includes more detailed information, such as the calculation methods used for computing the fund's results and the fund's audited financial statements.

Included in the data is a table that shows what a typical investment of $10,000 would be worth today had it been invested in the plan in a certain year. Also, several independent publications and services, such as Morningstar (Figure 7.3), Value Line Mutual Fund Survey (Figure 7.4), Lipper Analytical Services, and Wiesenberger Investment Company Service, provide useful and easy-to-understand summaries about investment companies. Each of the figures (7.3 and 7.4) shown provides the fund's investment objective; lists the composition and specific contents of the investment portfolio; ranks the fund's performance and risk; answers shareholders' questions about minimum initial investment, automatic investment, systematic withdrawal, telephone exchanges, etc.; gives the name (and sometimes an assessment) of the investment adviser; and provides other important information that can help an interested investor to select the fund most appropriate for his or her investment objectives.

*Money, Business Week, Forbes, Barrons, Consumer Reports,* and other magazines publish rankings of the performances of mutual funds. As part of its daily listing of mutual fund quotations, *The Wall Street Journal* publishes a "Mutual Fund Scorecard" by type of fund (equity income, growth, balanced, convertible securities, international, etc.). The scorecard states the investment objectives of funds in this group and then lists the 15 top performers and the 10 worst performers, ranked by the 12-month return (Figure 7.5).

Be aware that 12-month performance can be quite deceptive. Mutual funds are meant to be long-term investments. The Securities and Exchange Commission requires all funds to give 1-, 2-, 5-, and 10-year performance summaries in their sales literature. Thus, this year's hot fund may not be a good long-term investment.

# Franklin Growth

| Objective | Load | Yield | SEC Yield | Assets ($mil) | NAV |
|-----------|------|-------|-----------|---------------|-----|
| Growth | 4.00% | 2.6% | 1.42% | 561.1 | 14.25 |

Franklin Growth Series seeks capital appreciation. Current income is a secondary consideration.

The fund invests primarily in common stocks or convertible securities. It may invest in any shares traded on any national securities exchange. The fund may also write covered call options.

The fund charges a load on reinvested income distributions.

**Historical Profile**

| | |
|---|---|
| Return | Average |
| Risk | Below Avg |
| Rating | ★★★ |
| | Neutral |

Performance

Relative Strength

**Load-Adj Return %**
| | |
|---|---|
| 1 Yr | 2.97 |
| 5 Yr | 10.54 |
| 10 Yr | 12.14 |
| Alpha | -2.2 |
| Beta | 0.86 |
| R² | 88 |
| Std Dev | 10.08 |
| Mean | 13.22 |
| Sharpe Ratio | 0.89 |

## Total Return %

| | 1st Qtr | 2nd Qtr | 3rd Qtr | 4th Qtr | Total |
|---|---------|---------|---------|---------|-------|
| 1987 | 18.86 | 5.69 | 5.48 | -9.42 | 20.02 |
| 1988 | 4.77 | 4.60 | -2.48 | 2.12 | 9.14 |
| 1989 | 5.04 | 6.34 | 11.45 | -0.56 | 23.79 |
| 1990 | -0.04 | 6.66 | -12.73 | 9.71 | 2.07 |
| 1991 | 14.09 | -0.23 | 3.10 | 7.96 | 26.71 |
| 1992 | -1.75 | -2.19 | 2.01 | 5.03 | 2.96 |
| 1993 | -0.92 | 1.91 | 1.14 | — | — |

### Income $  Paid Annually
| | | | | | |
|---|---|---|---|---|---|
| 1991 | 0.00 | 0.00 | 0.00 | 0.35 | 0.35 |
| 1992 | 0.00 | 0.00 | 0.00 | 0.19 | 0.19 |
| 1993 | 0.00 | 0.18 | 0.00 | — | 0.18 |

### Capital Gains $  Paid Annually
| | | | | | |
|---|---|---|---|---|---|
| 1991 | 0.00 | 0.00 | 0.00 | 0.15 | 0.15 |
| 1992 | 0.00 | 0.00 | 0.00 | 0.07 | 0.07 |
| 1993 | 0.00 | 0.00 | 0.00 | — | — |

## Performance/Risk 09/30/93

| | Total Return % | +/- S&P 500 | % Rank All Obj | Growth of $10,000 |
|---|------|-------|-----|--------|
| 3 Mo | 1.14 | -1.44 | 91 90 | 10,114 |
| 6 Mo | 3.07 | 0.00 | 83 70 | 10,307 |
| 1 Yr | 7.26 | -5.71 | 85 88 | 10,726 |
| 3 Yr Avg | 13.49 | -4.58 | 52 90 | 14,617 |
| 5 Yr Avg | 11.45 | -3.27 | 43 81 | 17,192 |
| 10 Yr Avg | 12.60 | -2.12 | 34 48 | 32,759 |
| 15 Yr Avg | 12.62 | -2.48 | 59 82 | 59,493 |

| | Mstar Risk % Rank All Obj | Mstar Return 1.00 = Equity Average | Mstar Risk | Mstar Risk-Adj Rating |
|---|------|------|------|------|
| 3 Yr | 69 28 | 0.60 | 0.74 | ★★ |
| 5 Yr | 63 12 | 0.75 | 0.75 | ★★★ |
| 10 Yr | 51 14 | 1.03 | 0.76 | ★★★ |

Average Historical Rating: 2.8 ★s over 178 months

## Analysis  by Jim Coursey 10/29/93

Franklin Growth Series' investment strategy can be summed up in a single word: patience.

High-octane stock-pickers needn't consider this fund; it routinely lags both the S&P 500 Index and the growth-group average. More-conservative investors, however, should like its low risk; over the past 10 years, the fund has provided a smoother ride than 85% of its peers. That's because manager Jerry Palmieri only buys stable-earnings-growth companies selling at below-market multiples. When such securities grow scarce in the market, Palmieri simply sits tight (hence the fund's minuscule turnover rate) or allows cash to build up.

While not dynamic, this strategy has proved its value during such crisis periods as October 1987, when the fund weathered the crash with half of its assets in cash. Its performance also sparkled during recessionary 1990, when its blue-chip portfolio kept year-end returns in the black. The fund pays for its bear-market strength, however, with weak performances

during rallies. That's because Palmieri scoops his picks out of downtrodden sectors; when the fund's 20% pharmaceuticals stake suffered from a mid-1992 correction, for example, he simply added to the position.

Health-care stocks continue to lag this year, along with most of the other blue-chips held by this fund, but Palmieri intends to maintain more than half of assets in such struggling issues as Pfizer and IBM. While a strong showing from its 23% technology stake has kept the fund from dipping into the red, this position simply hasn't generated sufficient momentum to boost performance out of the group's bottom quintile. Indeed, the current cyclically focused market has been unkind to this fund's classic-growth fare; its three-year average return is lower than 90% of its peers'.

That said, investors will need an extremely long-term outlook to enjoy the benefits of this fund. After all, Palmieri's portfolio is designed to plod ahead, not sprint to the winner's circle.

| Year | 1982 | 1983 | 1984 | 1985 | 1986 | 1987 | 1988 | 1989 | 1990 | 1991 | 1992 | 09/93 | History |
|---|---|---|---|---|---|---|---|---|---|---|---|---|---|
| | 5.11 | 5.95 | 5.83 | 7.20 | 7.98 | 9.02 | 9.62 | 11.49 | 11.46 | 13.98 | 14.13 | 14.25 | NAV |
| | 45.73 | 17.89 | 0.79 | 26.43 | 14.72 | 20.02 | 9.14 | 23.79 | 2.07 | 26.71 | 2.96 | 2.12 | Total Return % |
| | 24.27 | -4.57 | -5.48 | -5.31 | -3.96 | 14.76 | -7.47 | -7.89 | 5.19 | -3.77 | -4.65 | -5.44 | +/- S&P 500 |
| | 2.13 | 1.44 | 1.73 | 2.64 | 2.00 | 4.34 | 2.45 | 2.00 | 2.34 | 3.17 | 1.36 | 1.27 | Income Return % |
| | 43.60 | 16.45 | -0.94 | 23.79 | 12.73 | 15.67 | 6.69 | 21.79 | -0.26 | 23.54 | 1.60 | 0.85 | Capital Return % |
| | 6 | 48 | 63 | 40 | 55 | 4 | 67 | 26 | 49 | 32 | 84 | 95 | Total Rtn % Rank All Funds |
| | 8 | 65 | 33 | 70 | 48 | 2 | 76 | 65 | 11 | 76 | 81 | 82 | % Rank Objective |
| | 0.05 | 0.06 | 0.10 | 0.13 | 0.13 | 0.35 | 0.22 | 0.21 | 0.27 | 0.35 | 0.19 | 0.18 | Income $ |
| | 0.00 | 0.00 | 0.06 | 0.01 | 0.12 | 0.19 | 0.01 | 0.20 | 0.00 | 0.15 | 0.07 | 0.00 | Capital Gains $ |
| | 1.05 | 1.01 | 0.85 | 0.87 | 0.87 | 0.81 | 0.77 | 0.76 | 0.73 | 0.70 | 0.66 | — | Expense Ratio % |
| | 1.72 | 1.78 | 2.34 | 2.13 | 2.12 | 2.34 | 2.27 | 1.94 | 2.74 | 2.58 | 2.06 | — | Income Ratio % |
| | 0 | 10 | 2 | 4 | 1 | 9 | 0 | 2 | 0 | 8 | 1 | — | Turnover Rate % |
| | 8.0 | 16.6 | 20.1 | 24.1 | 48.2 | 100.5 | 105.9 | 144.0 | 195.9 | 407.8 | 589.9 | 561.1 | Net Assets ($mil) |

## Investment Style

| | Stock Portfolio Average | Relative S&P 500 |
|---|---|---|
| Price/Earnings Ratio | 20.8 | 1.00 |
| Price/Book Ratio | 3.4 | 0.95 |
| 5 Yr Earnings Gr % | 13.5 | 1.32 |
| Return on Assets % | 10.0 | 1.36 |
| Debt % Total Cap | 18.1 | 0.63 |
| Med Mkt Cap ($mil) | 4923 | 0.38 |

# - figure is based on 50% or less of stocks
% Ranks: 1 = High, 100 = Low except Mstar Risk 1 = Low, 100 = High

## Portfolio  Total Stocks: 92  Total Fixed-Income: 0  as of 03/31/93

| Share Chg (12/92) 000 | Amount 000 | Security | Value $000 | % Net Assets |
|---|---|---|---|---|
| 0 | 175 | UAL | 21831 | 3.72 |
| 10 | 310 | AMR | 20150 | 3.44 |
| 35 | 225 | SCHERING-PLOUGH | 13500 | 2.30 |
| 0 | 250 | DELTA AIR LINES | 13219 | 2.25 |
| 15 | 120 | MINNESOTA MINING & MFG | 13140 | 2.24 |
| 0 | 221 | RAYTHEON | 12293 | 2.10 |
| 30 | 200 | AMP | 11975 | 2.04 |
| 0 | 140 | COMPUTER SCIENCES | 11113 | 1.89 |
| 0 | 90 | ATLANTIC RICHFIELD | 10451 | 1.78 |
| 0 | 300 | TIME WARNER | 10425 | 1.78 |
| 40 | 160 | PFIZER | 9960 | 1.70 |
| 150 | 150 | AMERICAN HOME PRODUCTS | 9919 | 1.69 |
| 40 | 160 | BRISTOL-MYERS SQUIBB | 9440 | 1.61 |
| 0 | 180 | AUTOMATIC DATA PROCESSING | 9405 | 1.60 |
| 72 | 155 | DUN & BRADSTREET | 9145 | 1.56 |
| 0 | 150 | AMERICAN GREETINGS CL A | 7819 | 1.33 |
| 10 | 90 | CABLETRON SYSTEMS | 7774 | 1.33 |
| 0 | 250 | BAXTER INTERNATIONAL | 7500 | 1.28 |
| 0 | 152 | PARAMOUNT COMMUNICATIONS | 7439 | 1.27 |
| 0 | 120 | UNION PACIFIC | 7275 | 1.24 |
| 0 | 180 | RAYCHEM | 7245 | 1.24 |
| 10 | 140 | IBM | 7123 | 1.21 |
| 0 | 210 | WMX TECHNOLOGIES | 7114 | 1.21 |
| 23 | 200 | MERCK | 7075 | 1.21 |
| 170 | 225 | SUN MICROSYSTEMS | 6750 | 1.15 |

### Stock Exchange/Index Allocation (% of stocks)
| | | | | |
|---|---|---|---|---|
| NYSE | 90.5 | Dow 30 | 10.1 |
| AMEX | 0.5 | S&P 500 | 83.5 |
| NASDAQ | 6.9 | S&P Mid-Cap 400 | 8.3 |
| Foreign | 2.1 | U.S. Small Cap | 6.2 |

### Composition %  as of 06/30/93
| | | | |
|---|---|---|---|
| Cash | 16.3 | Preferreds | 0.0 |
| Stocks | 83.7 | Convertibles | 0.0 |
| Bonds | 0.0 | Other | 0.0 |

### Tax Analysis
| | Tax-Adj Historical Return % | % Pretax Return |
|---|---|---|
| 3 Yr Avg | 12.46 | 92.4 |
| 5 Yr Avg | 10.42 | 91.0 |
| 10 Yr Avg | 11.51 | 91.4 |
| Potential Capital Gain Exposure (% of assets) | 18% | |

### Sector Weightings
| | % of Stocks | Relative S&P 500 |
|---|---|---|
| Utilities | 2.9 | 0.17 |
| Energy | 3.1 | 0.30 |
| Financials | 0.0 | 0.00 |
| Industrial Cyclicals | 11.2 | 0.97 |
| Consumer Durables | 4.6 | 0.66 |
| Consumer Staples | 1.4 | 0.13 |
| Services | 30.4 | 3.93 |
| Retail | 1.8 | 0.25 |
| Health | 22.2 | 3.00 |
| Technology | 22.6 | 2.31 |

| | | | |
|---|---|---|---|
| Address | 777 Mariners Island Boulevard San Mateo, CA 94403-7777 | Sales Fees | 4.00%L |
| | | Management Fee | 0.63% max./0.40% min. |
| Telephone | 800-342-5236 / 415-312-2000 | 3-,5-,10-yr Expense Projections | $60, $75, $119 |
| Portfolio Manager | V. Jerry Palmieri (1965) | Annual Brokerage Cost | 0.02% |
| Advisor | Franklin Advisers | Min Initial Purchase | $100 (Addt'l: $25) |
| Subadvisor | None | Min IRA Purchase | None (Addt'l: None) |
| Distributor | Franklin/Templeton Distributors | Min Auto Invest Plan | $25 (Systematic Inv: $25) |
| Ticker | FKGRX | Shareholder Report Grade | B |
| States Available | All plus PR | Date of Inception | 03/31/48 |

**MORNINGSTAR** Mutual Funds                    Reprint

---

Figure 7.3.  MorningStar Mutual Fund report sheet for the Franklin Growth Fund with explanation of key terms and information found in the report. Reprinted by permission of *Morningstar Mutual Funds*, Morningstar, Inc. 225 W. Wacker Drive, Chicago, IL 60606. 312-696-6000.

# The Morningstar Mutual Fund Report:
## An explanation of key terms and information found in each report

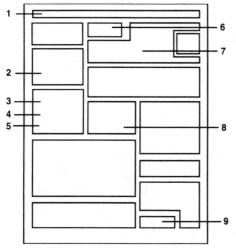

## 1 Yield

Yield represents a fund's income return on capital investment. There are two yield measures on the page, distributed yield and SEC yield. Morningstar computes distributed yield by summing all income distributions for the past 12 months and dividing by the previous month's NAV (adjusted for capital gains distributions). SEC yield is an annualized calculation based on the trailing 30-day period and is a standardized figure that the Securities and Exchange Commission requires funds to use when mentioning yield in advertisements.

## 2 Total Return

Total return is calculated by dividing the change in a fund's investment value, assuming reinvestment of income and capital-gains distributions, by the initial investment value. Total returns are adjusted for management, administrative, and 12b-1 fees, and other costs automatically deducted from fund assets. Total returns indicated here are not adjusted for sales load. Load-adjusted total returns are located in the upper right corner of the page.

## 3 Return

Return figures rate a fund's performance relative to its class based on total returns, adjusted for maximum front-end and deferred loads and redemption fees. The average Morningstar Return figure for any investment class is set at 1.00.

## 4 Risk

Morningstar Risk evaluates a fund's downside volatility relative to that of other funds in its class. This risk is calculated by adding the amounts by which the fund's returns trail those of the three-month Treasury bill, and dividing that sum by the number of months in the rating period. The average Morningstar Risk rating for any class is set equal to 1.00.

## 5 Risk-Adjusted Ratings

These star ratings represent a fund's historical risk-adjusted performance compared with the other funds in its class. If a fund scores in the top 10% of its class it receives 5 stars; the next 22.5%, 4 stars; the middle 35%, 3 stars; the next 22.5%, 2 stars; and the bottom 10%, 1 star. Ratings are recalculated monthly.

## 6 Historical Profile

This provides an overall assessment of a fund's historical returns and risk, and its overall risk-adjusted star rating. The three time periods (three-, five-, and 10-year) are combined as weighted average, with more weight given to longer periods.

## 7 Performance Graph

The top line of this graph expresses the fund's performance trend based on historical NAVs. Because past performance is adjusted downward for income and capital-gains distributions, performance reflected in the graph will be lower than the historical NAV figures reported in the table of annual data. The horizontal dotted line shows the fund's performance relative to its benchmark index (the S&P 500 Index for equity funds). When the dotted line slopes upward, the fund has outperformed its index; when it slopes downward, it has underperformed its index.

## 8 Style Box

This proprietary tool reveals a fund's true investment strategy, which may or may not match its stated objective. For equity funds, the vertical axis categorizes funds by size. Funds with median market capitalizations of less than $1 billion are small cap; $1 billion to $5 billion, medium cap; and more than $5 billion, large cap. The horizontal axis denotes investment styles: value-oriented, growth-oriented, or a blend of the two. A stock-fund portfolio's average price/earnings and price/book value ratios are computed relative to the averages of the S&P 500 Index (set at 1.00). Funds with a combined relative P/E and P/B figure of less than 1.75 are considered value funds; 1.75 to 2.25, blend funds; and more than 2.25, growth funds.

## 9 Tax Analysis

The tax-adjusted historical return shows the fund's average annualized after-tax total return for three-, five-, and 10-year periods. It is computed by diminishing each income and capital-gain distribution by the maximum tax rate in effect at the time of the distribution. Percentage pre-tax returns is derived by dividing after-tax returns by pre-tax returns. The highest possible score is 100% for funds with no taxable distributions. Potential capital-gain exposure gives investors an idea of the potential tax bite of their fund investment. This figure shows what percentage of a fund's total assets represent capital appreciation, either unrealized or realized. If unrealized, the fund's holdings have increased in value, but the fund has not sold these holdings; taxes are not due until the fund does so. Realized net appreciation (or realized gains) represents actual gains achieved by the sale of holdings; taxes must be paid on these gains. Unrealized appreciation may turn into realized gains at any time if the fund's management decides to sell profitable holdings.

---

**Figure 7.3.** *continued*

# FRANKLIN GROWTH FUND

**FRANKLIN GROWTH FUND** FKGRX

| INV. OBJECTIVE | YIELD | NAV | ASSETS(SMIL) |
|---|---|---|---|
| Growth | 1.2% | 14.72 | 560.8 |

| OVERALL RANK | RISK RANK | 5-YR RETURN |
|---|---|---|
| 4 | 2 | 11.7% |
| (Below Avg.) | (Lower Risk) | (Annualized) |

**FUND DESCRIPTION:** Franklin Growth Fund seeks long-term capital growth. Current income is not considered before making an investment commitment. The fund invests primarily in common stocks or securities convertible into common stock. The fund may hold certain levels of cash or cash equivalents for defensive purposes during certain economic conditions. The fund may also write covered call options for the purpose of hedging.

## PAST MARKET CYCLE PERFORMANCE

| | Fund | Peer | S&P 500 |
|---|---|---|---|
| Bull 10/90 - 10/93 | +48.4% | +77.4% | +69.0% |
| Bear 5/90 - 10/90 | -12.8% | -17.1% | -14.7% |

### SHAREHOLDER INFORMATION

| | |
|---|---|
| Min. Initial Invest: $100 | Syst. Withdrawal: Yes |
| Min. Subsequent Invest: $25 | Auto. Investing: Yes |
| Telephone Exchanges: Yes | Last Capital Gain: 12/1/92 |
| Tel. Redemption: Yes | Dividends Paid: Annually |

### FUND INFORMATION

Address: 777 Mariners Island Blvd., San Mateo, CA 94404
Distributor: Franklin Distributors Inc.

| | |
|---|---|
| Advisor: Franklin Advisors | |
| Sub-Advisor: None | Telephone: 800 632-2301 |
| # Shareholders: 91,121 | Date of Inception: 1/1/47 |
| Fiscal Year-End: September | # Funds in Family: 61 |

**ISSUE DATE** 1/11/94

### EXPENSE STRUCTURE

| | |
|---|---|
| Management Fee | 0.52% |
| 12b-1 Fee | None |
| 1st Yr. Red. Fee | None |

| Sales Load | Pct. |
|---|---|
| Maximum | 4.00 |
| at $25K | 4.00 |
| at $100K | 3.25 |
| at $500K | 2.00 |
| Minimum | 0.00 |

### Total Return
Performance of $10K Investment
Initial Investment 12/31/78: $10,000.
Value at 9/30/93: $61,124.
Fund
S&P500
Bottom Graph is Relative Strength of Fund Versus Peer.
Shaded areas indicate recessions.

Rising Line - Stronger Than Peer
Declining Line - Weaker Than Peer

## PORTFOLIO INFORMATION

### SECTOR WEIGHTINGS

| As of 11/30/93 | Port. % | Rel. S&P500 |
|---|---|---|
| Consumer Durables | - | - |
| Energy | 3.8 | 0.30 |
| Finance | 5.0 | 0.36 |
| Industrial Cyclical | 17.6 | 1.81 |
| Non-Durable | 8.1 | 1.11 |
| Retail Trade | 2.5 | 0.25 |
| Health | 17.7 | 1.66 |
| Services | 3.3 | 11.21 |
| Technology | 13.0 | 0.62 |
| Utilities | 1.5 | 0.17 |

### COMPOSITION %

| As of 9/30/93 | |
|---|---|
| Stock | 90 |
| Preferreds | - |
| Cash | 10 |
| Convts. | - |
| Bonds | - |
| Other | - |
| # Stocks | 98 |

### STATISTICS

| As of 11/30/93 | Port. Avg. | % Stock | Rel. S&P 500 | Rel. Peer |
|---|---|---|---|---|
| Price/Earnings | 20.66 | 70 | 0.99 | 0.95 |
| Price/Book | 3.68 | 85 | 1.09 | 1.14 |
| 5-Yr. Earn.Growth % | 14.09 | 71 | 1.39 | 0.82 |
| Avg.Mkt.Cap.($Mil.) | 11,171 | 90 | 1.67 | 1.11 |

### HISTORICAL ARRAY

| | 1979 | 1980 | 1981 | 1982 | 1983 | 1984 | 1985 | 1986 | 1987 | 1988 | 1989 | 1990 | 1991 | 1992 | 11/93 | |
|---|---|---|---|---|---|---|---|---|---|---|---|---|---|---|---|---|
| | 3.36 | 3.80 | 3.56 | 5.10 | 5.94 | 5.82 | 7.20 | 7.97 | 9.02 | 9.61 | 11.49 | 11.46 | 13.97 | 14.13 | 14.72 | Bid Price (NAV) |
| | 0.04 | 0.05 | 0.06 | 0.05 | 0.06 | 0.10 | 0.13 | 0.13 | 0.35 | 0.22 | 0.20 | 0.27 | 0.35 | 0.19 | 0.00 | Dividends ($) |
| | 1.14 | 1.26 | 1.48 | 0.94 | 1.00 | 1.63 | 1.73 | 1.54 | 3.67 | 2.19 | 1.60 | 2.24 | 2.40 | 1.29 | 1.24 | 12-Mo. Div. Yield (%) |
| | 0.00 | 0.00 | 0.00 | 0.00 | 0.00 | 0.06 | 0.01 | 0.12 | 0.19 | 0.01 | 0.20 | 0.00 | 0.15 | 0.07 | 0.00 | Cap. Gains ($) |
| | - | - | - | - | 1.01 | .85 | .87 | .87 | .81 | .77 | .76 | .73 | .70 | .66 | .64 | Expense Ratio (%) |
| | - | - | - | - | 0.98 | 0.77 | 0.77 | 0.74 | 0.62 | 0.54 | 0.54 | 0.52 | 0.51 | 0.49 | 0.53 | Exp.Ratio Rel. to Peer |
| | - | - | - | - | 10 | 2 | 4 | 1 | 9 | - | 2 | - | 8 | 1 | 2 | Turnover (%) |
| | - | - | - | - | 16.6 | 20.1 | 24.1 | 42.9 | 115.8 | 108.3 | 134.5 | 170.0 | 331.4 | 533.2 | 560.8 | Net Assets ($Mil.) |
| 8.6 | 14.8 | -5.0 | 45.4 | 17.9 | 0.6 | 26.2 | 14.5 | 19.7 | 9.0 | 23.6 | 2.0 | 26.5 | 2.9 | 4.2 | Total Return (%) |
| -9.9 | -17.6 | -0.1 | 24.0 | -4.6 | -5.7 | -5.9 | -4.0 | 14.5 | -7.8 | -7.9 | 5.2 | -4.0 | -4.9 | -4.6 | +/- S&P 500 (%) |
| -23.0 | -22.1 | -3.2 | 20.1 | -2.8 | 3.5 | -2.0 | -0.1 | 17.2 | -5.4 | -2.7 | 6.9 | -9.3 | -4.7 | -6.6 | +/- to Peer (%) |
| 5 | 5 | 4 | 1 | 4 | 2 | 4 | 3 | 1 | 4 | 4 | 1 | 4 | 5 | 4 | Quintile Perf. Rel. to Peer |

## PORTFOLIO HOLDINGS

### Top 20 Equity Holdings
As of 9/30/93

| | VL Rank* | Shares Held | Value ($000) | %Net Assets |
|---|---|---|---|---|
| UAL | - | 175000 | 24019 | 4.28 |
| AMR | 3 | 310000 | 20189 | 3.60 |
| SCHERING PLOUGH | 1 | 225000 | 14822 | 2.64 |
| MINNESOTA MNG & MFG CO | 4 | 140000 | 14403 | 2.57 |
| COMPUTER SCIENCES | 2 | 150000 | 13763 | 2.45 |
| RAYTHEON CO | 3 | 221000 | 13730 | 2.45 |
| AMP | 4 | 200000 | 13225 | 2.36 |
| DELTA AIR LINES INC DEL | 3 | 250000 | 13031 | 2.32 |
| DUN & BRADSTREET | 3 | 200000 | 12500 | 2.23 |
| TIME WARNER | 3 | 300000 | 12225 | 2.18 |
| PARAMOUNT COMMUNICATIONS | - | 152200 | 12005 | 2.14 |
| MITSUBISHI BK LTD JAPAN | - | 11250000 | 11225 | 2.00 |
| ATLANTIC RICHFIELD CO | 5 | 90000 | 10294 | 1.84 |
| AUTOMATIC DATA PROCESSIN | 2 | 200000 | 10050 | 1.79 |
| PFIZER | 2 | 160000 | 9520 | 1.70 |
| CABLETRON SYS | 2 | 90000 | 9450 | 1.69 |
| AMER GREETINGS CORP CL A | 3 | 300000 | 9375 | 1.67 |
| AMER HOME PRODS | 3 | 150000 | 9131 | 1.63 |
| BRISTOL MYERS SQUIBB CO | 3 | 160000 | 9000 | 1.60 |
| COASTAL | 3 | 300000 | 8213 | 1.46 |

*Latest available Timeliness ™ rank from Value Line Investment Survey.

### PORTFOLIO MANAGER
| Jerry Palmieri | 1965 |
|---|---|

### TAX STATUS 9/30/93
| Unrealized Apprec. % | 17 |
|---|---|

### Management Style
Large Cap ■
Small Cap
Value — Growth

### DIVIDENDS PAID

| Year | 1st Q | 2nd Q | 3rd Q | 4th Q |
|---|---|---|---|---|
| 1989 | -- | -- | -- | 0.20 |
| 1990 | -- | -- | -- | 0.27 |
| 1991 | -- | -- | -- | 0.35 |
| 1992 | -- | -- | -- | 0.19 |
| 1993 | -- | -- | -- | |

## PERFORMANCE (11/30/93)

| | Total Return | +/- % S&P 500 | +/- % Peer | Percentile Rank Peer | Value $10,000 Investment | Est. Taxes on $10,000 Investment | Value $10,000 +$100/Mo. |
|---|---|---|---|---|---|---|---|
| 3 MONTHS | 2.2 | 1.9 | -0.8 | 21 | 9,813 | - | 10,016 |
| 6 MONTHS | 2.3 | -1.7 | -4.8 | 76 | 9,820 | - | 10,335 |
| 1 YEAR | 5.4 | -4.7 | -7.3 | 72 | 10,120 | 49 | 11,265 |
| 3 YEAR | 12.0 | -4.3 | -6.7 | 88 | 13,477 | 218 | 17,353 |
| 5 YEAR | 11.7 | -3.0 | -3.1 | 76 | 16,704 | 448 | 24,071 |
| 10 YEAR | 12.6 | -2.2 | 0.2 | 46 | 31,312 | 1,368 | 53,495 |
| 15 YEAR | 13.5 | -2.2 | -2.2 | 82 | 64,373 | 3,043 | 117,857 |
| 20 YEAR | 10.0 | -2.8 | -3.4 | 86 | 64,825 | 3,332 | 164,859 |

### MPT
| | Fund | Peer |
|---|---|---|
| Beta | 0.84 | 1.04 |
| Alpha | -2.0 | 1.7 |
| R² | 84 | 87 |
| Std. Dev. | 9.83 | 11.85 |

### RANKINGS
| 1 (best) to 5 (worst) | | Fund | Peer |
|---|---|---|---|
| Overall | | 4.4 | 3.1 |
| Risk | | 2.8 | 3.2 |
| Growth | | 3.7 | 2.7 |
| Persistence | 5Yr. | 4.5 | 3.3 |
| | 1Yr. | | |

**ANALYSIS:** Franklin Growth Fund's manager, Jerry Palmieri, likes to play it safe. His simple overriding philosophy is to buy stocks with good growth prospects and reasonable prices. He will rarely buy high unless he expects an issue to have an unusual potential. Palmieri's stance is also somewhat defensive, buying stocks that he doesn't think will get knocked off too easily. Generally, these are companies that are leaders in their field. Palmieri is known for his exceedingly low turnover. His process is rather slow; he takes his time in shopping for what he wants. However, he won't hesitate to sell if a holding isn't working out. This strong buy-and-hold strategy has its good and bad points. The fund rarely loses money and expenses are kept low. On the flipside, the fund has trailed its peers in 11 of the last 15 years. Additionally, the fund hovered near the bottom of the growth category for the last three years. Palmieri attributes this to the fund's not holding many cyclical stocks, referring to it as more of a specialty fund where he tries to hold on to a stock for as long as possible. Palmieri agrees that the market is currently at a high. However, he feels his holdings have not been driven up as much in price and so are less vulnerable to declines.

The fund holds 18% in health care, particularly pharmaceutical companies. This sector was hit hard by health care uncertainties, and although some of these issues have rebounded from their August lows, this area has been the largest drag on the fund's performance. The second largest position is in transportation stocks, including Delta, American, and United Airlines, many of which were purchased at depressed prices. The outlook for the air transport industry has improved considerably, largely due to the group's return to profitability this past summer. With the larger airlines implementing aggressive cost-cutting moves, margins are expected to improve when business picks up. Franklin Growth may never dazzle investors with big numbers, but 12 straight years of positive returns is nothing to sneeze at. Although the fund's slow pace may not suit most growth investors, there is a small niche out there who wants growth with low risk. This fund seems to fit the bill just nicely as it carries one of the lowest Risk ranks in the growth category. As such, the fund offers an alternative for low-level thrill seekers.

---

**Figure 7.4.** Value Line Mutual Fund Survey sheet for the Franklin Growth Fund with explanation of key terms and information found in the report. © 1994 by Value Line Publishing, Inc. Reprinted by permission. All rights reserved.

# Value Line Mutual Fund Page:
## An explanation of key terms and information found on each page

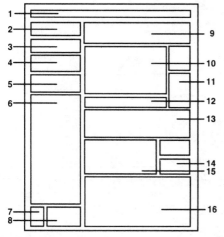

horizontal axis reflects the growth-value continuum as measured by the overall price/earnings and price-to-book value ratios of the portfolio's securities.

### 8 Dividends Paid
Quarterly dividend totals are shown for the past five years. The information provides an indication of the reliability of the fund's income stream.

### 9 Fund Description
The basic objectives and policies of the fund are explained.

### 10 Performance Graph
This graph illustrates the results of a $10,000 investment over the past 15 years (or life of the fund). For comparative purposes, results also are shown for the relevant index. For front-end load funds, the investment is assumed to be made at the current sales charge. The index assumes no sales charge. These data enable an investor considering a load fund to evaluate the effects of the sales charge on an actual investment over a long time period.

### 11 Expense Structure
A synopsis of the fund expenses, including maximum and minimum management fees, sales charges, etc.

### 12 Relative Performance
This graph shows the fund's performance relative to its peer group on a cumulative basis over the past 15 years (or the life of the fund, for younger funds). This relative-performance graph shows how well the fund has done over time compared to its peers. A rising curve indicates that a fund is outperforming its peers; a declining curve reflects underperformance.

### 13 Historical Array
Price per share, dividends, capital gains, expenses, assets, and performance are included for each of the past 15 years. The bottom row documents how well the fund has performed, on a relative basis.

### 14 Rankings
The fund's position within the rank. The number to the left of the decimal point represents the fund's broad rank on Value Line's scale of 1 (best) to 5 (worst), while the number to the right of the decimal point denotes the fund's position within that rank. For example, a fund that falls within the top tenth of all funds ranked 1 will show a rank of 1.0; a fund in the bottom tenth of all rank-1 funds will show a rank of 1.9.

### 15 Performance
The fund's total returns over various periods are shown in the first column. Results for periods longer than one year are expressed as average annualized rates. The second and third columns shows the percentage difference between the fund's performance and those of the relevant index and peer group, respectively. The fourth column indicates the percentile rank versus the fund's peers, with 1 the Highest and 100 the Lowest. The final three columns show what return a shareholder would have realized from a $10,000 investment. The first $10,000 illustration assumes that a lump sum was invested at the beginning of the period, at the current sales charge, and that no subsequent transactions were made. The last column shows the results of a $10,000 initial investment with subsequent investments of $100 at the end of each month during the entire period. This provides an illustration of dollar-cost averaging.

### 16 Analyst Commentary
A concise report on the fund's performance, management strategies, and future prospects.

### 1 Highlight Bar
The fund's name, ticker symbol, investment objective, dividend yield, latest NAV (net asset value) or price per share, and net assets.

### 2 Ranks
The Risk Rank shows each fund's level of risk relative to that of all other mutual funds. The fund's total-return performance (dividend and interest plus capital appreciation) is shown for the latest five years and is expressed as an average, annualized rate.

### 3 Past Market Cycle Performance
The fund's total return during the latest bull and bear stock markets. Total returns for the fund's peer group (those with a similar investment objective) and for the S&P 500 Index over the same periods.

### 4 Shareholder Information
Details about fees, minimum investments, special services, etc.

### 5 Fund Information
Companies servicing the fund, number of shareholders, when the fund began operations, the fund's address and telephone number, etc.

### 6 Portfolio Information
These details start with the percentage of assets in each of 10 broad equity-market sectors. The composition box shows the percentage of the fund's assets invested in common stocks, preferred stocks, other assets categories, and cash. The list of the 20 largest holdings of the fund is also listed. Concluding this section are the name and starting date for the individual(s) managing the fund and the fund's tax status, which includes "unrealized appreciation." This item indicates the percentage of the fund's current portfolio value that represents gains on securities. If and when these gains are realized through sale of the securities, the distributions to shareholders become taxable as capital gains.

### 7 Management Style
A representation of the fund's major orientation, within a two-axis grid. For equity fund, the vertical axis represents market capitalization of equities in which the fund invests; the

---

**Figure 7.4.** *continued*

## Mutual Fund Scorecard/Growth

INVESTMENT OBJECTIVE: Capital growth without regard for income; usually characterized by moderate portfolio turnover. Bull/Bear ratings are figured over the latest two rising and two falling market cycles

| ASSETS SEPT. 30 (in millions) | BULL MKTS | BEAR MKTS | FUND NAME | 4 WEEKS | 52 WEEKS | 5 YEARS |
|---|---|---|---|---|---|---|
| | PAST PERFORMANCE | | | TOTAL RETURN[1] IN PERIOD ENDING NOV. 24 | | |
| **TOP 15 PERFORMERS** | | | | | | |
| 418.1 | ** | ** | Putnam New Oppty A | −4.39% | 32.84% | **% |
| 1003.0 | ** | ** | Oakmark[2] | −0.91 | 32.27 | ** |
| 1730.5 | Hi | Med | New Economy Fund | −2.65 | 29.99 | 131.62 |
| 80.2 | Low | Low | Boston Co:Spec Gr Ret[2] | −7.27 | 29.95 | 130.41 |
| 27.1 | ** | ** | Alliance Port:Growth A[3] | −2.82 | 28.24 | ** |
| 6.4 | ** | ** | Brandywine Blue Fund[2] | −1.83 | 27.72 | ** |
| 86.4 | ** | ** | Alliance Port:Growth B[2] | −2.88 | 27.47 | 169.62 |
| 360.4 | Med | Med | Founders:Growth Fund[2] | −3.26 | 27.21 | 146.65 |
| 1143.0 | ** | Low | Fidelity Destiny II | −0.51 | 27.03 | 157.26 |
| 2973.5 | Hi | Low | Fidelity Destiny I | −0.69 | 26.56 | 146.90 |
| 3.6 | ** | ** | Boston Co Inv:Cont Ret[2] | −4.37 | 25.66 | 109.41 |
| 714.1 | ** | ** | Strong Common Stock[2] | −2.03 | 25.33 | ** |
| 31.2 | ** | ** | Crabbe Huson Equity[2] | 0.93 | 25.28 | ** |
| 30509.8 | Hi | Low | Fidelity Magellan Fund[3] | −2.28 | 25.17 | 144.95 |
| 487.6 | Hi | Low | CGM Cap Development[2] | −5.02 | 24.76 | 231.92 |
| **AVG. FOR CATEGORY** | | | | −1.82% | 9.64% | 100.19% |
| **NUMBER OF FUNDS** | | | | 455 | 372 | 212 |
| **BOTTOM 10 PERFORMERS** | | | | | | |
| 1.1 | ** | ** | Frontier:Equity Fund | 0.34% | −13.55% | **% |
| 700.8 | ** | ** | Dean Witter Cap Growth[2] | 0.23 | −9.54 | ** |
| 53.9 | ** | ** | Flag Inv Qual Growth Flag[3] | −0.63 | −8.47 | ** |
| 1.3 | ** | ** | Nottingham II:Hattrs Div[2] | −3.42 | −8.32 | ** |
| 558.2 | ** | Low | Pasadena Inv:Growth | −0.32 | −7.86 | 120.28 |
| 1.6 | Low | Low | Steadman Oceanographic[2] | −5.81 | −7.61 | −16.50 |
| 0.8 | Med | Med | Excel Value Fund[3] | −1.52 | −7.33 | −5.43 |
| 2.5 | ** | ** | Wasatch:Mid-Cap[2] | −3.83 | −7.19 | ** |
| 130.0 | ** | ** | Yacktman Fund[2] | 2.78 | −6.41 | ** |
| 6.6 | ** | ** | Ambassador:Core Gr Ret[3] | −2.86 | −5.99 | ** |

[1] Change in net asset value with reinvested dividends and capital gains  
[2] No initial load  
[3] Low initial load of 4.5% or less  
** Fund track record is too short

Hi = Top third  
Med = Middle third  
Low = Bottom third

*Source: Lipper Analytical Services Inc.*

**Figure 7.5.  Mutual fund scoreboard. Reprinted by permission of *The Wall Street Journal*, © 1993 Dow Jones & Company, Inc. All rights reserved worldwide.**

## Closed-End (or Publicly Traded) Funds

**closed-end fund:**

an investment company has a

While there are over 4500 mutual funds available in the market, there are only 900 *closed-end funds.*

Called "publicly traded funds," these companies assemble an investment portfolio and then issue shares to the public. The portfolio may or may not be diversified. After the initial public offering, a closed-end fund does not issue new shares or redeem old shares. The fund's shares thereafter trade on stock exchanges and in the over-the-counter market. Unlike mutual fund shares, closed-end fund shares are not redeemed by the sponsor. Instead, investors buy and sell them through brokers in the same way that common and preferred stock are traded. They also pay a commission for each trade.

The relationship between a closed-end fund's market value and net asset value is different from that of a mutual fund share. As Figure 7.6 shows, each closed-end fund share has an NAV. Like a mutual fund, this value changes daily depending on the market value of the shares that make up the investment portfolio. However, the fund's NAV is not the basis for computing the market value of the fund's shares. Because the shares trade like stock, their market value (labeled "stock price" in the listing) is determined by demand for the fund's shares themselves and not directly by the supply and demand for the stocks that constitute the portfolio. As a result, the market value of a closed-end fund may be higher than the NAV (trading at a premium), equal to the NAV, or lower than the NAV (trading at a discount).

Traditionally, the shares of a closed-end fund (especially closed-end equity funds) trade at a discount to their net asset value. This is true of newly issued funds also. After most new shares are sold in the primary market at their net asset value, they almost immediately trade at a discount in the secondary market to reflect the start-up costs of the fund. Thus, the purchaser has an immediate paper

one-time offering of a fixed number of shares to the public and then does not issue new shares or redeem old shares; the fund's shares are bought and sold like stock. Also called a "publicly traded fund."

# CLOSED END FUNDS

Unaudited Net Asset Values (NAV) of closed end funds, reported by the companies as of Friday's close. Each quote includes the closing stock exchange price or dealer-to-dealer asked price of each fund's shares, with the percentage of difference. For equity funds, the final column shows the 52-week percentage change in stock market price plus dividends. For bond funds, the final column shows dividends paid from income in the last 12 months, as of the prior month-end, as a percentage of the stock market price. The figure doesn't include capital gains distributions. N-New York Stock Exchange. O-Over-the-Counter. A-American. C-Chicago. T-Toronto.

| Fund Name | Stock Exch | NAV | Market Price | Prem /Disc | 52 week Market Return |
|---|---|---|---|---|---|
| **General Equity Funds** | | | | | |
| Adams Express | N | 19.67 | 18⅛ | -7.9 | 3.6 |
| Baker Fentress | N | 20.14 | 16⅝ | -17.5 | 9.4 |
| Bergstrom Capital | A | 95.00 | 96 | +1.1 | -24.7 |
| Blue Chip Value | N | 7.82 | 8 | +2.3 | 13.4 |
| Central Securities | A | 16.48 | 15¾ | -4.4 | 52.5 |
| Charles Allmon Tr | a N | 10.40 | 10 | -3.8 | 8.9 |
| Engex | A | 13.67 | 11¼ | -17.7 | 15.4 |
| Equus II | A | 21.15 | 14½ | -31.4 | 65.7 |
| Gabelli Equity Tr | N | 11.45 | 12⅛ | +5.9 | 33.0 |
| General American | N | 24.59 | 22⅛ | -10.0 | -15.0 |
| Inefficient Mkt | A | 12.24 | 10¼ | -16.3 | 5.6 |
| Jundt Growth | N | 15.67 | 14⅛ | -9.9 | -0.8 |
| Liberty All-Star | a N | 10.53 | 10⅞ | +3.3 | 9.8 |
| Morgan Gren Sm Cap | N | 12.78 | 11⅝ | -9.0 | -3.3 |
| NAIC Growth | O | N/A | 9¾ | N/A | 12.6 |
| Royce Value Trust | N | 14.33 | 13⅞ | -3.2 | 15.4 |
| Salomon SBF | N | N/A | 12⅞ | N/A | 9.6 |
| Source Capital | N | 41.00 | 44¼ | +7.9 | 2.4 |
| Spectra | O | 22.49 | 18 | -20.0 | 35.5 |
| Tri-Continental | a N | 27.38 | 23¾ | -13.3 | 3.4 |
| Z-Seven | O | 16.75 | 17 | +1.5 | 13.3 |
| Zweig | N | 11.69 | 13½ | +15.5 | 13.2 |
| **Specialized Equity Funds** | | | | | |
| ASA Limited | cv N | 48.15 | 46 | -4.5 | 42.2 |
| Alliance Glob Env | N | 10.85 | 9⅜ | -13.6 | 0.0 |
| Anchor Gold & Curr | C | N/A | 6 | N/A | 29.7 |
| BGR Prec Metals | cy T | 14.73 | 13¾ | -6.7 | 115.7 |
| C&S Realty Income | A | 8.94 | 9⅜ | +4.9 | 25.7 |
| C&S Total Return | N | 13.48 | 14⅜ | +6.6 | N/A |
| Central Fd Canada | c A | 4.66 | 5 | +7.3 | 38.2 |
| Counsellors Tandem | N | 17.51 | 14⅞ | -15.0 | 15.8 |
| Delaware Gr Div | N | 14.95 | 14⅞ | -0.5 | N/A |
| Dover Regional Fin | O | N/A | 6½ | N/A | 18.5 |
| Duff Phelps Ut Inc | N | 9.59 | 10⅛ | +5.6 | 6.0 |
| Emerging Mkts Tel | N | 20.21 | 24⅜ | +20.6 | 95.1 |
| First Financial | N | 19.35 | 17¾ | -8.3 | 43.9 |
| Global Health Sci | N | 12.01 | 11⅛ | -7.4 | -5.7 |
| H&Q Healthcare Inv | N | 18.61 | 17⅞ | -3.9 | -10.8 |
| H&Q Life Sci Inv | N | 13.52 | 12⅞ | -4.8 | -14.2 |
| New Age Media Fund | N | 13.71 | 14¾ | +7.6 | N/A |
| Patriot Global Dvd | N | 14.79 | 15⅛ | +2.3 | 15.1 |
| Patriot Pre Dvd II | a N | 12.42 | 11½ | -7.4 | 16.0 |
| Patriot Pref Div | a N | 13.42 | 12⅞ | -4.1 | N/A |
| Patriot Prem Divd | N | 10.43 | 10¼ | -1.7 | 10.4 |
| Patriot Select Dvd | N | 16.46 | 15¾ | -4.3 | 0.1 |
| Petroleum & Res | N | 29.27 | 27⅞ | -4.8 | 20.0 |
| Pilgrim Reg Bk Shs | N | 12.14 | 11⅛ | -8.4 | 8.2 |
| Preferred Inc Mgt | N | 14.27 | 14¼ | -0.1 | N/A |
| Preferred Inc Opp | N | 13.10 | 13 | -0.8 | 7.0 |
| Preferred Income | N | 18.32 | 18 | -1.7 | 4.9 |
| Putnam Divd Income | N | 12.48 | 11¾ | -5.8 | 0.8 |
| SthEastrn ThriftBk | O | 19.50 | 17¼ | -11.5 | 32.7 |
| Templtn Glbl Util | A | 14.95 | 15¾ | +5.4 | 24.0 |
| **World Equity Funds** | | | | | |
| Americas All Seas | O | 5.13 | 4⅛ | -19.6 | 4.6 |
| Argentina | N | 12.86 | 13¾ | +6.9 | 19.5 |
| Asia Pacific | N | 17.42 | 18⅜ | +5.5 | 75.7 |
| Asia Tigers | N | 13.97 | 15⅛ | +8.3 | N/A |
| Austria | N | 10.02 | 9¼ | -7.7 | 37.3 |
| Brazil | c N | 20.69 | 18⅞ | -8.8 | 63.4 |
| Brazilian Equity | c N | 15.10 | 14⅛ | -6.5 | 82.6 |
| Cdn Genl Inv Ltd | ay T | 41.06 | 34 | -17.2 | 27.4 |
| Chile | N | 37.15 | 36⅞ | -0.7 | 39.2 |
| China | N | 18.44 | 19½ | +5.7 | 39.7 |
| Clemente Global Gr | c N | 12.17 | 11⅛ | -8.6 | 43.2 |
| Emerging Mexico | c N | 21.78 | 23⅝ | +8.5 | 40.3 |
| Europe | N | 12.86 | 12¼ | -4.7 | 23.6 |
| European Warrant | c N | 13.81 | 13¼ | -4.1 | 110.5 |
| First Australia | A | 11.25 | 10½ | -6.7 | 55.1 |
| First Iberian | A | N/A | 7¾ | N/A | 41.7 |
| First Israel | a N | 15.69 | 15¼ | -2.8 | 33.0 |
| First Philippine | N | 20.75 | 17⅞ | -13.9 | 80.0 |
| France Growth | N | 12.23 | 12⅜ | +1.2 | 38.0 |
| GT Greater Europe | N | 13.88 | 13⅝ | -1.8 | 55.7 |
| Germany Fund | N | 12.42 | 11⅞ | -4.4 | 22.6 |
| Germany, Emerging | N | 9.56 | 8⅝ | -9.8 | 39.8 |
| Germany, Future Fd | N | 16.69 | 14¾ | -11.6 | 35.3 |
| Germany, New Fund | N | 13.82 | 12¼ | -11.4 | 32.9 |
| Global Small Cap | A | 14.65 | 14¾ | +0.7 | N/A |
| Greater China | N | 20.62 | 21⅛ | +2.4 | 64.1 |
| Growth Fd of Spain | N | 10.85 | 10 | -7.8 | 35.6 |
| India Growth | d N | 18.14 | 23⅛ | +27.5 | 49.6 |
| Indonesia | N | 12.10 | 13⅜ | +10.5 | 33.8 |
| Irish Investment | N | 9.67 | 8⅝ | -10.8 | 33.7 |
| Italy | a N | 8.79 | 9⅜ | +6.7 | 21.9 |
| Jakarta Growth | N | 9.21 | 9¾ | +5.9 | 45.6 |
| Japan Equity | N | 13.02 | 13 | -0.2 | 46.5 |
| Japan OTC Equity | N | 9.35 | 9½ | +1.6 | 20.6 |
| Jardine Flem China | N | 20.66 | 23⅛ | +11.9 | 79.6 |
| Korea | N | 14.92 | 17⅝ | +18.1 | 30.6 |
| Korea Equity Fund | N | 10.98 | 11¾ | +7.0 | N/A |
| Korean Investment | N | 11.79 | 14¼ | +20.9 | 35.8 |
| Latin America Eq | N | 20.47 | 22 | +7.5 | 79.7 |
| Latin America Inv | N | 24.71 | 27½ | +11.3 | 66.3 |
| Latin American Dis | N | 22.84 | 24 | +5.1 | 100.0 |
| Malaysia | N | 23.90 | 22¼ | -6.9 | 44.9 |
| Mexico | c N | 33.10 | 32 | -3.3 | 53.6 |
| Mexico Equity&Inc | c N | 21.15 | 21¼ | +0.5 | 44.6 |
| Morgan Stan Em Mkt | N | 25.06 | 27 | +7.7 | 66.0 |
| New World Inv | z | N/A | N/A | N/A | N/A |
| Portugal | N | 12.02 | 12⅛ | +0.9 | 71.0 |
| ROC Taiwan | N | 8.95 | 10⅜ | +15.9 | 9.4 |
| Scudder New Asia | N | 22.28 | 24⅛ | +8.3 | 69.0 |
| Scudder New Europe | N | 10.52 | 9⅞ | -6.1 | 30.8 |
| Singapore | c N | 17.01 | 17 | -0.1 | 77.7 |
| Spain | N | 9.69 | 9¾ | +0.6 | 20.4 |
| Swiss Helvetia | N | 20.25 | 19¾ | -2.5 | 42.9 |

**Figure 7.6. Closed-end funds (publicly traded funds) price quotations. This table shows the current market prices of domestic and international (e.g., Asia Pacific, Brazil, First Australia, Irish Investment Fund, Jakarta Growth) closed-end funds that invest primarily in equity securities. The list is published every Monday in *The Wall Street Journal*. It states the name of the fund, the market (exchange or over the counter [OTC]) in which it trades, the NAV per share, and the current market price (labeled "stock price") of each share. The last column—"% Diff"—indicates whether the fund's current price is at a discount (−) or premium (+) to its current net asset value. Notice that the majority of closed-end funds in the listing are trading at a discount. Reprinted by permission of *The Wall Street Journal*, © 1993 Dow Jones & Company, Inc. All rights reserved worldwide.**

loss. It should be kept in mind that closed-end funds are long-term investments. Over the long term, the market value of the portfolio should rise, thereby enabling investors to sell shares at a gain. Another strategy is to research the discount at which a fund usually trades. If the discount deepens appreciably, it may be a signal that the time is right to buy the fund.

Closed-end funds can trade at a premium. This is particularly true when the stocks that make up the investment portfolio are those of foreign companies in countries with bright economic futures and restrictive rules governing foreign investment, such as many Pacific Rim countries. The Korean Investment Fund is a good example. Notice in Figure 7.6 that it is trading at a 20.9 percent premium over its net asset value. The combination of a limited number of shares and the anticipated economic growth of the country frequently results in the shares' trading at a premium. This can be interpreted in one of two ways. First, the premium anticipates or indicates investor sentiment about the fund's future growth. Or, second, the fund provides an investment return that is higher than the current market rate of return.

Beginning investors should evaluate the possibilities of investing in closed-end funds just the same as they would investing in any other type of security, keeping in mind that each fund is essentially a package deal. Most international closed-end funds are either country funds or regional. It is rare that you will like the entire package of securities in the fund. On the other hand, if a fund has invested in an area or country where you may not be able to invest directly or obtain enough data to make an informed investment decision, then closed-end funds may be the only investment option.

# CHAPTER 8

# Indirect Investing in Stock: Rights, Warrants, and Options

**stock derivative:**
a security that
offers an investor
some but not all of
the benefits of
stocks, particularly
the capital gains
potential, usually at
a lower cost per
unit.

**N**ot all investors are interested in making money through the dividends that stocks pay. Many want only to profit from the rise and fall of a stock's price. And they want to do this without owning the stock and at the lowest possible cost. Rights, warrants, and options are appropriate investment vehicles for these individuals. Called *stock derivatives*, each of these securities can be thought of as a contract that offers its owner the possibility of buying (or selling) the underlying stock if he or she chooses. (Strictly speaking, rights and warrants are stock equivalents and options are stock derivatives. For the sake of simplicity throughout this chapter, I will refer to all three as stock derivatives.)

These derivatives have none of the traditional benefits of equity ownership. None entitles the owner to receive dividends. The holder has no voting rights or preemptive rights and no priority in the liquidation of a company. Their primary benefit is that the market price movement of each of these derivatives tends to parallel the price movement of the "real" stock that it represents—and the cost of purchasing them is usually a fraction of what it would cost to purchase the actual stock.

The owner of one of these stock derivatives typically has the right to purchase (or sell) the underlying stock for a predetermined price but only for a fixed period of time. Most equity derivatives do not have indefinite lives like the stocks they represent. On a designated expiration date, the security becomes worthless. During the period that an individual holds a right, warrant or option, its market value varies depending on the relationship between the derivative's fixed exercise price and the market value of the underlying stock. If, for example, a stock-derivative security gives its owner the right to buy the underlying common stock at $15 per share and the market value of that common stock is $25 per share, then the equity derivative has a "built-in" profit, or "intrinsic value," of $10 per share. If the market price of the stock is equal to or less than the derivative's fixed price, then the stock-derivative security would clearly have no intrinsic value for its owner—although it could have "time," or speculative, value.

The holder of any of these stock-derivative securities has a choice of three actions to take:

**1.** "Exercise" the contract by buying (or selling) the underlying stock. This is the choice if the investor wants the underlying stock or there is a built-in profit due to the difference between an equity derivative's fixed price and the underlying stock's market price.

**2.** Trade the equity derivative. This action takes advantage of the fact that the market price of the security tends to move in a direction similar to the price of the underlying stock. As the price of the underlying security increases, so does the price of the derivative security. The same price movement relationship holds for price decreases. An investor who buys an equity-derivative security can sell it at a profit when its market value increases. An investor who sells short a derivative can later cover the short position profitably by purchasing it.

**3.** Hold it to the expiration date, at which time it becomes worthless.

Like the stocks they represent, equity derivatives offer investors a high degree of liquidity. Rights and warrants trade on stock exchanges and in the over-the-counter market. These securities trade on the same exchange or in the same market where the underlying stock trades. Options trade primarily on exchanges: the Chicago Board Options Exchange, the American Stock Exchange, the Philadelphia Stock Exchange, the Pacific Stock Exchange, and the New York Stock Exchange. Unlike rights and warrants, most options do not usually trade on the same exchange where the company's stock is listed.

As the basic uses of rights, warrants, and options are explained in this chapter, we will look at different scenarios to illustrate how each works. The discussions and the accompanying examples are designed to provide beginning investors with a clear understanding of the rewards and risks associated with each security and strategy.

## RIGHTS

A preemptive right is a short-term security that gives existing common shareholders the first opportunity to purchase any additional common shares that a company may issue. This privilege, known as the "preemptive right" and granted in a company's charter, permits each common shareholder to maintain his or her proportionate ownership in a company. Unlike the common stock they represent, however, rights do not have an indefinite life. Usually you have 30 to 60 days to decide if you want to subscribe to the new shares or sell the rights to another investor.

It is customary to distribute one right for each share of a company's outstanding common stock. If you own 1000 shares of a company's stock, then you will receive 1000 rights during a rights offering. The number of rights needed to buy each new share of a company's stock is set by the board of directors. The ratio is determined using a simple calculation:

$$N = \frac{\textbf{Number of outstanding shares}}{\textbf{Number of new shares to be offered}}$$

$N$ = *number of rights needed to buy one new share*

If, for example, a company has 100,000 common shares outstanding and it plans to issue 20,000 new shares, then the number of rights needed to buy each new share is 5 (100,000/20,000). An investor who owns 1000 shares (1 percent) of the company's stock would have enough rights to buy 200 (1000/5) of the new shares. Upon subscribing to the new issue, the investor would own 1200 shares, or 1 percent of the total 120,000 shares now outstanding. The investor's proportionate ownership is maintained.

In order to be eligible to acquire the additional shares at the subscription price, you must own the stock on or before a specified date set by the board of directors. This date is known as the record date. Once the record date is announced, the exchange or the National Association of Securities Dealers uses this information to establish an appropriate *ex-rights date*. If you buy the stock at any time prior to the ex-rights date, you are buying the stock with the right included. In technical terms, the stock is described as

**ex-rights date:** by industry practice, the day after the distribution of the rights. The bid price of the stock is reduced by an amount equal to the value of the right.

**cum-rights:** literally, *with rights;* describes transactions in which the preemptive rights accompany the purchase (or sale) of common stock. Their value is included in the market price of the shares.

**ex-rights:** literally, *without rights;* describes transactions in which the preemptive rights do not accompany the purchase (or sale) of common stock. The rights at this time trade separately in the market.

**subscription price:** usually lower than a stock's current market price, the fixed price at which a company's existing shareholders can purchase new shares during a rights offering.

trading *cum-rights.* After the ex-date and until the end of the subscription period, the stock trades *ex-rights.* From this day forward, any purchaser no longer receives the rights with the stock.

In a rights offering, the company's board of directors does not expect the existing shareholders to subscribe to or buy the new shares at the same price at which the already outstanding shares are trading. Instead, they offer the shares to the stockholders at a *subscription price,* which is lower than the current market price. This is done primarily to make the new shares so attractive to the shareholders that they will buy all of the issue. It is the difference between the outstanding shares' market price and new shares' subscription price that gives the rights their value.

The "theoretical" value of one right when it is trading with the stock or separate from the stock can be determined using two formulas. The first, known as the "cum-rights value," is determined using the following formula:

$$\text{Cum-rights value} = \frac{M - S}{N + 1}$$

$M =$ *current market price of the outstanding shares*
$S =$ *subscription price of the new shares*
$N =$ *number of rights needed to buy one new share*

The following example shows how this formula can be used if you own 1000 shares (or 1 percent) of a company's outstanding 100,000 shares. The company has announced that it will issue 20,000 additional common shares. Each existing shareholder needs five rights (100,000/20,000) in order to be able to purchase each new share. The stock, which is trading at $50 per share, is offered at a subscription price of $35 per share. Using the cum-rights formula, the value of a right in this example is $2.50:

$$\text{Cum-rights value} = \frac{\$50 - \$35}{5 + 1} = \frac{\$15}{6} = \$2.50$$

After the stock goes ex-rights, its price is reduced by an amount equal to the value of one right. This is done because an investor who buys the stock as of this date does not get a right with it and therefore should not pay for it. The stock, whose price was previously $50.00, is reduced to $47.50 ($50.00 − $2.50) afterward. Now the rights are trading separate from the stock, as shown in Figure 8.1. Any investor who wants the rights can purchase them in the market just as he or she would buy the stock. Its ex-rights value is computed using a slightly different formula:

$$\text{Ex-rights value} = \frac{\text{Adjusted M} - \text{S}}{\text{N}}$$

*Adjusted M* = *adjusted market price of the outstanding shares after the stock "goes ex"*
*S* = *subscription price of the new shares*
*N* = *number of rights needed to buy one new share*

Using the same information from the previous example, we find that the ex-rights value is $2.50, the same as the cum-rights value:

$$\text{Ex-rights value} = \frac{\$47.50 - \$35.00}{5} = \frac{\$12.50}{5}$$
$$= \$2.50$$

This theoretical value is important for investors who want to sell their rights instead of exercising them. During the subscription period when the rights are being bought and sold by investors, their

## NEW YORK STOCK EXCHANGE

| 52 Weeks Hi | Lo | Stock | Sym | Div | Yld % | PE | Vol 100s | Hi | Lo | Close | Net Chg |
|---|---|---|---|---|---|---|---|---|---|---|---|
| 31 | 11 1/4 | BankBost pfA | | 3.51e | 12.5 | ... | 3 | 28 1/4 | 28 | 28 | – 3/8 |
| 30 1/8 | 10 3/4 | BankBost pfB | | 3.39e | 12.8 | ... | 5 | 26 1/2 | 26 3/4 | 26 1/2 | – 3/8 |
| 52 | 16 | BankBost pfC | | 6.15 | 12.7 | ... | z860 | 48 3/8 | 48 1/4 | 48 3/8 | – 3/8 |
| 39 1/4 | 13 1/4 | BankNY | BK | 1.52 | 4.8 | 20 | 3711 | 32 1/8 | 31 1/4 | 32 | + 3/8 |
| 37 | 24 1/8 | BankNY adj pfA | | 3.35e | 9.3 | ... | 9 | 36 | 36 | 36 | ... |
| 40 3/8 | 17 1/2 | Bank Amer | BAC | 1.20 | 3.0 | 10 | 5091 | 40 1/4 | 39 3/8 | 39 5/8 | – 5/8 |
| 88 3/4 | 54 3/4 | BauschLomb | BOL | 1.44 | 1.7 | 19 | 613 | 86 1/4 | 85 3/8 | 85 3/4 | + 1/4 |
| 15 3/4 | 7 1/8 | BearSterns | BSC | .60b | 3.8 | 13 | 3291 | 15 3/4 | 15 1/2 | 15 5/8 | ... |
| 56 1/4 | 39 1/2 | BellAtlantic | BEL | 2.52 | 5.6 | 13 | 5929 | 45 5/8 | 44 5/8 | 44 5/8 | – 5/8 |
| 8750 | 5500 | BerkHathwy | BRK | | ... | 25 | z270 | 575 | 8425 | 8500 | – 50 |
| 23 1/4 | 12 1/2 | Berlitz | BTZ | .50 | 2.9 | 31 | 8 | 17 3/8 | 17 3/8 | 17 3/8 | – 1/8 |
| 21 | 10 1/2 | BirmghamStl | BIR | .50 | 3.1 | 29 | 376 | 16 1/8 | 15 3/4 | 15 7/8 | ... |
| 7 5/8 | 5 1/8 | BluChipValFd | BLU | .74e | 10.0 | ... | 150 | 7 3/8 | 7 1/4 | 7 3/8 | ... |
| 68 | 47 3/4 | BritTelcom | BTY | 3.23e | 5.0 | 11 | 243 | 65 1/4 | 64 7/8 | 65 | ... |
| 12 1/2 | 6 1/8 | BrookeGp | BGL | .56b | 6.2 | 6 | 127 | 9 | 8 3/4 | 9 | + 1/8 |
| 2 3/8 | 1/2 | BrookeGp rt | | | ... | ... | 179 | 2 3/8 | 2 1/4 | 2 3/8 | ... |
| 6 5/8 | 3 3/8 | Playboy B | PLA | | ... | 65 | 4 | 6 | 5 7/8 | 5 7/8 | ... |
| 43 1/4 | 19 5/8 | Polaroid | PRD | .60 | 2.4 | 13 | 1305 | 25 3/4 | 25 1/8 | 25 1/4 | – 1/2 |
| 14 3/4 | 8 1/2 | PortugalFd | PGF | .12e | 1.2 | ... | 205 | 9 7/8 | 9 5/8 | 9 5/8 | – 1/4 |
| 37 3/4 | 16 7/8 | Primerica | PA | .40 | 1.3 | 9 | 3502 | 31 5/8 | 30 5/8 | 30 5/8 | – 1 |
| 91 1/4 | 70 1/8 | ProctGamb | PG | 2.00 | 2.4 | 17 | 5079 | 84 | 82 7/8 | 83 | – 3/4 |
| 8 1/2 | 6 1/2 | PropTrAm | PTR | .64 | 8.1 | 23 | 47 | 7 7/8 | 7 3/4 | 7 7/8 | ... |
| 25/64 | 3/32 | PropTrAm rt | | | ... | ... | 418 | 1/8 | 3/32 | 3/32 | – 1/32 |

Figure 8.1. Typical rights listing in a financial newspaper. Rights, highlighted in gray, are represented by the abbreviation "rt" in the listings. Notice that rights trade in fractions like the common shares they represent. Typically the minimum fluctuation is 1/8 ($.125); however, as the second example shows, they can also trade in units as small as 1/32 ($.03125) or less. Rights and the common stock they represent trade in the same market.

market value changes constantly with the value of the outstanding shares. In reality, the rights market value remains close to the theoretical value. The formula, therefore, calculates the approximate price at which an investor can sell his or her rights. If, as in our example, you choose to sell the 1000 rights you own, the total proceeds would be approximately $2500.00 ($2.50 × 1000). A person who holds an odd number of rights can sell those that he or she cannot use to subscribe to the issue. However, usually enough rights are lost so that the company will permit odd-right holders to round up to the next whole share number.

When selling rights, investors are faced with the classic investment timing question: "When do I sell my rights so that I get the highest price?" The prevailing sentiment regarding the best time to sell rights is captured in the phrase, "The early bird captures the worm." The logic behind this belief is that by disposing of the rights early in the subscription period, an existing shareholder gets a higher price because he or she sells before the other investors have decided what they will do. Once everyone begins to sell, usually near the end of the subscription period, the price almost invariably declines. This theory would certainly be true if the stock is in a downtrend or even a sideways trend. In an uptrend, however, the value of a right will increase during the subscription period. Investors get the best price by selling near the end of the period.

In the past, companies like AT&T used traditional rights offerings, like the one discussed, as a means of raising capital. Today, however, rights offerings are rarely issued by U.S. companies. When they are issued, they are usually associated with the recapitalization of a highly leveraged company following a takeover or merger. Some companies issue *long-dated rights*. These "poison pills" are automatically exercised when, during a hostile takeover, a company or an investor acquires a certain percentage of the shares, thereby diluting the takeover. When a traditional rights offering does appear in the financial news, it is most often being made by a British firm or by closed-end management companies.

Beginning investors are probably best advised

**long-dated rights:** a dilutive, antitakeover device in which rights are automatically distributed to existing stockholders during a hostile takeover.

to use rights to subscribe to the new shares. This means depositing additional funds to pay for new shares; however, the profitability that trading rights seems to offer is reduced by the commission costs charged for these transactions. In reality, investors would have to hold a large number of rights in order to make a reasonable profit after commissions have been paid.

## WARRANTS

**warrant:** a long-term security, usually attached to a bond or preferred stock, that gives the holder the right to buy a fixed number of a company's common shares at a price that is higher than the stock's current market price.

A *warrant* is a long-term security that gives its owner the right to buy a specified amount of common stock at a fixed price for a fixed period of time. The fixed price at which the stock can be purchased is at a substantial premium to the market value of the stock at the time the warrant was issued. There is usually a waiting period—typically a year—before the owner can exercise the warrant. Most warrants expire within 10 to 20 years, although some companies have issued perpetual warrants.

Warrants are rarely issued as stand-alone securities to the public. Most often, they are issued attached to a new bond or preferred stock. The combination of the new security and the warrant is often referred to as a unit and is designed to sweeten or increase the marketability of the speculative new issue.

When it is issued, a warrant usually has no intrinsic worth. It becomes valuable only when and if the market price of the common stock moves above the fixed price at which the warrant permits the investor to buy the stock. For example, a company has common shares outstanding that are trading in the market at $20 per share. The company issues a preferred stock with a five-year warrant that gives shareholders the right to purchase additional common shares at $35. If the price of the common stock rises to $50 per share during the

| NEW YORK STOCK EXCHANGE |||||||||||
| --- | --- | --- | --- | --- | --- | --- | --- | --- | --- | --- | --- |
| 52 Weeks || Stock | Sym | Div | Yld % | PE | Vol 100s | Hi | Lo | Close | Net Chg |
| Hi | Lo | | | | | | | | | | |
| 7 3/8 | 3 3/4 | Hanson wt | | | | ... | ... | 250 | 5 3/4 | 5 5/8 | 5 3/4 | + 1/8 |
| 23 1/4 | 17 | Hanson | HAN | 1.54e | 7.9 | 10 | 6378 | 19 5/8 | 19 3/8 | 19 1/2 | ... |
| 3 5/8 | 15/32 | HarBrJ | HBJ | | ... | ... | 773 | 5/8 | 9/16 | 9/16 | − 1/16 |
| 2 3/4 | 11/32 | HarBrJ pf | | | | ... | 3137 | 13/16 | 3/4 | 13/16 | + 1/16 |
| 41 1/8 | 29 3/8 | Heinz | HNZ | .96 | 2.5 | 18 | 2863 | 38 3/8 | 37 5/8 | 37 7/8 | − 1/4 |
| 57 1/4 | 37 | KnghtRidder | KRI | 1.40 | 2.5 | 21 | 597 | 57 1/2 | 56 7/8 | 57 | ... |
| 27 3/8 | 11 3/8 | KoreaFd | KF | 2.20e | 16.6 | ... | 84 | 13 1/2 | 13 1/4 | 13 1/4 | − 1/8 |
| 23 1/8 | 12 3/8 | LaZBoy | LZB | .56 | 2.4 | 18 | 67 | 23 1/8 | 22 7/8 | 23 | ... |
| 26 3/4 | 17 5/8 | MfrsHan pf | MHC | 2.74 | 10.4 | ... | 36 | 26 3/8 | 26 1/4 | 26 3/8 | − 1/8 |
| 2 | 9/16 | Manville wt | | | | ... | ... | 73 | 2 1/8 | 2 1/8 | 2 1/8 | + 1/8 |
| 7 1/2 | 4 | Manville | MVL | | | 9 | 316 | 7 1/2 | 7 1/4 | 7 3/8 | ... |
| 38 1/2 | 25 | McDonalds | MCD | .37 | 1.1 | 16 | 7575 | 35 1/8 | 34 3/8 | 34 5/8 | − 3/8 |
| 33 5/8 | 17 5/8 | Mellon BK | MEL | 1.40 | 4.6 | 11 | 786 | 31 3/8 | 30 | 30 3/8 | − 1 |
| 28 5/8 | 25 | Mellon Bk pf | | 2.80 | 10.1 | ... | 54 | 27 7/8 | 27 1/2 | 27 5/8 | − 1/4 |
| 19 5/8 | 15 1/2 | Mellon Bk pf | | 1.69 | 8.8 | ... | 4 | 19 1/8 | 19 1/8 | 19 1/8 | − 1/8 |
| 122 7/8 | 72 3/8 | Merck | MRK | 2.24 | 1.9 | 24 | 5347 | 117 | 115 5/8 | 116 1/4 | − 3/8 |
| 95 5/8 | 73 5/8 | MinnMngMfg | MMM | 3.12 | 3.3 | 16 | 3606 | 96 1/4 | 93 3/4 | 93 7/8 | −1 1/8 |
| 91 3/4 | 47 1/8 | MorganStan | MS | 1.50 | 1.7 | 11 | 503 | 89 1/8 | 88 1/2 | 88 1/2 | − 1/2 |
| 25 1/8 | 24 1/2 | MorganStan pf | | | ... | ... | 611 | 24 3/4 | 24 5/8 | 24 5/8 | ... |
| 44 1/4 | 16 7/8 | NCNB | NCB | 1.48 | 3.5 | 13 | 2258 | 42 1/4 | 41 1/2 | 41 3/4 | − 3/4 |
| 9 | 3 | NtlSemi | NSM | | ... | ... | 1845 | 7 3/8 | 6 7/8 | 6 7/8 | − 1/2 |
| 5/8 | 1/16 | NtlSemi wt | | | | ... | ... | 66 | 1/8 | 7/64 | 1/8 | ... |
| 40 1/2 | 20 | NtlSemi pf | | 4.00 | 10.1 | ... | 31 | 39 1/2 | 39 | 39 1/2 | ... |

Figure 8.2. Typical warrants listing in a financial newspaper. Warrants for several stocks are highlighted in gray. The symbol "wt" denotes warrants in financial newspapers. The minimum fluctuation is usually 1/8 ($.125), the same as the underlying stock. However, like rights, they can fluctuate in units as small as 1/64 ($.0156). Warrants and the common shares that underlie them trade in the same market.

five-year period, the warrant has an intrinsic value of $15 per share ($50 − $35). In cases where the warrant can be detached from the security, you can sell the warrant in the market and take the profit. In this case the warrant trades separately in the market as shown in Figure 8.2. You retain the security to which the warrant was originally attached.

You can also exercise your warrant, buying the

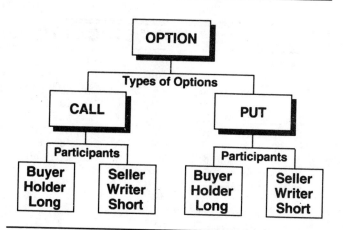

**Figure 8.3.   Types of options and participants in each transaction.**

**strike price:** the fixed price at which stock can be bought or sold when a call or put is exercised. Also known as the "exercise price."

**call option:** a security that gives its holder the right to buy 100 shares of a stock at a fixed price for a fixed period of time.

**put option:** a security that gives its holder the right to sell 100 shares of a stock at a fixed price for a fixed period of time.

shares at the specified price and depositing the required cash in your brokerage account. Sometimes in order to exercise the warrant, you must surrender the bond or the preferred stock. In this case, no additional money is required from you unless you must buy full shares to compensate for any fractional shares that result when the warrant is exercised. In effect, such "nondetachable" warrants are the equivalent of convertibles.

## OPTIONS

An option is a contract representing the right or obligation to buy or sell 100 shares of a stock at a specified price (called the *strike price*) at any time during a specified period. There are two types of options contracts: a *call option* and a *put option* (Figure 8.3). A transaction involving either type always involves two parties. The person who purchases the option contract is referred to as the "buyer," the "holder," or someone who is "long" the option. The person who sells the contract is referred to as the "seller," the "writer," or someone who is "short" the option.

## LISTED OPTIONS QUOTATIONS

| Option / Strike | | Exp. | – Call – Vol. | Last | – Put – Vol. | Last |
|---|---|---|---|---|---|---|
| **Baxter** | 22 1/2 | May | 30 | 12 1/8 | ... | ... |
| 34 7/8 | 25 | May | 20 | 9 1/2 | 4 | 1/16 |
| 34 7/8 | 25 | Aug | 22 | 9 3/4 | ... | ... |
| 34 7/8 | 30 | May | 40 | 4 1/2 | ... | ... |
| 34 7/8 | 30 | Jun | 15 | 5 | ... | ... |
| 34 7/8 | 30 | Aug | 8 | 5 | 2 | 1/2 |
| 34 7/8 | 35 | May | 4 | 1/2 | 5 | 5/8 |
| 34 7/8 | 35 | Jun | 12 | 1 1/4 | 16 | 1 7/8 |
| 34 7/8 | 35 | Aug | 26 | 2 1/2 | 24 | 2 3/8 |
| 34 7/8 | 40 | Aug | 7 | 5/8 | ... | ... |
| **Boeing** | 35 | Aug | ... | ... | 24 | 1 5/8 |
| 47 1/8 | 40 | May | 60 | 7 3/8 | ... | ... |
| 47 1/8 | 40 | Aug | 106 | 8 | 19 | 7/16 |
| 47 1/8 | 45 | May | 64 | 2 3/8 | 17 | 3/16 |
| 47 1/8 | 45 | Jun | 120 | 3 1/4 | 26 | 3/4 |
| 47 1/8 | 45 | Aug | 90 | 4 1/4 | 30 | 1 3/4 |
| 47 1/8 | 50 | May | 181 | 1/8 | 86 | 3 1/8 |
| 47 1/8 | 50 | Jun | 21 | 13/16 | ... | ... |
| 47 1/8 | 50 | Aug | 21 | 13/16 | 197 | 4 1/8 |
| 47 1/8 | 55 | May | 76 | 1/16 | 207 | 8 1/8 |
| 47 1/8 | 55 | Aug | 479 | 8 1/8 | ... | ... |
| **CBS** | 150 | Aug | ... | ... | 238 | 4 7/8 |
| 159 7/8 | 160 | May | 196 | 1 15/16 | 267 | 2 |
| 159 7/8 | 165 | May | 47 | 9/16 | 200 | 5 3/8 |
| 159 7/8 | 165 | Jun | 50 | 4 1/4 | ... | ... |
| 159 7/8 | 165 | Aug | 40 | 8 5/8 | ... | ... |
| 159 7/8 | 170 | Jun | 50 | 2 7/8 | ... | ... |
| 159 7/8 | 190 | Aug | 20 | 2 | ... | ... |
| **Coke** | 40 | May | 47 | 14 7/8 | ... | ... |
| 54 5/8 | 45 | May | 67 | 9 1/2 | ... | ... |
| 54 5/8 | 45 | Aug | ... | ... | 14 | 3/8 |
| 54 5/8 | 50 | May | 122 | 5 1/8 | 16 | 1/16 |
| 54 5/8 | 50 | Aug | 356 | 10 3/8 | ... | ... |
| 54 5/8 | 55 | May | 166 | 3/4 | 42 | 1 1/8 |
| 54 5/8 | 55 | Jun | 338 | 2 1/4 | 21 | 2 1/8 |
| 54 5/8 | 55 | Aug | 351 | 2 3/4 | 76 | 2 3/8 |
| 54 5/8 | 60 | May | ... | ... | 26 | 6 1/8 |

**CALL** ◀
1 Boeing Jun 45 Call @ 3 1/4

**PUT** ◀
1 CBS May 165 Put @ 5 3/8

**Figure 8.4. Typical options listing in a financial newspaper.**

The other terms of an options contract can be found by examining a typical newspaper listing such as the one illustrated in Figure 8.4. Using Boeing options as an example, we see that beneath the stock's name, the price 47⅛ is repeated. This is the price at which Boeing's common shares closed on the New York Stock Exchange (or another exchange) on the previous day. The next column shows the different strike prices of the option contracts. The strike price is the fixed price at which the option can be exercised. In this case, they occur in $5.00 intervals— $35.00, $40.00, $45.00, $50.00, and so on. This interval may be smaller ($2.50) or larger ($10.00) depending on the market price of the underlying security. The next column, labeled "Exp.," shows the expiration month of the option contract. The columns with the headings "–Call–" and "–Put–" show, respectively, the trading volume and the closing market price (called the *premium*) of the option contract whose strike price and expiration are presented at the beginning of the line. The premium prices are always stated per share. An investor wishing to buy the June call with the 45 strike price would pay $3¼ per share, or a total of $325. (Remember that each option represents 100 shares of the underlying stock.) Conversely, the investor who sells the same call would receive $325.

**premium:** the market price of a call or a put option.

Throughout this discussion on options, we will use the terms "holder" and "writer" to describe the two parties involved in each type of option contract in order to reduce potential confusion. We assume you are the holder most of the time although you can be either party in reality.

## Call Option

You as the holder of a call have the right, but not the obligation, to buy 100 shares of the underlying stock at the option's strike price at any time until the option's expiration date. You pay the total amount of the option's premium for this right. The writer of a call is obligated, on demand, to sell 100 shares of the underlying stock to you at the strike price if and when you exercise the option. For assuming this obligation, the writer receives the premium that you paid. Importantly, the premium is

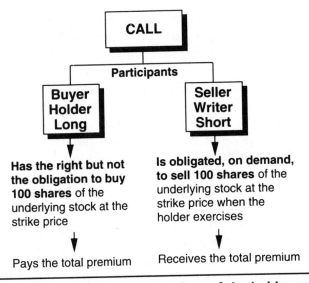

**Figure 8.5.   Rights and obligations of the holder and writer of a call.**

a one-time, nonrefundable payment by the holder of the option to the writer. The premium is not part of the exercise price. (Figure 8.5 shows the rights and obligations of the holder and writer of a call.)

Using the Boeing call cited in Figure 8.4, 1 Boeing June 45 Call @ 3¼, we will discuss both parties' potential risks and potential rewards. When you as the holder buy this call, you pay the total premium, $325.00 ($3.25 × 100 shares), for the right to buy 100 shares of Boeing at $45.00 per share any time up through the option's expiration date. You want the price of the underlying stock to rise above a total cost per share equal to the strike price plus the premium you paid for the option. At any point above this amount, you make a profit. You can then exercise the call, buying the stock at the call's strike price, when the market price is higher.

If the market price of Boeing common stock rises to $65 per share, you can exercise the option, buying 100 shares at $45. This action produces an immediate gain of $20 per share ($2000 total) on the stock transaction. However, you paid a $325 premium for the call; therefore, your net profit on the entire trade is $1675. (Commission costs are not included in these examples because the percentage charged varies among brokerage houses.)

If the price of Boeing common falls below the call's strike price ($45), then you would not exercise the option because it would be unprofitable to do so. You would let the option expire, losing $325, the total premium paid for the contract.

The writer of an option receives the premium that you as holder paid. The writer cannot exercise the call. (For the purposes of exercising, think of the relationship of the holder and the writer in psychological terms. The writer is in a "passive" position, while the holder is in an "active" position.) The writer of a call wants the market price of Boeing stock to stay flat or decline. You as the holder would not exercise the option, and the writer would keep the premium—$325 in our example.

If the price rises to $65 per share and you as holder exercise, the writer is obligated, under the terms of the options contract, to deliver or sell 100 shares of Boeing at $45 per share. If the writer does not already own the stock, then he would have to buy it at its current market value of $65, incurring a loss of $20 per share ($2000 total). Remember, however, that the writer received the premium when he or she wrote the option. The loss would therefore be partially reduced by the amount of the premium received, leaving the writer with a net loss of $1675. (Figure 8.6 summarizes these expectations, rewards, and risks of holder and writer of a call option.)

Most of these investors are not interested in owning the stock that underlies the option. They simply want to profit from the rise and fall of the stock's value. Given this objective, most holders

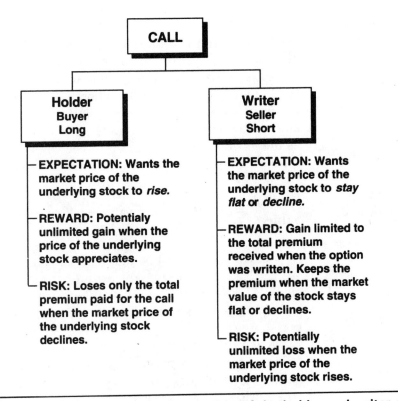

**Figure 8.6.** Summary of rewards and risks of the holder and writer on a call option.

are not interested in exercising the option. Nor are writers interested in being exercised. Neither party wants to incur the additional transaction fees and margin calls that must be paid when an option is exercised. Instead, each wants to trade the contracts: buy and sell them based on changes in the premium. A holder of a call wants to buy the option at a low premium and later sell it at a higher premium. The writer of a call wants to sell the option at a high premium and then buy it back at a lower premium. This is possible because the value of the premium on a call changes in direct relationship to several factors, including the market price of the underlying security and the time remaining to expiration.

**in the money:** the relationship between the market price of the underlying security and the strike price of the option is such that exercising would yield a profit to the holder.

**intrinsic value:** part of the value of an option's premium reflecting the amount by which an option is in the money.

**at the money:** the market price of the underlying security and the option's strike price are the same.

**out of the money:** the relationship between the market price of the underlying security and the option's strike price is such that the holder (buyer) would not exercise the option because it would result in a loss.

**time value:** the amount of an

A call is profitable to a holder only when the market price of the underlying security is above the option's strike price. As the stock's market price increases, it becomes more and more profitable for the holder to exercise a call. When this occurs, the option is described as being *in the money*. The amount by which the call is in the money is known as the *intrinsic value*. A call's intrinsic value is computed using the following formula:

$$\text{Intrinsic value} = \text{Stock's market value} - \text{call's strike price}$$

Returning to our Boeing example (Figure 8.4) we can see that the market price of the common stock, 47⅛, is above the call's strike price, 45. This call is in the money and has intrinsic value of 2⅛ per share or $2.125.

When the market price of the stock equals the strike price of the option, a call is said to be *at the money*. When a stock's market price is below a call's strike price, the option is described as being *out of the money*. Both at the money and out of the money options have no intrinsic value. (The concept of negative intrinsic value does not exist.)

*Time value* is the price that investors pay for the likelihood that the option will move in the direction they want before the expiration date. Time value can be computed using the following formula:

$$\text{Time value} = \text{call's premium} - \text{call's intrinsic value}$$

The premium on the June 45 call is 3¼, and the intrinsic value, which we just computed, is 2⅛. The time value is 1⅛, or $1.125 per share. The more time an option has until its expiration, the greater the time value. As an option approaches its expiration date, this value decreases. On the expiration date, no time value remains. Thus, options are said to be "wasting assets." If an option has any value on this date, it will be solely intrinsic value. The typical life of a listed option is about eight months, although there are long-term options with one-year and two-year expirations. These long-term options are called LEAPs—the acronym for Long-term Equity Appreciation Products. These are available only on the most actively traded stock options.

As the price of the security underlying a call increases in value—i.e., moves more and more in the money—the increasing intrinsic value is directly reflected in the premium almost dollar for dollar. Rather than exercising the call as we showed earlier, you as the holder can sell or offset it on an exchange at close to its intrinsic value. Your net profit will closely equal what you would have obtained by exercising the option, and the total transaction costs will be substantially less. If the stock's price moves below the strike price, you simply let the option expire, losing only the total premium paid.

The writer of a call profits only when the option remains at the money or moves more and more out of the money. The option will not be exercised, and the writer keeps the premium. When the option moves in the money, the writer begins to lose. This investor cannot exercise the option but can buy it back at a higher premium, incurring perhaps a smaller loss than he would if he were forced to wait until you as holder exercised.

### Strategies for Buying Calls

There are two basic strategies that beginning investors in stocks can use for buying call options. We will use an example to illustrate how each of these strategies works.

*option's premium that exceeds its intrinsic value, representing the price investors place on the time an option has until its expiration. If an option is out of the money, all of the premium represents time value.*

**1. Buying calls to profit when a stock's price is rising.** Our example using Boeing illustrates this strategy. Rather than buying 100 shares of the stock and paying $4712.50 if they were paid in full or $2356.25 if they were bought on margin, you buy one Boeing call for substantially less—$325.00 for the total premium. If the market price of Boeing shares appreciates, so will the market value of the Boeing call. In theory, when the stock advances from $47⅛ per share to $65, the option would move in the money by an additional $17⅞ per share and this would be reflected in the premium. In reality, the premium would probably increase by a bit more if the upward price momentum of the underlying stock were strong. You as holder would be able to sell the call at a higher premium than you paid for it, earning a profit. If, however, the market price of the stock declines, your total loss is limited to the price paid for the option contract.

**2. Buying calls to protect profits on a short stock position.** You sold short 100 shares of IBM when the price of the stock was $76 per share. The price has declined to $55 per share, and you are worried that the price may turn around and wipe out the $21 per share gain. To protect the profit, you buy one IBM call option with a $55 strike price. If the price of IBM shares rise, your profits are protected. Every dollar lost on the short stock position is offset by every dollar gained on the long call. Also, you can exercise the call, buying 100 shares at $55 each, and then use the shares to cover the short sale. On the other hand, if the market continues downward, you continue to make money on the short position. The call moves out of the money, and you lose only the premium paid for the call. In technical terms, this is one of many hedging strategies. An investor uses the call as "insurance" to protect the profits on an existing stock position without liquidating the position.

### Strategies for Writing Calls

Strategies involving writing options are commonly called *income strategies* because the writer of a call receives the premium. This terminology does not consider the fact that when writing an option, an investor may have to deposit margin approximately equal to 20 percent of the market value of the underlying security. The writer of an *uncovered option*—a call or a put—must deposit the required margin. The writer of a *covered option* deposits no margin. Instead, he or she owns enough of an offsetting position that eliminates the risk that a naked writer faces. The covering position can include:

1. Owning the underlying common shares
2. Owning a preferred stock or bond that can be converted into the underlying common shares
3. Owning enough warrants that can be used to acquire the underlying common shares.

These are sophisticated strategies and should be attempted only after you have a solid understanding of the risks associated with them.

The two basic income strategies involve writing uncovered calls and writing covered calls. As before, examples will be used to illustrate both scenarios.

**1. Writing uncovered calls to profit in a flat or declining market.** This is one of the most speculative option strategies because the investor is exposed to unlimited risk. You must deposit margin with the broker in order to establish this position. Recall that in our initial example, an investor wrote 1 Boeing June 45 Call, receiving a premium of $325. As long as the price of the stock remains at or below the option's strike price, you, as the holder, will not exercise the option, and the writer will keep

**income strategies:** in options, any strategy in which the investor receives more options premium than he or she pays.

**uncovered option:** term used to describe a call or put writer who is unprotected against the maximum possible loss on a short option position.

**covered option:** term used to describe the writer of a put or a call who holds another security position that protects against or offsets the risks of a short option position.

the premium. If the price rises, the writer will be exercised, forced to deliver or sell 100 shares to you (the holder) at $45 per share, the call's strike price. Since the writer does not own 100 shares of Boeing common, he is forced to go into the market and buy it at whatever the prevailing market price is at the time, which could be $65 per share, $85 per share, or $105 per share. Since a stock's price can rise potentially an unlimited amount, the writer of an uncovered or naked call is subject to unlimited risk. The writer's gain is limited to the premium received for selling the option.

**2. Writing covered calls to increase returns from stock during a flat market.** There is much less risk for an investor who writes covered calls. This strategy is used to increase income and to protect a stock position. Covered call writing is a popular strategy among investors who hold portfolios of blue chip stocks, whose prices are reasonably stable. It is used to increase total returns from the portfolio. In addition, the customer does not have to deposit any margin on the option positions because there is little or no risk.

The following example demonstrates how this strategy works. (In this case, you, the reader are the writer of the call *not* the holder.) Say you own 500 shares of Commonwealth Edison stock that you originally purchased at $25 per share and is currently trading at $40 per share. The stock's price is relatively stable, offering you little opportunity for capital gains. Although you are reasonably satisfied with the dividends the company pays, you want to increase your return from the shares you own. You write 5 CWE June 40 calls @ 3, receiving a total premium of $1500. As long as the price of Commonwealth Edison remains relatively flat (i.e., the stock does not rise above $40 per share) you will not be exercised and will get to keep the total premiums.

If the price rises above $40, the option will be exercised (by the holder) and the stock called away from you. But you still profit. Because the price at which you are obligated to sell the shares—the call's $40 strike price—is higher than the price you originally paid for Commonwealth Edison ($25), you make $15 per share on the share transaction. Additionally, you keep the $3 per share earned for the writing call. The total profit is $9000 ($18 × 500 shares). If you wanted to keep the stock, you could go back into the marketplace and repurchase it.

If the price drops below $37 per share, then you lose because the total loss on the value of the 500 shares of Commonwealth Edison exceeds the premiums received for writing the call. There would still be a gain on the 500 common shares that you own; however, you would not have achieved your goal of generating additional income by writing covered options.

## Put Option

The holder of a put has the right, but not the obligation, to sell 100 shares of common stock at the option's strike price at any time through the option's expiration date. The holder pays the premium for this right. The writer of a put is obligated, on demand, to buy 100 shares of the underlying stock at the strike price if and when the holder exercises the option. (Remember that only the holder can exercise the put.) For taking on this obligation, the writer receives the total premium paid by the holder. (Figure 8.7 summarizes the rights and obligations of both parties.)

Using the CBS put highlighted in Figure 8.4, 1 CBS May 165 Put at 5⅜, let us examine the rewards and risks of the holder and the writer. You

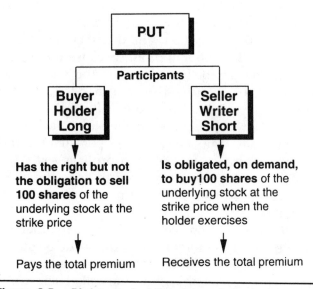

**Figure 8.7.  Rights and obligations of the holder and writer of a put.**

as holder of this CBS put pay a total premium of $537.50 ($5⅜ × 100 shares) when you purchase the option. You want the market price of CBS common shares to decline. If this occurs, you can exercise the put, selling short 100 shares of CBS at the strike price, knowing that you can cover the position by purchasing the stock at the lower market price. Before you can make any profit, the price of the stock must fall below the strike price by an amount that exceeds the premium paid for the option.

If, for example, the price of CBS common stock falls to $140 per share, you as holder of the put can exercise the option, selling short the stock at $165 per share. You can then cover this short sale by purchasing the stock in the market at $140 per share. The result is a gain of $25 per share or $2500 total on the stock transaction. However, you had already paid $537.50 for the option, so your net profit on the transaction is $1962.50. The firm's commission would be deducted from this gain. The further a stock's price declines, the more it profits the holder of a put.

If the price of the stock rises after you have purchased the put, then it would be unprofitable for you to exercise it. If you did, you would sell 100 shares at a price lower than you could buy it in the market—not a prudent action. You would probably hold the put until it expires, losing the total premium paid—$537.50 in the CBS example. This is the maximum risk for you, the holder of this put.

The writer of a put profits only when the price of underlying stock stays flat or rises. When this occurs, it is not profitable for the holder to exercise the put. Hence, the writer does not have to fulfill the contractual obligation to buy 100 shares of CBS from the put holder at the strike price. The option expires, and the writer keeps the premium that was paid to him or her. In the CBS example, the writer of a put would make $537.50 if the price of the common shares stays at or above $165.

The writer loses when the price of the underlying shares declines. As we have shown, when the price of CBS declines below the strike price, you as holder of the CBS put will force the writer to buy the stock at the option's strike price—$165 per share. Since the market price of CBS stock is only $140 per share when the option is exercised, the writer has an immediate loss of $25 per share, for a total of $2500. This loss is then partially reduced by the total premium that the writer received ($532.50) when the put was sold. The writer's net loss is therefore $1967.50. The brokerage house's commissions are added to this loss. (Figure 8.8 summarizes the expectations, rewards, and risks for the holder and writer.)

As with calls, the holder and writer of a put are not interested in exercising the options or being exercised. They too prefer to trade the option based on the rise and fall of its premium. Like a call, a

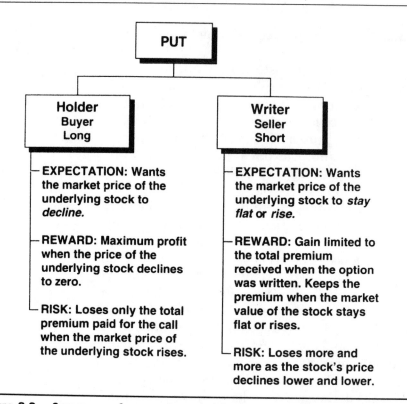

**Figure 8.8. Summary of rewards and risks for the holder and writer of a put option.**

put's premium is influenced by the option's intrinsic value and its time value. The intrinsic value is the amount by which an option is in the money. A put is in the money when it is profitable for the holder to exercise the option. This occurs when the market price of the underlying stock is below the option's strike price. The formula for computing the intrinsic value of a put is:

$$\text{Intrinsic value} = \text{Put's strike price} - \text{stock's market price}$$

Using the CBS put in Figure 8.4, we see that the market price of the stock is 159%, and the put's strike price is $165. This put is clearly in the money with an intrinsic value of 5⅛. As the price of the underlying stock decreases, the put's intrinsic value will increase by almost the same amount. The put's premium will also increase. Instead of exercising the put, you as holder can simply trade it—sell the put—and reap close to the same amount of profit. By trading the put instead of exercising it, you also save on transaction costs and do not have to meet the initial margin call on the short stock position. If the market price of the common stock moves above the option's strike price, the put is described as being out of the money. The option would have no intrinsic value and it would not be profitable for you to exercise. You would let the put expire, losing only the total premium paid.

The holder loses as the option moves out of the money or stays at the money; the writer profits in both situations. The holder will most likely let the put expire, and the writer will keep the premium. As the put moves in the money, the writer, knowing that there is increasing likelihood that the option will be exercised, can buy it back at a higher premium prior to being exercised. Not only would her obligation to the holder be removed, but the writer may, depending on the price at which the position was closed out, retain part of the premium she originally received or sustain a smaller loss than she would have if she had to wait for the holder to exercise.

### Strategies for Buying Puts

Investors can buy puts to profit from the underlying stock's price decline or to protect the profits on an existing long stock position. Two basic strategies are described below.

**1. Buying a put to profit when a stock's price is falling.** Instead of selling short a stock to profit from a price decline, you can buy a put. As the example using CBS showed, the holder of a put makes money when the price of the underlying stock falls. More important, the investor's risk is substantially reduced. When you sell short a stock and the price of the stock increases, you are potentially subject to an unlimited loss and a maintenance margin call. If you do not liquidate the position, you will have to deposit more and more money in the account as the stock's price appreciates. If you buy a put, the only risk you face is the loss of the premium paid. An adverse price move would not result in a margin call.

**2. Buying a put to protect profits on a long stock position.** Known as hedging, this strategy permits investors to lock in profits that have been made on an investment and still maintain the stock position. For example, you purchased 200 shares of CBS stock when the price was $125 per share. At a current price of $160 per share, you have a $35 per share gain. You believe that the price of CBS shares is about to fall. You want to protect the $7000 profit ($35 × 200 shares) but do not want to sell off the stock. You buy 2 CBS puts with a $160 strike price. You have locked in the profit. The price of this "insurance" is the premium you pay for the put. If the price of CBS common stock falls, as you believe it will, then every dollar lost on the long stock position is offset by every dollar made on the put. If the price of CBS increases, you continue to make money on the 200 shares of CBS common stock and lose the premium on the put. Perhaps of equal importance, you have been able to maintain holdings in CBS common stock, benefiting from any dividends that may be paid during this time.

### Strategies for Writing Puts

Like the writing strategies for calls, these are also called income strategies because the investor receives the premium. They are equally complex and should be attempted only after you have a clear understanding of the risks involved.

**1. Writing uncovered puts to profit in a rising market.** In our initial example, involving an investor who wrote 1 CBS June 165 Call @ 5⅞, the person profited when the price of CBS common shares rose above the option's strike price or stayed close to it. The writer kept the premiums. There is, however, substantial risk for the writer when the price of the stock declines. Once she is forced to buy CBS when you as holder exercise, she may be able to sell the stock in the market only at a price less than what she has paid for it.

**2. Writing uncovered put as a means of buying a stock at a lower price.** This is a conservative strategy. Normally when you want to buy a stock at a price that is lower than its current market price, you would use a buy limit order. (This was discussed in Chapter 3.) The same objective can be accomplished by writing a put whose strike price is at or near the price you wish to buy the stock. Imagine that CBS is trading at $160 per share. You believe the price will decline and want to buy 300 shares of the stock only when the price is at $150 or lower. You write 3 CBS Jun 150 puts and receive the premium. If the price declines below $150, the holder of the put will exercise it, forcing you as writer to buy 300 shares of CBS at $150 per share. The cost of buying the stock is further reduced by the premiums that you received when the option was sold. If the price of the stock rises, you keep the premium. This is a decided advantage over simply using a limit order. With this order if the price of the stock rises, the order could not be executed and you would not receive the premium as compensation. You are still subject to the risk that the price of the stock will continue to fall after you have been forced to purchase it when the put was exercised.

**3. Writing covered puts.** An investor who writes a put is covered only by simultaneously holding another put whose strike price is the same or higher and whose expiration date is the same or longer than the one written. This strategy is done primarily so that the investor will have to deposit no margin. Because stocks or other equities are not directly involved in this strategy, it is not appropriate to the scope of this book and will not be discussed here. Investors interested in covered put writing strategies should consult another book in this series, *Getting Started in Options*, or one of the many advanced books on options available in bookstores.

## THE EFFECT OF STOCK SPLITS AND STOCK DIVIDENDS

Many beginning investors do not consider the effect that a stock split or a stock dividend can have on equity-equivalent securities. Without the proper protections, each event could adversely affect the value of the investment.

If the common shares that you own entitle you to the preemptive right, then each new share will have one right when the company splits its stock or pays a stock dividend. You can still choose to maintain a proportionate ownership in the company when it issues new shares.

If the common stock that the owner of a warrant may acquire is split or if the company pays a stock dividend, the exercise price of the warrant is reduced in proportion to the split or the dividend. This adjustment protects the warrant holder against dilution. It gives him or her the ability to acquire enough additional shares to compensate for the change.

With options, the adjustment depends on whether the split or dividend results in a round lot or an odd lot. Splits or dividends resulting in a round lot cause an increase in the number of option contracts and a proportional reduction in the strike price. If you own 1 Boeing Jun 60 Call and the underlying stock splits two for one, you will own 2 Boeing June 30 Calls afterward.

If a split or dividend results in an odd-lot number of shares, then the number of options contracts remains the same, but the number of shares underlying it increases. The strike price is decreased proportionately to the percentage of the change. For example, Boeing declares a 20 percent stock dividend, and you own 1 Boeing June 60 Call. After the dividend, the number of shares underlying the one option would be 120 instead of 100. The option's strike price would decrease. Recall that the total value of the shares underlying the original option is $6000 (strike price × 100 shares). After the split, the total value of the shares remains the same ($6000); however, there are now more shares underlying the option. By dividing the total value by the new number of shares, you get the adjusted strike price: $6000/120 = $50. After the dividend, you will own 1 CBS June 50 Call. In all cases, the fixed prices at which these equity-related securities can be exercised are unaffected by the payment of cash dividends.

CHAPTER **9**

# International Investing in Stocks

The Pacific Rim, Spain, Portugal, Eastern Europe, and now the newly formed commonwealth of republics that was once the Soviet Union have been cited as markets having great potential for economic growth and investment profit. Most investors who read the analyses and predictions in various financial and investment publications media assume that investing abroad is beyond their financial means and, perhaps more important, far beyond their risk tolerance. Another widely held belief is that this type of investing is only for experts or big players. Both of these ideas are incorrect and serve only to limit the gains that investors—small or large—can make as the securities marketplace becomes increasingly international.

Today, you cannot ignore the gains in market share, product development, and profits that some international companies have made during the past several years—many of them greater than gains posted by the largest and most successful U.S. companies. A handful of these companies' names are familiar to many U.S. households: Honda, Sony, Nissan, Samsung, British Petroleum, British Airways, Nestlé, Royal Dutch, and Bayer for example. Also, in the 1970s the United States was the largest issuer of stock in the world. During the 1980s, the balance shifted. Now more than 60 percent of the total dollar value of all stock in the world is issued by non-U.S. companies.

How do you go about investing in these foreign companies and markets? What are the risks associated with these investments? What percentage of your investment portfolio should be in foreign stock? This chapter answers these questions and serves as a primer for beginning investors who are interested in this increasingly important part of the equities market.

One important distinction must be clarified at the outset: the difference between international investing and global investing. "International investing" denotes the buying and selling of the securities of foreign companies—those located outside the United States. "Global investing" refers to trading the securities of any company with a broad international presence (in other words, a multinational corporation), whether its primary office or headquarters is located outside or within the United States. Thus, an "international" portfolio might consist of Telemex, British Airways, Toyota, and Sony stock. A "global" portfolio could consist of the same companies but might also include Coca-Cola, GM, IBM, and Gillette—U.S. multinational companies that earn a substantial part of their revenues in foreign markets.

## INVESTING IN COMPANIES OVERSEAS

There are four ways to invest in companies located abroad. Figure 9.1 lists these investment vehicles in order of the easiest to the most complicated.

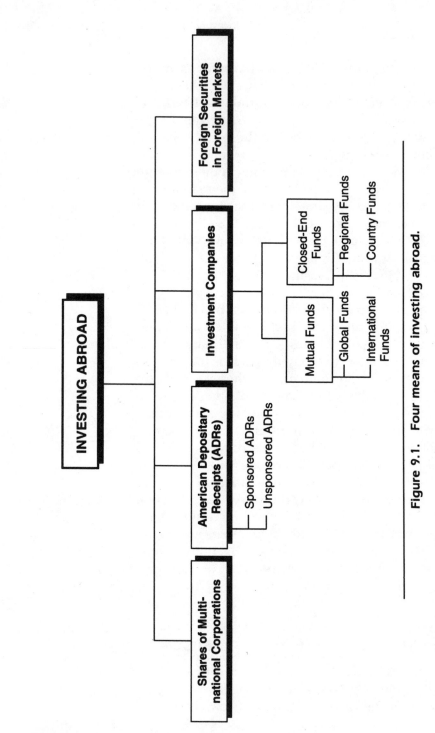

Figure 9.1. Four means of investing abroad.

## U.S. Multinational Corporation

Many large U.S. companies actually sell more of their products in foreign markets than they do in the United States. Coca-Cola is one of the best examples of this. (See the second page of Figure 5.1.) Perusing several of the company's annual reports, one discovers that a substantial portion—more than 50 percent—of its sales and profits comes from its operations in Europe, Asia, and Latin America. Gillette is another company with a huge international presence and sales. If you are traveling overseas, you can find Gillette razor blades in any pharmacy or department store in the world, except in the most remote or closed countries. As new markets open in other countries, Gillette will not only promote its basic shaving products but will doubtlessly make strong marketing efforts for its other lines, such as the Oral-B dental products.

These large multinational companies are often the first to establish trade and sales agreements in the emerging markets of newly accessible countries. As each country's economy improves, it becomes increasingly receptive to sales of the multinational companies' products. For beginning investors, this is perhaps the least risky way to invest abroad. Of course, investing in multinational, publicly held corporations is not what most people have strictly in mind when they think about investing overseas. This approach is decidedly indirect. Usually the companies that have substantial visibility and sales in foreign markets are among the largest and most successful in the United States—3M, IBM, GM, Coca-Cola, McDonald's, Exxon (known as Esso abroad), and Procter & Gamble, to name just a few. For the average investor, many of these companies' names are synonymous with blue chip investments. Hence, the risks associated with buying their common stock are substantially lower than the risks associated with buying the stock of a company located in a foreign country.

Although the connection between buying the shares of multinational U.S corporations and investing abroad is more tenuous than the other methods discussed here, this strategy offers beginning investors an opportunity to learn about the international markets as they read through the quarterly or annual reports of these companies. In short, purchasing stock in U.S.-based multinationals exposes investors to the international investment marketplace in a very limited and protected way.

**American Depositary Receipts (or Shares):** negotiable securities representing ownership of the common or preferred stock of a foreign company that are being held in trust. Commonly known as ADRs or ADSs.

## American Depositary Receipts or Shares

*American depositary receipts* (ADRs) or *shares* (ADSs) is the easiest way for U.S. residents to invest directly in the stock of foreign companies. An ADR or ADS is a negotiable receipt representing the common stock in a foreign corporation. An ADR is not a common stock. Rather, it is backed by those common shares of a foreign company held for this purpose in trust by a bank in the corporation's home country. In essence, each ADR is a certificate representing a percentage ownership of the securities being held in trust. The ADR is priced in U.S. dollars and trades like U.S. stock.

Importantly, one ADR does not always represent one share of the common stock held in trust. Each ADR can be backed by any number of the corporation's common shares. These terms are negotiated at the time that the trust is established and the ADRs issued.

ADRs are divided into two groups: sponsored and unsponsored. An ADR is said to be sponsored if the foreign company is directly involved in its issuance in the U.S. markets. In this case, the issuer chooses a bank to serve as the depository for its shares. The foreign company is responsible for registering the ADRs with the Securities and Exchange Commission and with the securities agencies in the states in which the ADRs will be offered and sold to U.S. residents. It also selects the U.S. brokerage firms that will be involved in the distribution of the shares. Like shareholders of publicly held U.S. corporations, holders of sponsored ADRs have all of the usual rights of common shareholders, including the rights to receive dividends and to vote (including by proxy). The bank is responsible for converting the company's dividend payments into U.S. dollars and distributing them to shareholders. Additionally, the foreign corporation must provide U.S. shareholders with quarterly and annual reports in English. Sponsored ADRs trade on the exchanges (e.g., Sony, Honda, British Airways, Telefonos de Mexico, Daimler Benz, Glaxo) or in the over-the-counter market (DeBeers, Fuji, Toyota). (Increasingly the term "American depositary share" is being used to denote a sponsored ADR.)

If the foreign company is not directly involved in the issuing of its ADRs, then the issuance is described as unsponsored. In this case, a bank, acting for itself, is the depository and issuer. After first determining that there is sufficient interest in the foreign company's stock in the United States to warrant the issuance of ADRs, a bank purchases a predetermined number of the foreign company's common shares and places them in trust. The bank handles all of the U.S. registration requirements, including paying all of the associated expenses, and then offers and sells the ADRs to the public through U.S. brokerage firms. Because the foreign company is not involved in the issuance of the ADRs, the bank is considered to be the owner of record of the common shares. The holders of the unsponsored ADRs have only the right to receive dividends, which are converted into dollars and distributed by the bank. These shareholders have no voting or proxy rights. As the owner of the shares, the bank has the right to vote. If there is a rights offering, the bank sells the rights and distributes the proceeds to the ADR owners. Additionally, the bank is not required to provide shareholders with quarterly and annual reports in English. Instead, they receive only an annual report in the language of the issuer's home country. Unsponsored ADRs do not trade on stock exchanges. They trade solely in the over-the-counter market.

When ADRs were first issued, there was essentially no difference between sponsored and unsponsored ADRs except for the reporting requirements and voting rights. One was not necessarily riskier than the other. This remains true of the large issues already outstanding; however, unsponsored ADRs issued today tend to be smaller and are not very active. Consequently, the majority of them are listed in the over-the-counter pink sheets. Sponsored ADRs are becoming more and more the preferred choice of large foreign corporations seeking to tap into the U.S. capital markets. These offer the same liquidity as the common stock of U.S. companies.

Today, nearly 900 ADRs trade in the U.S. market; the largest issuer is the Bank of New York. Purchasing an ADR is as easy as purchasing the common stock of a publicly held U.S. corporation. When you buy an ADR, it is usually held in street name, although certificates in your name may be requested. Current trading and price information is widely available in the financial press. In fact, the information is included in the same column and format as the reports on U.S. stocks. Usually, no special notation is used to highlight or distinguish ADRs in these listings.

## International Investment Companies: Mutual Funds and Closed-End Funds

Like investment companies that buy and sell domestic securities, investment companies that invest in the common stock of corporations located abroad provide investors with many of the same advantages: convenience, professional management, diversification, and lower costs. The foreign stocks that comprise a portfolio are selected by professional portfolio managers who research and evaluate the individual companies, as well as the economies of the countries or regions in which they are located. All that you have to do is select the fund that best meets your financial objectives. (The process of selecting the appropriate investment company was discussed in Chapter 7.)

Investment companies that buy and sell foreign securities can be divided into four categories: global funds, international funds, regional funds, and country funds. The first two are usually set up as mutual funds; funds in the last two are usually organized as closed-end funds.

**global fund:** a mutual fund or closed-end fund that invests in the negotiable securities of corporations located in the United States and abroad.

A *global fund* establishes an investment portfolio that consists of the stock of both U.S. multinational corporations and foreign corporations. The securities can be traded in either the U.S. or foreign stock markets. This is perhaps the most diversified type of fund available. The combination of domestic and international securities enables investors to diversify across the market on a global scale.

An *international fund* invests in the common stock only of foreign corporations whose stock

**international fund:** a mutual

fund or closed-end fund that invests only in the negotiable securities of companies located outside the United States.

**regional fund:** a mutual fund or closed-end fund that invests in the negotiable securities of companies located in a specific geographical area.

**country fund:** usually a closed-end fund that invests in the securities of companies located in one country, whose name the fund bears.

trades on foreign exchanges. This fund is suitable for you if your current investment portfolio consists solely of domestic securities. By placing some of your investment dollars in an international fund, you can achieve the diversification that is already built into a global fund.

A *regional fund* invests only in a specific geographical area of the world. When organized as a mutual fund, a regional fund becomes a type of specialty fund. However, many of these funds are also closed end, as shown in Figure 7.6. Among the regional funds listed in the figure are the Europe Fund, the Asia Pacific Fund, and the Latin America Investment Fund. A regional fund is less diversified than an international fund. Nonetheless, it gives investors who believe that certain areas of the world will grow more than others an opportunity to focus their investment dollars in that region only.

A *country fund* invests in only one country. The chart in Figure 7.6 lists many of these—among them, the Chile Fund, the Indonesia Fund, the India Growth Fund, and the Greater China Fund. The majority of country funds are closed end. Many countries restrict foreign investment in local corporations. Hence, these funds may represent the only vehicle for investors outside the country to benefit from the economic growth of businesses located within the country. Country funds are perhaps the riskiest of the investment companies that buy and sell securities abroad.

## Buying Foreign Company Shares on Foreign Exchanges

Trading shares on foreign exchanges is probably not suitable for beginning investors. Although the types of investment risks are the same as for the other investment tools, the degree of risk is much greater. Many factors—the differences in language, trading regulations and procedures, reporting systems, different (and high) fee structures, often no degree of investor protection or legal recourse, and many, many others—could place small investors at a disadvantage and also in serious danger of losing all of their investment.

## WHAT ARE THE RISKS ASSOCIATED WITH INVESTING ABROAD?

Two primary risks face anyone who invests in the international markets: foreign exchange fluctuation and political instability.

Foreign exchange risk (also called "currency risk") is that risk associated with a change in the value of the foreign currency relative to the dollar. When the value of the dollar rises on the foreign exchange market, a foreign currency is worth less. Conversely, when the value of the dollar declines, a foreign currency is worth more. A foreign company pays dividends in its home currency. If the value of the dollar rises relative to the foreign currency, the dividends (and capital gains) an investor earns will result after conversion in fewer dollars for the investor. In response, the price of the foreign company's securities falls because there will be a decline in demand for the securities by U.S. investors. However, when the exchange rate for the dollar declines, the foreign currency becomes more valuable. In this case, the dividends and capital gains will result in more dollars after conversion. The demand for the foreign securities increases, and so do the prices.

Another risk associated with foreign investment is political turmoil. When investing overseas, particularly in countries with histories of political instability, there is always the risk that a change in government could bring about a change in the investment climate. The threat of a civil war, for example, could devastate the business investments in a country. Also, although some governments favor foreign investments and try to make the path easier, others restrict it. The greatest risk that investors face is the possibility that a new government could nationalize all business, which generally would leave U.S. and other foreign investors with no legal recourse. They would lose all of their investment dollars.

The risks that result from the differences in language and securities industry regulations are significant. It is therefore important to have access to good information when investing overseas. For beginning investors, this type of information is most easily obtained from an investment adviser or investment advisory firm. The cheapest way to obtain this professional advice and avoid many of the hassles of foreign markets is to buy shares of a global fund, international fund, or regional fund. However, remember to investigate the skill and expertise of the fund manager. It is that person's access to information and expertise that ultimately determines the returns that investing overseas will provide.

## WHAT PERCENTAGE OF A PORTFOLIO SHOULD I INVEST IN FOREIGN SECURITIES?

Consider investing abroad only if you are willing to take the heightened risk for a chance to obtain a better return. It is definitely not suitable for risk-averse investors. Experts recommend that no more than 10 percent of an investment portfolio be allocated to foreign securities.

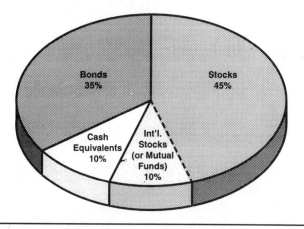

**Figure 9.2.   Traditional asset allocation mix including investing abroad.**

Figure 9.2 shows how the traditional asset allocation mix looks when the recommended percentage of international investments is included. For a beginning investor, this 10 percent would be made up of shares of a mutual fund or a closed-end fund. Even if the majority of the securities in the "stocks" category are mutual funds that invest in the stocks of domestic companies, an investor who anticipates the emergence of foreign markets as important economic forces might consider shifting into one of the international, global, or regional funds that are usually a part of every mutual fund's family of funds.

# Epilogue: The Psychology of Investing

**T**oday's markets have shown that stocks are indeed appropriate investments for most people. Now that you have a basic knowledge of stocks—the different types, how they work, what investment opportunities each provides—you must now ask yourself this question: "Do I have the temperament to invest in stocks?"

Accurately answering this question is essential. Knowing that stock and equity mutual funds are volatile is not the same as knowing whether or not you are able to *handle* that volatility. You need to determine whether you are able to endure emotionally the stock market's periodic declines—some of which are more precipitous than others. Can you keep your long-term goals in focus through a relatively short period of sharp volatility? Or will every rise and fall result in a sleepless night or a knot in your stomach?

As the three investor profiles in the Introduction demonstrate, individuals' attitudes toward their money and the stock market are as varied as their investment goals. To begin determining how you "feel" about money, ask yourself—and answer honestly!—the following questions:

- How and on what do I spend my "extra" money?
- Do I save regularly, and how much do I save?
- In what vehicles—certificates of deposit, securities, or objects (art, coins, baseball cards, furniture, pottery, and other collectibles)—do I "invest" my extra money?
- Do I believe that money and other financial matters simply "take care of themselves" or "the less time I think about money, the better"?
- Do I frequently worry when buying anything— clothing, furniture, a computer, or securities— that "it won't be the right or perfect" use of the money?
- Am I so concerned about every penny, nickel, or dime, that I feel more secure knowing exactly where my money is and what it is worth?
- Do I make my money work for me—to let me enjoy life, to treat myself well occasionally, to live today and plan for the future?

To gain some insight into how you "feel" about the stock market, ask yourself:

- Do I have a healthy respect (and skepticism) for the investment markets or will I attempt to try to outsmart them?
- Do I have the discipline to take the profits in hand or will I want more and hold a stock too long?
- Do I have the discipline to sell an investment on which I have lost money, or will I wait, hoping for a recovery?
- Do I want someone else to make the investment decisions for me through a mutual fund?

While these questions are somewhat "touchy-feely," their purpose is simply to lead you toward a clearer—not perfect—statement of your investment goals, in terms of your comfort level with money and the stock market, as well as your financial suitability for investing. The clearer your thinking, the better you will be able to communicate your financial goals to the investment professionals who provide your individual stock or mutual fund recommendations.

Having now read the entire book and determined your attitude toward your "hard-earned dollars" or "your nest egg" and the stock market itself, **go back and re-read Chapter 1.** With your new knowledge and understanding of the points you must consider before investing, you will undoubtedly see the information and questions presented in sections of this chapter from a slightly different vantage point—one that is better informed and based on greater self-awareness. It should be easier for you to state clearly your investment objectives, set the time-frame of those objectives, and determine the amount of risk you are willing to take— and can tolerate—to achieve those objectives.

Always remember: Understanding how various stock investments work and how each matches your personal "money characteristics" is an essential component in your becoming a successful investor.

# Glossary

**account executive** an individual who is employed by a broker/dealer to give advice to the public about investing in securities, to solicit buy and sell orders for securities, and to handle customer accounts. This person must be registered with the National Association of Securities Dealers or an exchange and be licensed to sell securities in the state. Also known as a "broker" or "registered representative."

**adjustable rate preferred (ARP)** a preferred stock whose dividend is adjusted periodically to reflect changing interest rates.

**aftermarket** a collective term for the markets—exchange and over-the-counter—in which stocks are bought and sold after they are issued to the public. Proceeds from trades in this market go to the previous holder. Also called the "secondary market."

**agent** anyone who acts as an intermediary in the purchase or sale of a security for the account of a customer and charges a commission for the service. The term is used for both the member firm acting as an agent and for the registered representative or account executive acting as an agent.

**American depositary receipts (ADRs)** a negotiable receipt representing ownership of a foreign company's stock that is being held in trust by a U.S. bank. ADRs give the holder the right to receive dividends and capital gains.

**American depositary share (ADS)**  usually synonymous with American depositary receipt, but the term is evolving to denote those ADRs whose issuance is sponsored by the foreign company that issued the common stock rather than by the bank that holds the shares on deposit.

**annual report**  an abbreviated version of Form 10K, which all reporting corporations (those with 500 or more shareholders) are required by the Securities and Exchange Act of 1934 to print and distribute to their shareholders annually. Contains audited financial statements, as well as other information about the company's performance and business plans. *See also* **Form 10K**.

**arbitrage**  the simultaneous purchase and sale of securities in different markets in an attempt to profit from short-term price disparities.

**asked price**  the lowest price at which a market maker offers to sell stock to a buyer. Also known as the "offer price."

**asset allocation**  the systematic and thoughtful placement of investment dollars into various classes of investments, such as stock, bonds, real estate, insurance, and cash equivalents.

**asset allocation fund**  mutual fund that invests in stocks, bonds, and cash equivalents and adjusts the mix in response to changing market conditions. The advantage of this type of fund is diversification and flexibility. The disadvantage is that its success depends almost entirely upon the fund manager's skill. *See also* **asset allocation**.

**at the money**  the market price of the underlying security and an option's strike price are the same.

**auction market**  a phrase used to describe how trading is performed on a stock exchange. In reality, the exchange is a double auction market in which buyers call out successively higher bids and sellers call out successively lower offers until a trade is arranged at a price satisfactory to the successful buyer and seller.

**auction rate preferred**  preferred stock whose dividend is adjusted periodically by the issuer; however, the shareholders (usually large corporations) must agree to the rate before it goes into effect. If they do not, the issuer continues to offer other rates until one is accepted. The term "Dutch auction" is also used. *See also* **adjustable rate preferred.**

**authorized shares**   the maximum number of common and preferred shares that a company is authorized to issue by its corporate charter.

**average**   a composite measure that gives insight into the movement of the overall market or of a particular industry. Typically it consists of a small number of stocks and is usually not capitalization weighted.

**averaging down**   a strategy in which an investor lowers the average price paid for each share of stock by purchasing more shares as the price declines.

**back-end load**   the fee charged when an investor redeems mutual fund shares. It is the same as a contingent-deferred sales charge. *See also* **contingent-deferred sales charge.**

**balance sheet**   a constantly changing snapshot of a company's financial position that shows all of its assets, liabilities, and net worth.

**bear market**   a period during which the overall prices of common stocks are falling. The term is less frequently used for bond prices.

**below-investment grade bond**   *See* **junk bond.**

**beneficial owner**   the investor who owns securities held in street name.

**Beta**   the relative volatility of a particular stock relative to the overall market as measured by the Standard & Poor's 500 Index. If a stock's Beta coefficient is 1, it means that its price rises and falls in direct relationship to the movement of the S&P index. A Beta that is less than 1 indicates a stock is less volatile than the overall market; a Beta greater than 1 indicates that a stock is more volatile.

**bid price**   (1) for stocks, the highest price at which a market maker offers to purchase a stock from a seller; (2) for mutual funds, the net asset value.

**Big Board stocks**   a popular name for stocks that trade on the New York Stock Exchange.

**blue chip stock**   the shares of stable, profitable, and well-known public companies that have a long history of steady revenues and dividend payments.

**Blue-sky laws**   commonly used name for the state laws that govern the securities industry under the Uniform Securities Act.

**board of directors**   individuals elected by a company's shareholders to set the firm's management policies, including setting the amount of the dividend that common shareholders will receive.

**bond**   a long-term debt security in which the issuer (a corporation, a municipality, or the U.S. government) promises to pay the holder a fixed rate of interest at regular intervals and to repay the face value of the security at maturity. *See also* **zero coupon bond.**

**book entry**   securities for which no certificates are issued. The names, addresses, and holdings of investors are listed only in the records of the issuer or registrar.

**book value**   the theoretical value of the company that remains if all the assets of the company were liquidated at the values carried on the balance sheet and then all liabilities paid off. Intangible assets such as goodwill, patents, and copyrights are excluded from the total assets.

**box**   the physical location where securities are held for safekeeping at a brokerage firm. Evolved from a time when firms held certificates for securities in a large box.

**breadth of the market**   the number of individual stocks traded out of the number of stocks listed.

**breakout**   a price rise above a resistance level that results in a substantial advance or a price decline below a support area that results in a substantial price decline. Breakouts usually establish new support and resistance levels.

**breakpoint**  the dollar level at which a mutual fund investor qualifies for a lower sales charge on either a lump-sum purchase or under the right of accumulation.

**bull market**  a period during which the overall prices of securities are rising.

**cabinet stock**  exchange listed stock, usually preferred, that trades in 10-share round lots and does not have an active trading market.

**call feature**  a provision that permits the issuer to repurchase preferred stock, usually at a premium to its par value.

**call loan rate**  the interest rate that banks charge brokerage firms for loans collateralized by marginable securities.

**call option**  a security that gives its holder the right to buy 100 shares of common stock at a fixed price for a fixed period of time.

**call protection**  the period of time following the issuance of a security when it may not be called.

**capital appreciation**  an increase in the market value of a security over the adjusted cost of acquisition. If realized, this gives rise to a capital gain.

**capital gain**  the profit that results if the proceeds from the sale of a security are higher than the security's cost basis. (*Compare* **capital loss**.)

**capital loss**  the loss that results if the proceeds from the sale of a security are less than the security's cost basis. (*Compare* **capital gain**.)

**capital risk**  the risk that an investor can lose the money invested in a security. This risk is made up of several different types of risks, including business risk, liquidity risk, systematic risk, inflationary risk, and political risk.

**capitalization**  that part of a company's funds raised by issuing stocks and bonds.

**cash account**  an account in which an investor buys securities by paying for them in full or sells securities that he or she owns fully paid.

**cash balances**  cash deposits in an account at a brokerage firm that are uninvested or awaiting investment.

**cash dividends**  part of a company's after-tax earnings that its board of directors decides, usually quarterly, to distribute to the shareholders.

**cash equivalents**  short-term investments that are virtually cash because of their high liquidity and safety.

**cash flow statement**  a statement of the sources and uses of cash by a business for a period of time.

**charting**  capturing the patterns of a stock's price and volume movements on a line, bar, point and figure, or moving average graph.

**chartist**  a technical analyst who uses charts to capture a stock's price and volume movements and then analyzes this information as a basis for making buy and sell recommendations.

**churning**  excessive trading in a customer's account by a broker in order to generate commissions.

**closed-end fund**  an investment company has a one-time offering of a fixed number of shares to the public and then does not issue new shares or redeem old shares; the fund's shares are bought and sold like stock on the exchanges and in the over-the-counter market. Also called a publicly traded fund. *See also* **publicly traded fund.**

**closed-end management company**  legal name for a **closed-end fund**.

**commercial paper**  short-term unsecured debt issued by a corporation with a usual maturity of 270 days. It is sold at a discount and redeemed at face value.

**commission**   the fee charged by a broker or agent for executing an order for a customer.

**common stock**   an equity security that usually gives the holder the right to receive dividends and vote on company issues.

**confirmation**   a notice sent from a broker to the customer on the day following the trade date that gives the details of the execution of an order, including price and number of units.

**consolidated tape**   an electronic display of trades of all listed securities on all exchanges and in the over-the-counter market. Currently, the consolidated tapes consist of two networks. Network A displays trades of all New York Stock Exchange–listed stocks, and Network B displays trades of all American Stock Exchange–listed issues.

**constant-dollar plan**   an investment method in which a person maintains a fixed-dollar amount of a portfolio in stocks, buying and selling shares periodically to maintain the fixed-dollar amount.

**constant-ratio plan**   an investment method in which a person maintains a fixed ratio between stocks and bonds throughout the investment period, with regular adjustments made to compensate for different levels of price increases and decreases.

**contingent-deferred sales charge**   a fee that is charged when an investor redeems shares within a relatively short period of time after purchasing them. Also called a **back-end load.**

**contrary indicators**   information used to establish the bullish or bearish sentiment of the market. In general, the indicator provides an opposing insight. For example, the put/call ratio is a classic contrary indicator because it measures index options, the typical instrument professional money managers use to hedge portfolio positions. If the managers are bullish, they buy stocks and buy puts to hedge. Therefore, an increase in the put/call ratio is bullish. If they are bearish, they sell short stocks and buy calls to hedge. A decrease in the put/call ratio is therefore bearish.

**conversion ratio**   the number of common shares that an investor receives when converting a preferred stock or convertible bond.

**convertible preferred**   preferred stock that shareholders can convert into a fixed number of common shares.

**cost basis**   the price, for tax purposes, paid for a security, including commissions, markups, and other cost adjustments.

**country fund**   usually a closed-end fund that invests in the securities of companies located in one country, whose name the fund bears. Mutual funds can also be country funds.

**covered option**   term used to describe the writer of a put or a call who holds another security position that protects against or offsets the risks of a short option position.

**covering**   eliminating a short position by buying the shares that have been sold short and delivering them to the lender.

**cum-rights**   literally, *with* rights; describes transactions in which the preemptive rights accompany the purchase (or sale) of common stock and their value is included in the market price of the shares.

**cumulative preferred**   if dividend payments are missed, holders of these shares have a right to receive all back dividends before any dividend payments can be made to common shareholders.

**cumulative voting method**   a procedure whereby a shareholder can place his or her votes on directorships in any combination he or she chooses.

**curb market**   an anachronistic name for the American Stock Exchange (AMEX) that is still used today. It refers to the fact that the AMEX was called the New York Curb Exchange until 1921.

**current ratio**   a measure of a company's ability to pay its current expenses and obligations from its current assets. The formula is current assets divided by the current liabilities.

**current yield**   the annual dividend or interest on a security divided by its current market price.

**day order**   an order to buy or sell securities without a time notation; if it is not executed or canceled, it expires at the end of the trading session during which it was placed.

**dealer**  a member firm that makes a market in an over-the-counter stock. Also called a "principal" or a "market maker."

**debenture**  an unsecured corporate bond that is backed by the full faith and credit of the issuer.

**debit balance**  the balance owed to the brokerage firm by a customer who purchases securities on margin; generally used for margin purchases.

**debt ratio**  a measure of the percentage of bonds that comprise a company's total capitalization.

**declaration date**  the day on which the board of directors announces the terms and amount of a dividend payment, rights offerings, or stock splits.

**discount**  the amount by which the market value of a preferred stock or a corporate bond is below its par value.

**diversification**  investing in different securities, different industries, or a mutual fund portfolio containing various securities in order to diminish the risk associated with owning too few stocks.

**dividend**  that portion of a corporation's after tax earnings that its board of directors distributes to stockholders. Dividends are usually distributed quarterly.

**dividend reinvestment plan**  a plan whereby a company's existing shareholders choose to have their cash dividend payments automatically reinvested in additional shares of the company's stock; often abbreviated DRIP.

**dollar-cost averaging**  a strategy whereby a person invests the same amount of money at regular intervals in a stock or a mutual fund without regard for the price fluctuations of the security.

**downtrend**  the downward movement of a security's price, or of the market, as measured by an average or index over a period of time.

**earnings per share (EPS)**  that portion of a company's profit that is allocated to each outstanding common share after operating expenses, bond interest, taxes, and preferred dividends have been paid. A company's board of directors decides what portion of the EPS is distributed as a dividend.

**economy of scale**    a reduction in the ratio of expenses to assets as the size of a mutual fund increases.

**EPS**    *See* **earnings per share**.

**equity fund**    a mutual fund that invests primarily in common and/or preferred stocks. In practice, the term is used for both stock and bond funds and balanced funds as opposed, for example, to a money market fund. Funds that invest only in stocks tend to be called "common stock funds."

**equity security**    more commonly called a share or a stock, it is a security representing a proportionate ownership of a business and the right to receive dividends.

**ex-dividend date**    the day, set by the National Association of Securities Dealers or an exchange, on which the bid price of the stock is reduced by the dividend amount. Anyone purchasing the stock on that day or later will not be eligible to receive the upcoming cash dividend.

**ex-rights**    literally, *without* rights; describes transactions in which the preemptive rights do not accompany the purchase (or sale) of common stock. The rights at this time trade separately in the market.

**ex-rights date**    by industry practice, the day after the distribution of the rights. The bid price of the stock is reduced by an amount equal to the value of the right.

**family of funds**    a group of different funds with portfolios made of different securities or having different investment objectives all managed by the same investment adviser.

**financial profile**    an assessment of an investor's assets, liabilities, investment objectives, and willingness to bear risk.

**floor broker**    an exchange member and an employee of a member firm who executes buy and sell orders on the trading floor of an exchange.

**flow of funds indicators**   statistics that enable analysts to determine in which markets—money markets, stock, bonds, savings accounts—individual and institutional investors are most likely to invest their money during given economic conditions or periods of time. Also used for cash balances held by mutual funds and pension plans.

**Form 10K**   the detailed report that all companies with 500 or more shareholders must file annually with the Securities and Exchange Commission. The information contained in the report is made public so that investors can use it to evaluate their investment. *See also* **annual report.**

**forward P-E ratio**   the P-E (price-earnings) ratio calculated using the earnings per share reported from the two most recent quarters plus the estimated earnings for the next two quarters.

**front-end load**   a sales charge that is applied when an investor buys a mutual fund share.

**fully diluted earnings per share**   a calculation of the earnings per share using all of the common shares currently outstanding plus any additional shares that could result from the conversion or exercise of any outstanding convertible preferred stock, convertible bonds, rights, or warrants.

**fundamental analysis**   evaluating a company's balance sheet and income statement as a means of predicting the future, long-term price movement of its stock.

**global fund**   a mutual fund or closed-end fund that invests in the negotiable securities of corporations located in the United States and abroad.

**growth stock**   stocks of new, expanding companies whose market values are expected to appreciate rapidly.

**GTC**   a time notation on an order meaning "good 'til canceled." Subject to periodic renewal, the order remains in the market until it is executed or expires. *See also* **open order.**

**hedging**   protecting against or limiting losses on an existing stock position by establishing an opposite position in the same or an equivalent security.

**high-yield bond**   a more attractive, less emotionally charged synonym for a junk bond. *See also* **junk bond.**

**holder**   buyer of an option contract.

**holder of record**   the person whose name appears as the owner of the security on the company's records, usually as of the record date.

**hot issue**   a newly issued stock that immediately begins trading in the secondary market at a price higher than its initial offering price.

**hypothecation agreement**   *See* **margin agreement.**

**in the money**   in option trading, a phrase that describes an option that has intrinsic value. Specifically, an option is in the money when the relationship between the market price of the underlying security and the strike price of the option is such that exercising would yield a profit to the holder (buyer).

**income statement**   a profit-and-loss statement showing all of the income and expenses of a business for a period of time.

**income stock**   the shares of companies that make regular and substantial dividend payments to investors.

**income strategies**   in options, any strategy in which the investor receives more options premiums than he or she pays.

**index**   a composite measure of the movement of the overall market or of a particular industry that consists of a large number of stocks and is usually weighted by other factors, such as capitalization.

**initial margin requirement**   under Regulation T, the percentage of a stock's market price that must be deposited when initially buying or selling short stock on margin.

**initial public offering (IPO)**   the first time that a company sells its stock to the public.

**international fund**   a mutual fund or closed-end fund that invests only in the negotiable securities of companies located outside the United States.

**intrinsic value**   that portion of an option's premium reflecting the difference between the market price of the underlying security and the strike price of an option. *See also* **in the money.**

**investment adviser**   the financial professional who manages the investment portfolio of a mutual fund and charges a management fee for these services. Often called a "portfolio manager."

**investment advisory services**   companies or individuals registered with the Securities and Exchange Commission who in the course of business provide investment advice or money management regarding nonexempt securities for a fee.

**investment banker**   a securities firm that assists businesses in raising capital through issuing securities. Also called an underwriter. *See also* **underwriter.**

**investment company**   generic name for one of the many companies whose primary business is investing and reinvesting in securities for the accounts of others. These companies include mutual funds, closed-end funds, variable annuities, and unit trusts. Neither banks nor holding companies are included in this definition.

**investment planning**   defining an investment objective and establishing the systematic approach to achieve it.

**IPO**   *See* **initial public offering.**

**issued and outstanding**   authorized shares that have been distributed to investors and that may trade in the market.

**junk bond**   low-quality, high-risk, long-term debt security. Any bond with a rating of BB by Moody's, Ba by S&P, or lower is considered to be "junk." To avoid the negative associations of the word "junk," more and more firms use synonyms such as high-yield bond, non-investment grade bond, and below investment grade bone.

**leverage**   the purchase (or sale) of a large amount of a security using a large percentage of borrowed money—for example, buying stock on margin.

**limit order**   an order to buy stock (buy limit) at a specified price or lower or to sell stock (sell limit) at a specified price or higher.

**listed stock**   a company whose stock meets the listing requirements of one of the exchanges and has been accepted by the exchange to trade on its floor.

**load**   the sales charge that an investor pays when buying a mutual fund share.

**load fund**   a mutual fund that charges its purchasers an up-front sales charge.

**long position**   phrase denoting ownership of a security, which includes the right to transfer ownership and to participate in the rise and fall of its market value.

**long-dated rights**   a dilutive, antitakeover device in which rights are automatically distributed to existing stockholders during a hostile takeover. *See also* **poison pill.**

**maintenance call**   a demand from a brokerage firm that an investor deposit enough cash or securities in a margin account to restore the account to the minimum maintenance margin. *See also* **margin call.**

**management company**   one of the three types of investment companies defined under the Investment Company Act of 1940. This investment company manages by objectives and, depending on its structure, is described as either an **open-end management company** or a **closed-end management company**.

**management fee**   a percentage of a mutual fund's total assets that the fund's portfolio manager charges for his or her services. It is typically the largest expense of a mutual fund.

**margin account**   an account in which an investor buys (or sells short) securities by depositing part of their market value and borrowing the remainder from the brokerage firm.

**margin agreement**   a document an investor must sign when opening a margin account. By signing it, the investor pledges the securities purchased as collateral for the margin loan. The agreement also details the terms of the margin loan, including the interest rate and how it will be computed. Also called a "hypothecation agreement."

**margin call**   a demand from a brokerage firm for an investor to deposit enough cash (or securities) in a margin account to meet the Regulation T initial margin requirement. *See also* **maintenance call.**

**margin department**   a division of a brokerage firm that computes an investor's equity in a margin account daily and sends out margin or maintenance calls, as appropriate.

**marginable security**   a security that can be bought or sold in a margin account. These include all stocks registered (listed) on exchanges and any over-the-counter stock that appears on the Federal Reserve Board's margin list.

**mark down**   the amount or percentage subtracted from the bid price when the customer sells over-the-counter stock to a market maker or principal firm.

**marked to market**   the process by which a brokerage firm computes the value of the shares in an investor's account based on the daily closing price.

**market maker**   a firm that is a member of the National Association of Securities Dealers that disseminates bid and ask prices at which it stands ready to buy or sell stock for its own account and risk. Synonymous with "dealers."

**market not held order**   abbreviated MKT (NH), a market order in which an investor gives the floor broker discretion as to the time and price at which the order may be executed. These orders are used typically for large or complex trades.

**market order**   an order to buy or sell stock immediately at the best available market price.

**market value**   the price of a stock determined by the forces of supply and demand in the marketplace.

**markup**    the amount or percentage added to the ask price when a customer buys an over-the-counter stock from a firm acting as a principal or market maker in the transaction.

**merger**    the joining of two companies, under either friendly or hostile terms.

**minimum maintenance margin**    set by the New York Stock Exchange and the National Association of Securities Dealers, the minimum equity that a customer must maintain in a margin account. Below this percentage or amount, the customer gets a call to restore equity in the account to the maintenance margin level.

**money market preferred**    adjustable rate preferred whose dividend is adjusted to reflect short-term interest rates of money market instruments such as treasury bills and commercial paper.

**mutual fund**    common name for an open-end management company that establishes a diversified portfolio of investments. These companies issue new shares or redeem old shares representing ownership in the portfolio.

**NASD**    abbreviation for the National Association of Securities Dealers, the self-regulatory organization of the over-the-counter market.

**NASDAQ**    acronym for National Association of Securities Dealers Automated Quotation System, an interdealer computer system that provides brokers, traders, and market makers with current bid and asked quotes for over-the-counter securities.

**NASDAQ National Market Issues**    the approximately 2700 most active and best capitalized over-the-counter stocks.

**NASDAQ Small-Cap Issues**    the approximately 1500 stock trading on NASDAQ that do not meet the listing requirement set for the National Market Issues. The small caps have lower assets and revenues, and an average per share price of about $1.60.

**negotiable security**    a security whose title can be readily transferred when it is bought or sold.

**net asset value (NAV)** the market value of each share of a mutual fund, computed by subtracting the fund's liabilities from its total assets and dividing the remainder by the total number of outstanding shares. A mutual fund must calculate its NAV at the end of each trading day.

**net transaction** a trade, such as the purchase of a new issue, in which the buyer or seller is not charged a commission or additional fee.

**net worth** (1) also called **stockholder's equity**, the amount of a company's total assets that exceeds its total liabilities on the balance sheet; (2) the difference between the total value of a person's assets and possessions (e.g., home, land, savings accounts, investments) and total indebtedness (e.g., mortgage, credit cards, school loans).

**new issues** securities offered for sale for the first time by an issuer in the primary market (for example, an **initial public offering**).

**no-load fund** common name for a mutual fund that does not add a sales charge to its net asset value when investors purchase shares of the fund.

**non-investment grade bond** *See* **junk bond**.

**not held order** *see* **market not held order**.

**OCC** abbreviation for the Option Clearing Corporation, a clearing organization owned by the exchanges that issues all option contracts and guarantees the performance or obligation of both the option buyer and seller under the terms of the contract.

**odd lot trade** a trade involving between 1 and 99 shares. *See also* **round lot trade**.

**offer** synonym for **asked price**.

**open order** order that remains valid until it is executed or canceled. Same as a **good til canceled order**.

**open-end management company**   legal name for a **mutual fund**. An investment company that, after the initial public offering of shares to the public, continually issues new shares and redeems outstanding shares.

**OTC**   common abbreviation of the **over-the-counter market**.

**out of the money**   in option trading, a phrase that describes an option with no intrinsic value. Specifically, an option is out of the money when the relationship between the market price of the underlying security and the option's strike price is such that the holder (buyer) will not exercise the option because it would result in a loss.

**over-the-counter (OTC) market**   a decentralized, negotiated market in which many dealers in diverse locations execute trades for customers over an electronic trading system or telephone lines.

**overbought market**   usually interpreted as an indicator of a future price decline, a technical term used to describe a stock (or market) whose value has risen quickly and unexpectedly and thus may represent a price far above its actual worth.

**oversold market**   usually interpreted as an indication of an impending price rise, a technical term to describe a stock (or the market) whose value has fallen quickly and sharply, far below its actual worth.

**par value**   (1) for common stock, an arbitrary (and meaningless) value assigned the stock at the time it is issued; (2) for preferred stock, the fixed value upon which dividend payments are based.

**parity**   when the total market value of the common shares into which a security can be converted equals the market value of the convertible security.

**participating preferred**   a rarely issued stock that pays the shareholder a fixed dividend and part of the earnings that are distributed to common shareholders.

**payable date**   the date on which a cash dividend or stock will be paid to an investor who has purchased the stock before the appropriate ex-date.

**P-E ratio**   *See* **price-earnings ratio**.

**Pink Sheets**   a sheet listing the bid and ask prices of certain thinly traded over-the-counter stocks—mostly low-priced and foreign issues. Named for the color of the paper and published each business day by the National Quotations Bureau.

**point**   the price movement on an individual stock equal to one dollar. On bonds, a point represents 1 percent of face value.

**poison pill**   jargon used to describe a security whose features are specifically designed to defend against a hostile takeover. *See also* **long-dated rights.**

**preemptive right**   an entitlement giving existing stockholders the right to purchase a proportional amount of new common shares before they are offered to other investors.

**premium**   (1) the amount by which the market value of a preferred stock exceeds its par value; (2) the market price of a call or a put option.

**price**   in technical terms, the point at which supply (sellers) and demand (buyers) meet and a trade occurs.

**price-earnings (P-E) ratio**   a ratio in which a stock's current market price is divided by its annual earnings. It is a measure of the number of times that a stock's price exceeds its earnings. Also called the "multiple."

**primary issue**   another name for a new issue of securities.

**primary market**   the market in which the issuer and underwriter first offers and sells securities to the public, with proceeds from the sale going to the issuing corporation. *See also* **aftermarket.**

**prime rate**   the short-term interest rate that commercial banks charge their most credit-worthy business customers.

**prior preferred**   sometimes called a senior preferred, it receives dividends before all other preferred stock.

**prospectus**   a printed summary of the Securities and Exchange Commission–filed registration statement that discloses the details of a particular offering of securities, including the company's business history and that of its management, its future business plans, and its intended use of the proceeds from the issue. The prospectus must contain enough material information for the investor to judge the merits of the issue. *See also* **registration statement.**

**proxy**   a form by which an investor votes *in absentia* by transferring voting authority to another party.

**public offering price**   (1) for stocks, the price at which new shares are sold to the public by the issuer or underwriters; (2) for mutual funds, the asked price at which an investor purchases a mutual fund share.

**publicly traded fund**   *See* **closed-end management company.**

**put option**   a security that gives its holder the right to sell 100 shares of common stock at a fixed price for a fixed period of time.

**random walk theory**   contrary to technical analysis, the theory asserts that stock prices do not move in predictable patterns in response to information in the market; therefore, an investor who chooses stock at random has as much opportunity to make money as one who does elaborate analysis.

**realized gain**   the cash profit resulting from the liquidation of a stock position.

**record date**   the deadline date, set by a corporation's board of directors, on which an investor must be recorded as an owner of the stock in order to be eligible to receive the dividend payment or stock distribution.

**red herring**   jargon for the preliminary prospectus, an abbreviated version of the final prospectus, which is often used to get an indication of the public's interest in a security before the price is set and the security issued.

**redemption fee**   a fee that some mutual funds sometimes charge investors when they liquidate their shares.

**regional fund**   a mutual fund or closed-end fund that invests in the negotiable securities of companies located in a specific geographical area.

**registered securities**   (1) securities that are registered and held in customer's name at a brokerage firm; (2) securities that are registered with the Securities and Exchange Commission.

**registrar**   usually a commercial bank that is responsible for maintaining an accurate list of the names and addresses of a company's stockholders.

**registration statement**   the disclosure document that companies planning to offer nonexempt securities to the public are required to file with the Securities and Exchange Commission under the Securities Act of 1933. The registration statement must be filed before the securities can be issued, and it must contain full and fair disclosure of the company's business history, financial status, management, and planned use for the proceeds from the sale of the new securities. *See also* **prospectus.**

**regular way settlement**   the normal settlement method for stock transactions in which the securities must be paid for or delivered no later than five business days after the trade date.

**Regulation T**   the Federal Reserve's regulation that gives it the power to set the initial margin requirement on most corporate securities and thereby governs the amount of credit that brokerage firms can extend to their customers.

**resistance level**   a price level to which a stock or the market rises and then falls from repeatedly. Selling increases as a stock's price approaches this level.

**retained earnings**   the portion of the earnings per share that the board of directors does not pay out as dividends to the common stockholders. Retained earnings are reinvested in the company. *See also* **dividend; earnings per share.**

**right of accumulation**   a reduction in the sales charge on all subsequent purchases when the value of an investor's shares and current purchases reaches a breakpoint.

**rights offering**   an offering of new shares to existing shareholders. The method and terms by which preemptive rights are distributed to existing shareholders are explained in the prospectus that accompanies the offering. *See also* **preemptive right.**

**risk arbitrage**   the simultaneous purchase and sale of the shares of two companies in anticipation of or upon the announcement of a merger or acquisition.

**round lot trade**   a trade involving 100 shares of common stock.

**sales charge**   a fee, included in a mutual fund's public offering price, that an investor pays, when buying a fund share. Also called a sales load. *See also* **load; load fund; back-end load.**

**secondary market**   *See* **aftermarket.**

**Securities and Exchange Commission**   established in 1934 as the regulatory authority of the securities industry, the SEC is responsible for interpreting, supervising, and enforcing compliance with the provisions of the various securities acts.

**selling long**   selling or liquidating stock positions that an investor owns.

**selling short**   strategy investors use to profit from a price decline; involves selling securities that the investor has borrowed with the intention of repurchasing them later at a lower price.

**sentiment indicators**   statistics used to measure the bullish or bearish mood of the market and its investors.

**settlement date**   the date on which cash and securities are exchanged following a purchase or sale.

**short against the box**   a strategy used to lock in a gain on securities that an investor owns and defer taxes to the next year. The investor sells short the same security that he or she owns and later uses the long position to cover the short sale.

**short interest**   the total amount of a company's outstanding shares that have been sold short and have not been covered or bought in.

**short interest ratio**   a calculation (a stock's short interest divided by its average daily trading volume) used to determine the number of days it would take to cover or buy in the number of shares that investors have sold short.

**short margin account**   a margin account in which an investor sells stock short.

**sinking fund provision**   a feature that permits a company to deposit funds regularly into an escrow account that will eventually be used to redeem or repurchase the outstanding preferred issue or bond.

**SIPC**   acronym for Securities Investors Protection Corporation, a government-sponsored private corporation created in 1970 that provides insurance protection for the customers of broker/dealers that go bankrupt. Each customer's account is covered for up to $500,000, of which no more than $100,000 may be for cash.

**SMA**   abbreviation for **Special Memorandum Account**.

**socially responsible fund**   mutual funds that do not invest in any company that has holdings in politically or environmentally incorrect sectors of the world.

**Special Memorandum Account (SMA)**   an account used to show the excess equity or line of credit that an investor has in a margin account.

**special situation fund**   a mutual fund that invests in companies that are candidates for takeover or those that are emerging from bankruptcy.

**specialist**   an exchange member located at the trading post, responsible for maintaining a fair and orderly market in the stock(s) assigned to him or her.

**spread**   (1) the compensation that an underwriter receives for distributing a new issue; (2) the difference between the bid and asked prices for a security.

**statement**   a summary of all transactions in an investor's account, as well as the current value of all long and short positions being held in the account. Statements are sent monthly for active accounts and quarterly for inactive accounts.

**Statement of Additional Information**    an addendum to a mutual fund's prospectus that includes more detailed information, such as the fund's audited financial statements and the calculation methods used for computing the fund's results.

**statutory voting method**    a procedure whereby a shareholder divides his or her total votes equally among the directorships being decided; the standard voting method in most corporations.

**stock**    a security representing ownership of a company and entitling its owner to the right to receive dividends. *See also* **equity security.**

**stock derivative**    a security that offers an investor some but not all of the benefits of stocks, particularly the capital gains potential, usually at a lower cost per unit.

**stock exchange**    an auction market in which exchange members meet in a central location to execute buy and sell orders for individual and institutional customers.

**stock index fund**    a mutual fund that invests in a group of securities whose performance reflects the performance of a particular stock market index, such as the Standard & Poor's 500 Index or the New York Stock Exchange Composite.

**stock option**    *See* **call option; put option.**

**stock power**    usually a separate document attached to a stock or bond certificate and signed by the stockholder, it is a power of attorney giving the brokerage firm the right to transfer ownership to another party, such as to the securities firm when the securities are pledged or to another individual when the securities are sold.

**stock split**    an increase or decrease in the number of a company's authorized shares that results in no change in the total value of the investor's holdings.

**stockholders' equity**    a synonym for **net worth**, the equity that remains after a company's total liabilities have been subtracted from its total assets.

**stop order**   an order that becomes a market order to buy (buy stop) or to sell (sell stop) when the stock trades at a specified price, known as the "stop price." Also called a **"stop-loss order."**

**stop-loss order**   *See* **stop order**.

**straight preferred**   synonym for "nonconvertible preferred."

**street name**   industry term describing securities owned by an investor but registered in the name of the brokerage firm.

**strike price**   the fixed price at which stock can be bought or sold when a call or put is exercised. Also known as the "exercise price."

**subscription price**   usually lower than a stock's current market price, the fixed price at which a company's existing shareholders can purchase new shares during a rights offering.

**support level**   a price level to which a stock or the market falls (and then rises from) repeatedly. Demand for the security increases as the price approaches a support level.

**technical analysis**   (1) research that seeks to predict the future price movement of a stock or the overall market by using price and volume as indicators of changes in the supply and demand for a stock; (2) using charts of a stock's past price and volume movements to predict its future, short-term, or intermediate-term price movements.

**tender offer**   a limited time offer by a company to purchase its own shares or another company's outstanding shares, usually at a premium to their current market value.

**thin market**   a market in which there are few buyers or sellers for a security and which is characterized by increased price volatility. Also called an "illiquid market."

**tick**   the minimum price move of a stock. On most stock, a tick is 1/8 of a point, or $0.125.

**ticker**   the electronic display that continuously shows the stock symbols and prices at which each successive order is executed. Also called the "ticker tape" or the **consolidated tape**.

**time value**   the amount of an option's premium that exceeds its intrinsic value, representing the price investors place on the time an option has until its expiration. If an option is out of the money, all of the premium is considered to present time value. *See also* **out of the money.**

**timing**   attempting to buy or sell a security at the optimum moment in its price movement.

**tombstone**   an advertisement published in financial newspapers and periodicals announcing the public offering of securities by its underwriters.

**total capitalization**   the total long-term debt, preferred stock, and common stock that makes a company's capital structure.

**total return**   the percentage return, including both dividends and capital appreciation, on money invested in a stock.

**trading post**   the designated place on the exchange floor where a particular stock trades.

**trailing P-E ratio**   the P-E (price/earnings) ratio calculated using the previous year's earnings per share.

**transfer agent**   usually a commercial bank, a firm appointed by an issuer of a security that is responsible for canceling old certificates and issuing new ones.

**treasury stock**   outstanding stock that has been repurchased by the corporation that issued it.

**trend**   in technical terms, the up, down, or sideways movement of the overall market (as reflected in an average or index) or a stock's price over a period of time, usually longer than six months.

**12-b-1 plan**   a mutual fund that charges investors distribution fees and a portion of the advertising cost to attract new investors. Normally the costs are borne by the fund.

**uncovered option**   term used to describe a call or put writer who is unprotected against the maximum possible loss on a short option position. *See also* **covered option.**

**underwriter**   a brokerage firm that assists the issuer of a new security in setting the offering price and in marketing the securities to the public. Also known as an **investment banker.**

**unlisted stocks**   virtually synonymous with over-the-counter stocks, a term used to describe any stock or other security that does not trade—is not listed—on an exchange.

**unrealized gain**   the profit resulting from an increase in the value of a security position that is still being held.

**uptrend**   the upward movement of a stock's price or of the market as measured by an average or index over a period of time.

**venture capital**   money invested in a new, unproved and risky business or enterprise.

**volatility**   the relative amount or percentage by which a stock's price rises and falls during a period of time.

**volume**   the total number of shares traded in a given period of time.

**voting trust**   a trust, usually having a maximum life of 10 years, established to control the voting shares of a corporation.

**voting trust certificate (VTC)**   negotiable certificates showing that investors have deposited common shares into a voting trust and consequently have forfeited their right to vote.

**warrant**   a long-term security, usually attached to a bond or preferred stock, that gives the holder the right to buy a fixed number of a company's common shares at a price that is set higher than the stock's current price at the time of issuance.

**wasting asset**   a security that becomes worthless on a predetermined expiration date. Rights, standard warrants, and options are securities that are wasting assets.

**wealth building**   an investment strategy designed to increase one's net worth over time.

**weighting**   the method for determining the worth of each company's stock relative to the value of the overall index.

**when-issued security**    a security that is sold to the public and trades in the market before the physical certificates are available for distribution.

**writer**    seller of an option contract.

**yield**    the percentage or rate of return that an investor makes on capital invested in a security or in a portfolio of securities.

**zero-coupon bond**    a bond sold at an original issue discount that pays interest in a lump sum at maturity. *See also* **bond.**

# Index